Blaise

The
Interviews

ESSENTIAL WRITERS SERIES 45

**Canada Council
for the Arts**

**Conseil des Arts
du Canada**

**ONTARIO ARTS COUNCIL
CONSEIL DES ARTS DE L'ONTARIO**

an Ontario government agency
un organisme du gouvernement de l'Ontario

Canadä

Guernica Editions Inc. acknowledges the support of the Canada Council
for the Arts and the Ontario Arts Council. The Ontario Arts Council
is an agency of the Government of Ontario.

We acknowledge the financial support of the Government of Canada.
Nous reconnaissons l'appui financier du gouvernement du Canada.

Clark Blaise

The Interviews

Edited by J.R. (Tim) Struthers

GUERNICA
EDITIONS
TORONTO · BUFFALO · LANCASTER (U.K.)
2016

J.R. (Tim) Struthers, editor
Michael Mirolla, general editor
Joseph Pivato, series editor
Cover and interior design: David Moratto
Front cover image: Ron Shuebrook
Guernica Editions Inc.
1569 Heritage Way, Oakville, (ON), Canada L6M 2Z7
2250 Military Road, Tonawanda, N.Y. 14150-6000 U.S.A.
www.guernicaeditions.com

Distributors:
University of Toronto Press Distribution,
5201 Dufferin Street, Toronto (ON), Canada M3H 5T8
Gazelle Book Services, White Cross Mills,
High Town, Lancaster LA1 4XS U.K.

First edition.
Printed in Canada.

Legal Deposit—Third Quarter
Library of Congress Catalog Card Number: 2015959610
Library and Archives Canada Cataloguing in Publication
Clark Blaise : the interviews / edited by J.R. (Tim)
Struthers. -- First edition.

(Essential writers series ; 45)
Issued also in print and electronic formats.
ISBN 978-1-77183-114-7 (paperback).--ISBN 978-1-77183-115-4
(epub).--ISBN 978-1-77183-116-1 (mobi)

1. Blaise, Clark, 1940- --Interviews.
I. Struthers, J.R. (Tim), 1950-, editor II. Series: Writers series
(Toronto, Ont.) ; 45

PS8553.L34Z56 2016   C813'.54   C2015-905899-6   C2015-905900-3

The cover art for this volume is derived
from a drawing by Ron Shuebrook,
Site of Discourse #2 (2013),
inspired by table talk with Will Alsop,
designer of the Sharp Centre for Design
at OCAD University in Toronto

Clark Blaise: Essays on His Works
and
Clark Blaise: The Interviews
are dedicated with gratitude to
JOHN METCALF
for the more than fifty years
he has ardently spent
creating and defining and championing
the very best in Canadian writing

Contents

ix

Part of the Myth:
An Interview with Clark Blaise
[1992]

J.R. (Tim) Struthers

TS: There's an old saying that you have to give a little to get a little. So here's a bit of a gift. My father was born in Sarnia, Ontario. He lost a twin brother at birth.
CB: Identical?
TS: I don't know. Sometime afterwards, he was put up for adoption and taken in by a couple who lived in Winnipeg — where your mother lived intermittently, including her college years and her final years. A little later, when his sister was born, she was taken in by the same family in Winnipeg. Yet the details of my father's birth and adoption and childhood remained unknown to me, or at least unaccepted by me, until after I myself became a father — through falling in love, upon her arrival to do Ph.D. work like me at Western, with Marianne Micros, then recently widowed and the mother of a nearly five-year-old daughter, Eleni Alexandra Kapetanios. Interestingly, Eleni is now, in 1992-93, a fourth-year Creative Writing and English student at Concordia University in the very program in which you taught for a dozen years before leaving Montreal in 1978. So it wasn't until after, and in terms of some matters well after, Marianne and Eleni entered my life in September 1974 — the same month that I met Alice Munro, when she came to Western to serve as writer-in-residence for a

year — that certain very important details of my father's life became known to me. And indeed, many details of my father's life are unknown to me, or at least undeciphered by me, even now.

I recall my mother telling me, when I was a teenager, that my father was adopted. At the time, I thought my mother was criticizing him in some way to me. But she may have meant something entirely different. Perhaps she was trying to explain something about him to me and I misunderstood her intention completely. But I didn't trust the information at the time. Moreover, I don't think I ever heard it from his own lips. And I only accepted it as fact when I learned from Marianne that he had told this to Eleni and to her. I believe my father was trying to offer Eleni some emotional support since her first father had died after an automobile accident when she was not quite thirteen months old. I believe my father wanted Eleni to have confidence that our new family would work — and would continue to work when we became a family of four with the birth of our younger daughter, Joy, in 1978 — and he decided it might be reassuring to tell Eleni about his success adjusting to changes during his own childhood.

My father died on November 25th, 1991, at the age of seventy-nine, died happily after a fairly short illness. He had played eighteen holes of golf the day before he became ill and was sick at home and in hospital for only five and a half weeks. So he lived a long and hardy and devoted life. A few months earlier, we had played a round of golf together on his birthday, August 19th, at a course on the Bluewater Highway immediately north of Bayfield, Ontario. I'd just finished my summer teaching — my schedule at the University of Guelph includes winter and summer teaching, then the fall for research

— and as we were walking down the first fairway together after hitting our drives I told him that I'd recently
received a letter from the Dean of Arts thanking me for
my past year's work and advising me of my salary for
the coming year. My dad was overjoyed: I'd achieved
the success — by which he would have meant the secu-
rity and the salary — that he had dreamed of my achieving. I appreciated the pride that he felt in me, yet there
was much more that I still didn't know about him. It
was only after he died that I learned he had been a twin.
And it was only after he died that I learned his birth
name. I was forty-one years old at the time. His birth
certificate gave his father's and mother's surnames as
Jones and Smith. His birth name, Harry Jones, struck
me as pure invention. Or maybe you could say part joke
and part invention.

Some of my favourite memories of my father are
from his days with Trans-Canada Air Lines, later re-
named Air Canada, which he joined in 1947, the company's eleventh year. He spent twenty-three years, all in
London, Ontario, working for the company. And for
many years, right up to his forced retirement in 1970 at
age fifty-seven — Air Canada having elected to cut, if I
remember correctly, three hundred executives from
coast to coast — he held the top position, locally, as Dis-
trict Sales Manager. So my father, like yours, was a
salesman — though I actually think of him more as
someone who gave his life to public service. And I, like
you, am a salesman's son. And also, like you, an only
child, an only son.

As a kid, in the 1950s, I would ask my father to take
me down to the CPR station in London, Ontario because I liked to watch the trains come in. This proved
to be quite comic because men would come up to my

dad and say, "Well, if it isn't Jack Struthers. What are you doing here? Couldn't you get the planes off the ground today?" And I can remember my dad on innumerable occasions introducing himself with a big smile and a firm handshake and saying, "Hi, I'm Jack," or else just giving his name, "Jack Struthers." He *wasn't* "Jack" by birth, he wasn't "Jack Struthers," but that's certainly what he became.

What I'm getting to, what I want to tell you, is how deeply I was moved by a passage from the closing segment of autobiography in *Resident Alien* that describes your mother's family and the traits particularly of the men in her family. You're talking about Winnipeg and you say, "Right now, it is still a hard, Siberian winter day. Winnipeg should not exist, except as an urban planner's act of defiance, an experiment on the heartless Russian model. Yet it does exist, like Edmonton exists, like Montreal exists, and the effects of that anomaly — the intense communalism, the isolation, the pride, the shame and absurdity of carrying on normal life at forty below zero — create a population of stubborn, sceptical survivalists, hungry for recognition and certification, a people born with the ache of anonymity and the conviction that they'll always have something to prove. All of which leads to that bone-proud prairie loneliness, the suspicion of anyone who's had it easier — east, west, or south. In my mother's family, self-reliance was a creed; bottled-up and bitten-back, no grief was exposed, no help asked for, though none was refused."

My father didn't explain much to me about his background, didn't explain much to me about Winnipeg, for example — though once or twice when I was still a kid we did spend a day or so there when my father took me north for a week to a friend's fishing lodge on Waterbury Lake in northern Saskatchewan. Something that I'm sure you would appreciate based on your own experiences of going fishing with your father. And my father may have pointed out various things about himself to me then, and on other travels together, that I was too young to interpret, or perhaps even too young to recognize as important, things that I seem to have forgotten. But I wanted to mention these details, these correspondences, in order to convey the depth to which that passage of yours struck home for me, in order to suggest how much it explained about my father's attitudes and conceivably some of mine.

Another bit of synchronicity between us is that when my dad was still a boy — in the early to mid-1920s I suppose — his father took his family to live for a short time in Florida. I know nothing about this. And my only knowledge of the American South — other than a tourist's view of Florida that I acquired when my parents and I flew down there a couple of times for a short vacation while I was very young, then later when Marianne and I drove down there once for a few days at Christmastime the year we met — has come through reading Southern writers, in which company, in some respects, I would include you. I know that you spent a hugely formative period, roughly from age six to age ten, living in north-central Florida during the mid- to late 1940s. I was wondering if you would describe the sense that you formed then, the sense that you carry now, of that landscape — the importance of that landscape to you as an artist.

CB: First of all, what you say about your own background and Winnipeg and the feeling that your father disguised himself in a sense all of his life seems to me to be part of the myth that is enacted between fathers and sons universally. I can think of no father who really confesses the important things of his life to his son. So that even a father who was seemingly in essence a good father, a warm and supportive father, has withheld from you the vital statistics of his life — his name, his origins — as did my father. So that in a sense every son has to invent his own father, every son is left with this void of who his father really was. Part of it is shame because no father wants to tell his son of the women, the world, that pre-existed his son's birth. And part of it is the son's feeling that the father didn't really exist before he came along anyway, that the father is not allowed to have a life before he became a father, when he was just another guy knocking around.

The myth of Canada and Florida is, I think, easy to explain. These are the attractions of polar opposites, quite literally polar opposites, North to South — in my case also compounded by French to English. We love and fear, are attracted to and repulsed by, those forces that we consider to be opposite to our own. We feel somehow that we can draw strength from them.

I clearly am my mother's son and yet, while not rejecting her and her background, I find, as you can see even from the part that you read from *Resident Alien*, they are alien people to me. I am not at all part of their self-reliance and their hardiness and their pride and their isolation and their defiant impregnability. I'm not that at all and I'm not attracted to those kinds of people. Even as much as I might admire them, I'm not attracted to them particularly. And as much as I love and respect my mother, or the memory of my mother and what she went through and what she survived, I feel that her very quality of survival was really her greatest weakness. Her strength was her weakness. The fact that she was so obviously capable of surmounting difficulty almost guaranteed that she would be given a huge helping of disaster in her life. Catastrophe stalked her, largely because she could prove that she could surmount it so often. Her life became an evidentiary show of her ability to survive.

My mother told me everything about herself. I think there's really nothing from her life that she left secret. It was all laid out for me. I had all the tools, all the details. She was a wonderful storyteller. And she told me all the stories of her life. My father told me *nothing*, nothing at all, including his earlier marriages, his name, his upbringing. If I'd known anything about any part of his life, I think it would have unravelled him as a person because I would have started asking him questions. Sooner or later the whole terrible history of French Canada at the turn of the twentieth century, his marriages, his brutality, his divorces, his women would have all come tumbling out and it would probably have been horrendous.

So I think it's true that your story, while it's dramatic and illustrative, and my story, while it's dramatic and illustrative, are probably no different, except in the more lurid colours, from the stories of most boys and their fathers of our generation or of the generation immediately afterwards. I think now, with the prevailing ethos of male vulnerability and friendliness and openness and all these things that are probably the result of the new kinds of child-raising techniques, perhaps that world of mysteries might be a little bit less available, or less inevitable.

Certainly I come from a generation of people who were secret to the world, and in many ways to themselves, and who could not share even the first level of intimacy. All the desire for intimacy, or the desire to explain oneself, then, took the form only of sexuality, or of criminality in my father's case, or of aggressive salesmanship, so that he was in a sense saying to the people he sold furniture to, his customers, not "Do you want a sofa?" but "Who am I? Tell me who I am. Confirm to me, by buying this sofa, that I exist."

TS: It was his work and his ambitions that took you down to Florida.

CB: Well, I think in an overt way it was. But I think in a covert way it was something else. His ambitions took him as far south as Atlanta in 1946. He quit Sears, which had been his employer for eight years in various parts of the States — North Dakota, where I was born, and Cincinnati, and Pittsburgh. Sears did not give much money at all as a salary, but it did have a very generous parting package. So he took his accumulated money from eight years' wartime service to Sears and invested immediately in a little showroom he started in Atlanta which failed within a very short time. Then he was obliged to go back on the road as a travelling salesman and the only territory that opened up for him was in Florida. Florida at that time was not an attractive place to be. Florida was the back of beyond in some ways in the mid-forties, especially since he was not allowed to do any selling in the territory of Jacksonville or Miami or Tampa. He was given south Georgia, south Alabama, and north Florida.

And so he simply established himself. I don't know how it came about that he established himself in Leesburg, Florida, but that's where he rented a little second-floor-rear apartment in a small Southern town in 1947. That was the first place I remember with *real* vividness. I was back there just a few months ago giving a reading at the University of Central Florida, which is in Orlando — it's a fairly new university — and the professor who had invited me, Anna Lillios, and I went back to Leesburg where I was able to point out to her every single building, every single street.

We went to the very house that I had lived in and talked to the people who are living in it now. The street has not changed. It has been paved, but other than that it hasn't changed. The houses are exactly as they were — typical Florida thirties or twenties construction, with screened-in porches and bungalows on stilts and everyone keeping hound dogs tied up against the stilts. And there was an old toothless woman with a big chaw of tobacco in her mouth, reading, if she could read — I don't remember if she was reading, maybe she was listening, maybe she was being read to by her grandchild — out on the very porch that I as a kid had lain on. I was asking her about the names of people. I remembered vividly all the names of all the people in all the little houses. And she kept going back, saying, "Well, I been here since 1953 and ain't never seen nothin' like that here." And I would say to her, "Well, I was here in 1947." She may have looked the role of the Big Mama from Florida and she may have looked like and sounded like a typical Florida Cracker but actually I pre-dated her there and I was the Cracker if anyone was.

And the professor who was with me was so amused that I was telling this old remnant of the Old South more things about her neighbourhood than she knew. She was denying them. But I said, "No, if you go back there, you'll find there's an old fish pond that has obviously now been filled in, and this particular laundry house in the back is where my mother had her spontaneous abortion that I wrote about in my novel *Lunar Attractions*."

You know, in the sense that "I own this land out of memory and blood more than you do." In the Faulknerian sense. "Even though you've been living here unbrokenly for forty years, I was here forty-five years ago."

TS: A more general question has to do with the entirety of a writer's inheritance. You've been speaking about your family inheritance — on your mother's side, English-Canadian from Western Canada, and on your father's side, French-Canadian from Quebec. Something else that I'm interested in is the inheritance you gained from your formal education. As an undergraduate you studied geology, didn't you?

CB: Geology and English and religion, as a matter of fact. I could have taken a degree in either English or geology, depending on the comprehensive exam. I had the hours for either. Since the trend in my life at the time was towards English and away from science, I chose to do my comprehensive exam in English and not geology.

TS: That's very interesting. To use a geological metaphor, however, what I'm wondering about more broadly are the various layers of a writer's inheritance. But maybe "layers" isn't exactly the right metaphor. Maybe something spread out in space would be better. Specifically, what I want to ask is how you as a writer, and a teacher of creative writing, would describe a writer's inheritance: a writer's family inheritance and geographical landscape, any religious beliefs that have come down through a writer's upbringing, any literary influences derived from a writer's formal education and personal reading, any cultural influences in later life — through marriage, for example. You married a Bengali-born woman, Bharati Mukherjee. I married an American woman of Greek descent. I'm wondering how you would describe the different dimensions — maybe that's the word I want — of a writer's inheritance.

CB: Well, that's really the subject of the book I have coming out in the spring of 1993, called *I Had a Father*, which is trying to deal with the whole bundle of Quebec and Catholicism and the dark mysterious forces of death and doom and fatalism and Jansenism. And all of that obviously formed my father and, by extension, formed a lot of myself. Because I'm also trying to deal with the genetic impulse of a son who never *really* knew his father, nevertheless growing older and realizing that he is enacting the father's life almost helplessly. I don't know if it's inherited. In fact, I have a riff on the word "inheritance." I have a paragraph where I quote a Thoreau line, "Books are the treasured wealth of the world, the fit inheritance of generations and nations." And I talk about the word "inheritance" having a kind of dual nature — that is, it's both what comes down to you and what you leave behind. So "inheritance" is one of those forward-looking, backward-looking, Janus-like words. I don't know what an inheritance is. It's as much what I leave behind as what I have picked up.

The image I use is not of layers, the metaphor I use is not of layers, it's from astronomy: the idea that we who could train our telescopes on the planet Neptune at the turn of the twentieth century, studying the orbit of Neptune, knew that there was something out there beyond Neptune that was causing what they called a perturbation in the orbit of Neptune. In other words, we knew where it was, we knew how big it was, but we couldn't see it because we didn't have the technology, the light-gathering devices. So I say in this book that we knew the geography of ontogeny but we didn't yet see it and it wasn't until the technology or the statistics or the documentation came in that we were able to find Pluto. And so Pluto completes the cast of characters of the solar system.

In many ways that's how I think of parents. They are the things that perturb your own orbit and make you not quite the smooth, friction-free, spinning orb in the universe that you would like to be. Instead you have gravitational affinities that you cannot explain or cannot escape. It's because they are out there, the dark stars of your parentage or of your inheritance, bumping you out of a smooth orbit.

TS: Are there consolations in this? [Laughter.]

CB: Constellations or consolations? [Laughter.] I think perhaps the main consolation is that you realize that you are only such things as they made you. You are born with the illusion of being free and being able to create your own life and being utterly your own agent in the world. And you realize as you grow older and older that you were never free and that the tribe, the language, the country, the culture you were born into, however much you define yourself against them, are in fact what define you. Whether you conform to their expectations or fight against them, it doesn't matter: you are them.

In the case of a son, he almost inevitably becomes the father — no matter how much he had fought against the father, no matter how much he had defined himself against the father. I don't know a single man my age who has lost his father years before who wouldn't want him back, who doesn't miss the connection. No matter how much they fought, or how little they had in common, that relationship is the vital one in their lives. So that's a consolation.

Another consolation, I suppose, is simply that it doesn't matter how ragged or how imperfect the relationship was. Age will in some way perfect it and in fact will make you more or less identical to the father. And I suppose the sad thing is that it doesn't matter how good your relationship was. Age will in a sense darken it, age will roughen it up a bit. If the relationship was a perfect image of father-son solidarity in wonderful communal wholeness, the son will break away. If the relationship was a ragged and fractured one, the son will heal it.

TS: You seem equally capable of rendering that sort of archetypal situation between father and son as a horrifying scene in fiction and as a delightful scene in fiction. To me, one of your most moving descriptions is the long paragraph at the end of the title story of your first book, *A North American Education*, where Frankie Thibidault sits with his father for an hour on a bench at a beach in Florida, with a hurricane breaking offshore, after his mother has returned to the car ...

CB: "What a day it was, what a once-in-a-lifetime day it was."

TS: Yes. And in this context, it seems to me, it would also be interesting to look at a couple of scenes from your autobiographical writing. In "Tenants of Unhousement," the long essay or memoir which you published in *The Iowa Review* in 1982 and which you told me you had hoped to include with related material in *Resident Alien*, you describe a scene at Lac Mégantic in Quebec, the one scene your father revealed to you from his past ...

CB: His father skating out on Lac Mégantic with his arms out in the buffalo robe.

TS: Yes. And somehow — in terms of positive father-son scenes — I connect this with the wonderful passage, in the opening segment of autobiography in *Resident Alien*, in which you describe your mentor, Bernard Malamud, coming down to Boston to the bookstore where you worked for several months before starting your MFA at Iowa.

CB: Signing his books and saying, "A deposit on Blaise's freedom ..."

TS: "... for the afternoon." Then taking you out for a walk.

Certainly I find interviews to be, for myself, very much that sort of special occasion. In a way I dread them in that I doubt whether I'm going to be well enough prepared. I think that despite all my years of study of the writer's work, and my love for the writer's work, I will arrive with far too modest knowledge and understanding. But I also live for interviews. And I think that they are among the best moments of my intellectual and my personal life.

The Sense of an Authentic Randomness: An Interview with Clark Blaise [1988]

Catherine Sheldrick Ross

CSR: Because I am writing a biocritical introduction to your papers held in Special Collections at The University of Calgary Libraries, I am interested in the biographical aspect of your work. Perhaps you can help me by filling in some gaps. One is your mother.

CB: She died last year, 1987, on February 5th I think it was, in Winnipeg.

CSR: I got the feeling from the story "Meditations on Starch," which you read last night at the conference on the Canadian short story Tim Struthers is hosting here in Guelph, that your mother was a much stronger presence in that story than she had been allowed to be in some of the others.

CB: I wanted to do justice to her, to the extraordinary person she was. I think I was feeling very strongly the full terrors of Alzheimer's disease. For someone who had seen as much of the century as she had and who had absorbed so much of it—to see that all of that is lost. There is not a more profound loss in the universe than blown brain cells, which is what happens to people with Alzheimer's. It's the cruellest parody of loss for a person who asserted her independence against a very strong and patriarchal family and simply demanded that she be independent and worked so hard to achieve it and

15

did all of the things that are not permissible. To see that she became nothing — there's the tragedy of that which I felt someone had to demark. And I also feel that it's probably going to be my fate as well.

CSR: There's a similar theme in *Resident Alien*.

CB: There I took on the disease of epilepsy, which I don't have. I wanted to give a very provisional sense of sanity or health.

CSR: You were saying last night that the book you would like to write next is the one in which identity is stripped back, layer by layer. That is really the process of Alzheimer's disease.

CB: Yes. Right. You just keep falling from ledges. You're on a plateau for a bit and you fall off that plateau and back and back and back.

CSR: Your mother was born in North Battleford, Saskatchewan?

CB: No. Wawanesa, Manitoba. But North Battleford was part of her childhood. Her family went from Wawanesa to North Battleford.

CSR: Could you give me a quick sketch of what she did, because I think I have a lot of gaps there.

CB: She was born in Wawanesa. Her father was the town doctor and he was a horse breeder and also a fruit breeder. He was in the first class of the University of Manitoba medical school. His father was born in England and came to Canada as a child. He left Kincardine, Ontario and went west to be a master carpenter and work on the houses of parliament in Winnipeg. Much of the interior of the Manitoba parliament was done by him.

So my mother was born in Wawanesa, a tiny little town on the Souris River, south of Brandon near the North Dakota and Saskatchewan borders. Those were my mother's most pleasant memories. She was the eldest of ten children. There were two boys and one died in infancy.

There have been many tributes written about my grandfather. He was a very famous man. I have a few of them framed at home because he was very much "The Canadian Century" and embodied the best of that breed. He became President of Wawanesa Mutual. He was the man who took it from prairie co-op into national insurance company.

CSR: And his name was Vanstone.

CB: Yes. Charles Morley Vanstone. There were a number of little towns that they lived in where he had a medical practice. But it was horse breeding that he really loved — the importing of Clydesdales and selling them to American farmers. That was what made him very wealthy.

Then when the Depression came, it destroyed him. By age fifty or so, he was hundreds of thousands of dollars in debt to his breeders in Scotland. That's when he went into Wawanesa Mutual as Chief Executive Officer and brought it around and brought himself around and once again became a prosperous person. He was a man of rectitude and honour.

I never knew him. His Alzheimer's disease had taken him totally away by the time I saw him. I saw him frequently, but he never knew who I was or who my mother was or who he was. He was just this tyrannical figure running around the house in Winnipeg.

CSR: You give an image of this figure in *Resident Alien*.

CB: Yes. Underlining newspapers. It was a tragic thing, because my mother was more attached to him than to any person, aside from myself, in her life.

My mother went to Wesley College, what is now the University of Winnipeg, and graduated in 1927 in art —

I think Canadians are not fond of people who leave. There's still that strong nationalist sense that if you're not on the scene contributing to the culture, you don't count. In Canada, we have such a cozy community. It's very moving to see. When you are in Canada and with your tribe of writers — Margaret Laurence called it that — you realize what a supportive and wonderful and warm bunch of people they are. You can step right into it — although there are always new names coming up — and you have a place, you have a niche. I don't have that niche in the States.

I know an awful lot of writers in the world. I know all of them in Canada and I have a comparable file of friends, writers, down in the States. But there's no community of writers there. That sense of a tribe of writers or a community of writers is not present. Everyone is an individual with their own career in mind. There's not a sense that you are creating the consciousness of your race.

CSR: What difference do you think this is going to make to your own writing?

CB: I can only think it will be disastrous. Catastrophic. Just like a stroke. I really do feel cut off. I don't have an audience.

As I was saying last night, when you are writing for an audience that is already half-creating the work for you, that already knows where you are coming from and what you are saying and is already a participant in your work, it makes it very easy. Sometimes it worries me that it's too easy — at its worst, you end up playing the game of a writer, simply pushing buttons and pulling levers. But I think one is always buoyed up by an audience, like any performer, like any artist.

You work hard to create an audience, to create a world that is recognizably your own and that people respond in art teaching. Her father absolutely forbade any kind of artistic career. So she worked for three years teaching in prairie towns: Guernsey, Saskatchewan and Dauphin, Manitoba and Minnedosa, Manitoba — places that sound like a Margaret Laurence story. She had some pictures of the main street of Guernsey, Saskatchewan that would break your heart.

Then in 1930 she said, "I'm going to Europe to be an artist" and by that time he couldn't stop her. She was twenty-seven years old and she went to Germany. She was there in Dresden and Dessau. She was studying design in Dresden and making frequent trips to Dessau to audit classes at the Bauhaus. To me it's an extra-ordinary thought that she was this girl from prairie Canada in the midst of the Bauhaus studying interior design with high functional modernism. Also at the same time she was drawing those heavily ornamental German cathedral doors and Dresden pottery and Meissen ware and porcelains that come out of that area of now East Germany — Leipzig-Dresden, that area.

She was there in 1933 when Hitler came to power. She fled, like everyone else in that school, and went to Prague, where she lived for a year by doing sketching and models for fashion design. Then she went to London where she worked for two years as a fashion designer before being called back to Montreal to be head deco-rator at Eaton's. In 1937 she came to Eaton's and that's how she ran into my father, who was a furniture sales-man on the floor.

CSR: The word "accident" comes to mind. I get the sense that a lot of your stories are about accident. It's a reso-nant word in your work.

CB: Yes. How else can I put it? I want to write a fiction which is sufficiently broad to contain random, chaotic, accidental qualities. There's nothing more moving in fiction to me than the sense of an authentic randomness. I want to create a fiction that is sufficiently broad so that it can contain the notion of all of the accidents and contradictability that are part of life itself. If I can do that, I'll be happy. My own life has not at all been a series of predictable turns.

CSR: When I think about your work, even the novels read to me like short stories. Yet from what you're saying, you have an interest in doing novels. You're not like, say, Alice Munro, who tried to write novels and then said, "I guess I'm not a novelist. I'll do short stories or inter-locked stories." You have an interest still in the novel.

CB: For me, the short story is an expansionist form, not a miniaturizing form. To me, the novel is a miniaturizing form. I think of the story as the largest, most expanded statement you can make about a particular incident. I think of the novel as the briefest thing you can say about a larger incident. I think of the novel as being far more miniaturist — it's a miniaturization of life. And short fiction is an expansion of a moment.

CSR: So you want to be able to keep writing both those forms.

CB: I would like to keep both those options open.

CSR: We've been talking a bit about accident. One of the themes that I keep coming across in reading your stories is that moment when the character discovers that his name is not what he thought it was. He thought it was Porter but it's Carrier. He thought it was Desjardins but it's Gardner. In your case it was ...

CB: From Blais to Blaise.

CSR: Was this in fact a striking moment for you, the way it was for your characters?

CB: No. Well, I think it probably was. Yes. It seems to me

like an entirely different universe — Blais as opposed to Blaise. Blais does look truncated and, in a sense, inexpressible: Bluh, Bleh, Blah. There are all sorts of possible variants in pronunciation. I regretted not being able to claim myself as part of that community of Blais — the pages after pages after pages in the Montreal phone book of the very commonest French-Canadian name. The only Blaises were Max and Rudi, the two Swiss-German Protestant Blaises. I wasn't part of their world either. In New York, there are a lot of Blaises and they're all Haitians — French West Indian names.

CSR: But it does come back to the business of identity.

CB: Yes. Of course. And having it tampered with in some profound way.

CSR: Yesterday at the conference Tim Struthers mentioned the statement you made to Geoff Hancock after the publication of your first novel, *Lunar Attractions* — that you were going to take up questions very removed from autobiography and first-person explorations of identity. But what you've been saying about your more recent work sounds like it's still first-person ...

CB: Well, many of the stories in this new book of stories are not first-person and none of them is what I would call autobiographical. The one I read last night, "Meditations on Starch," is very intertwined with what's really autobiographical and what's not. My mother didn't have any of those experiences. She's not of that background. My younger son is not that son. My younger son is very profoundly aware of the twentieth century and what it means. But it's true that my wife has a cousin in Vienna that we stayed with. And it's true that I went one day with my son and his cousin to the Freud Museum. There's no more autobiography in that than in most writers' stories. I have a large number of stories in this book that are totally invented and they are in third-person.

I really don't feel that I'm writing in the least autobiographically anymore. I'm not seeking to complete myself in these stories or to exploit parts of myself. I'm not adding anything to my personal myth. These are stories that may use the autobiographical form or an autobiographical voice or tone, if I'm writing in first-person, but I'm not fooled for a minute that they have anything to do with me. They're art; they're not me. I have a story called "Did, Had, Was" that is an Alzheimer's disease story from the inside. The point of view is very difficult, because everything that is presented as fact is perhaps fantasy. What he projects as having happened to other people may have happened to him.

CSR: It's like the difficulty of trying to do a Benjy in Faulkner's *The Sound and the Fury*.

CB: Yes. Except that it's not a first-person story; it's not that close to being inside him. It's a limited third-person story. But it jumps around a lot in his mind. The only thing that is autobiographical in it is I've projected the kind of tragedy that I feel Alzheimer's is. The wiping out not only of the individual life but the wiping out of a culture — in the sense that each individual is a separate culture. The culture of this particular individual is the culture of a French-Canadian journalist who has been stationed in Asia. He's coming home to take over the Deanship of a School of Journalism in Ottawa. No one realizes that they have bought into some very damaged goods. By the time he gets back after a slow progress from Hong Kong to Paris to Ottawa, although he has good intentions to do a lot of things, he will never be able to pull it all together.

CSR: One of the things I've been trying to piece together

is just where you have been. It gets harder after you leave Canada. Can you tell me what happened to you after you left Toronto in 1980?

CB: I went to Saratoga Springs, New York. In 1980-81, I taught at Skidmore College. We had a house there, a mansion actually. With our Toronto money, it was very easy to buy real estate. We had an alternating contract, my wife and I. I would be on for one year and she would be on for one year. So she started out in 1979-80 at Skidmore. And I came there in 1980-81. Then in 1981-82 she was at Skidmore. At that time I was at the University of Iowa teaching in the Writers' Workshop. The boys and I went to Iowa City in 1981-82. They loved it and they hated Saratoga Springs. The school there was a terrible school — it was Appalachia north.

By that time our older boy, Bart, was a senior in high school and the younger one, Bernard, was in grade eight or grade nine. The younger one said, "We've never lived more than two years in one place." And that was true. We hadn't, after his first few years in Montreal. He said, "I don't want to move again. I want to stay here." Seeing the pattern that had been my father's pattern, I agreed. The Writers' Workshop offered Bharati a job the following year, 1982-83. I had to go back to Saratoga Springs for my last year at Skidmore. But the kids stayed. We rented a very small place. Bart graduated from high school and then started at the University of Iowa. We stayed until 1985, until our younger son, Bernard, graduated from high school. He graduated a year ahead of his class in November. So he went on to Vienna for the rest of the year and got a certificate in German at the University of Vienna, staying with the cousins.

We were in Iowa City then with no money. We had no jobs. For three years we lived really on the proceeds from the sale of our house in Saratoga Springs plus the writing. I wrote *Lusts* there and *Lusts* came out then.

Then in the winter of 1984 Bharati got a job — an offer right out of the blue, one of those accidents that saves your life. She got a request from Emory University to come down as writer-in-residence for a semester in Atlanta. She hadn't published a book in six years and she was in a very desperate psychological state. She was very, very low, very depressed. The whole Canadian experience had devastated her. I had gotten a job at the David Thompson University Centre in Nelson, British Columbia. One semester, in the fall of 1983, I was up there in Nelson sending money down so that we could survive — Canadian money and not very much of it, so that money was very, very tight. The next semester Bharati was off to Atlanta sending money back, while I was in Iowa City with the kids. So someone always stayed with the kids. At Emory, she wrote almost all of the stories in *Darkness* in a burst of energy.

CSR: Yes. She says that in the introduction to *Darkness*.

CB: Yes. Right. It saved her life. It saved her creative and psychological life. Then Montclair State, New Jersey offered her a job. She went out to Montclair State the following fall and started there and was writing more. She was starting to write the stories that came out in *The Middleman.* I had to wait in Iowa City until our younger son graduated from high school in 1985. As soon as he graduated, we sold that house and moved to New York. By that time it was the fall of 1985. We interrupted the writing that we were doing to do the Air India book. We got a little apartment in Long Island City, and by that time Columbia had asked me to teach in the graduate program.

Bharati was teaching at Montclair State, New Jersey

and I was going up to Toronto every week to interview people. As soon as my contract with Columbia was over, I came up to Canada to finish the interviewing of the victim families in Toronto. Then I went out to Vancouver and hooked up with the terrorists themselves. Then I went to Ireland in the summer of 1986 to interview the hospital people and to be there during the one-year memorial service. We finished the book in 1986.

Then I saw a sign saying "Sublet a Columbia Professor's apartment." So we were able to take that for a year in 1986-87. And then, when the sublet year was over in August 1987, we had to find a place that we could buy. With the money that was in my mother's account when she died, about $20,000, we were able to buy the tiny little apartment that we have now. I've had two terms as writer-in-residence at Emory. I followed the semester after Bharati and for the past few summers I've been the Director of the summer writing programs at Emory. So Atlanta has become a kind of secondary home — not a "home," but it's a familiar world and we have a whole set of friends down there that we reactivate every summer.

Bharati has become a very, very major force in American writing. And I have not. I have none of that visibility on the American scene at all. It's a total reversal of what our situation was in Canada, where she had no presence in the Canadian scene during the fifteen years that we were here and I had it all. Now it's a reversal.

CSR: Like crossing a mirror.

CB: Yes. America has given her the power to write and has freed her imagination because she has found an audience. Whereas Canada had done that for me.

CSR: So you feel that you've lost something.

CB: I've lost it. I think I really have lost it. I'm now a historical footnote in Canada. I'm someone who left and to. It takes many, many years to do that. I gave it many, many years. But that world doesn't always export; it doesn't always transport. So I don't have that audience in the States. I don't have that readiness of an audience to know who I am or what I am or what it is I'm talking about.

Relatively speaking, the message that I have for Canada is very central to the central dilemma of being Canadian. Identity and all of its tortures. The question doesn't arise and doesn't exist in the States. My personal agony is mirrored as a national concern in Canada. It becomes nothing more than a crazy guy who doesn't know who he is in the States.

CSR: Whereas Bharati's experience, which is the immigrant experience, is a more resonant story for Americans.

CB: Yes. Exactly. The idea of becoming American is very appealing and very moving in the American mythology.

CSR: A writer from the Caribbean was interviewed on CBC Radio. He had come here and had become very successful as a writer.

CB: Neil Bissoondath, probably.

CSR: Yes. That's right. It was. And what struck me was his comment that Canada says to the immigrant, "You can still keep your community. We aren't a melting pot. We want multiculturalism." He said, "That's no good. That's not really a country." I get the same feeling with Bharati that she resented ...

CB: Very strongly. She hated it. She very much rejects the notion of the mosaic. The mosaic is something created by Pierre Trudeau. It's not a fundamental part of Canadian consciousness. It was a political expediency, a political sop thrown to the western ethnic, namely the Ukrainian. To say that if you are going to force French down the English gullets in the West and force English down the French gullets in Quebec, then what about this third force out here that is neither French nor English. So they created this multiculturalism notion. I think it fed everybody's desire in Canada to say that we have something that is not American. It served an awful lot of agendas simultaneously.

CSR: What I seem to be hearing is that the experience you had in Canada was the shadow side of the Canadian identity. We like to think that multiculturalism is a good thing. Yet in the experience of the people who are marginalized by it, it can become another form of racism.

CB: Yes. It becomes very much a form of racism. Also it creates petty little tyrants. It creates warlords. It creates people who become spokespeople for their community so that you end up with all of these hyphenated-Canadians and with money going to those who can identify themselves as the spokespeople for their group.

That's fundamental to what happened in the Air India tragedy. We have marginalized people who have not a hope of joining the mainstream, who have neither the skills nor the language, and who are alienated by the mainstream. They are nevertheless protected and patronized by spokespeople within their group, the Punjabi-Canadians, who control the lives and destinies of dozens, if not hundreds, of the fundamentalist faithful in the interior of B.C. and on Vancouver Island. These are the people who do the dirty work.

CSR: What made you decide to do the Air India book?

CB: Very much from reading in the ethnic press, the Indian press, in the United States what was being said by November 1985, four months after the crash, by the bereaved members of the families about the people who had been lost. They said that had this not been an

Air India tragedy, the Canadian government would have responded more sympathetically and with greater alacrity — the government would have seen it as a Canadian tragedy. They said, "Our losses are not being taken seriously."

The Canadian government denied that this was ever on their minds. And so we thought, "Is it so or not?" That's what started it. But by the time we finished, the government admitted that they had been very slow to respond. Had it been an Alitalia plane, or had it been a British Airways plane bombed by an Irish-Canadian cell, there would have been all hell to pay. Canadians would have seen it as an attack on Canada. This was seen as alien or foreign, even though everyone who was lost and everyone who did it was Canadian.

CSR: So this is the "unhousement" of the tragedy.

CB: Yes. And it's very much a function of multiculturalism going terribly wrong. As soon as you start saying there's multiculturalism and the mosaic, then some people are more Canadian than others. If you want to be an anti-Semite in Canada, then the government is going to take you on, as in the Ernst Zündel case in Alberta. If you want to be anti-French in Manitoba, the government is going to take you on. But if you want to be anti-Indian in the Punjabi press in Vancouver, the government is not going to give a shit. When people complained that there were actual newspaper articles published in the Punjabi press saying, "Go out and kill this person, an enemy of the faith," and when they wanted to have protection, the cops would patronizingly say, "You guys settle it." They were decidedly treating it as a less serious matter.

CSR: It sounds as if, to do this book back in Canada, both of you had to confront some painful experiences.

CB: Yes. It was the most painful book that one could possibly imagine. It was very painful, even if we were not personally involved. It was very painful spending hours and hours and hours interviewing people who had lost their wives, their children. It's that empathetic pain — pity and rage. But also there's the confrontational fear when you are actually being taken into the homes and temples of people who are gleeful about what they did.

CSR: In *Resident Alien,* you use the word "emblematic" to refer to your experience.

CB: I feel as though we're both emblematic characters. Bharati is always ahead of her time, an emblem of someone who emigrated and married and did all sorts of things that are against the rules in a very structured society. By the same token, I've tried to reverse the natural flow of things. My parents anticipated that they had created an American. I encounter people all the time who say, "My parents are from Canada," but who have never been to Canada. To them, Canada is like Idaho is, some alien part of the United States.

I don't know what it is that made Canada so real to me that it became a compulsion to go back to it. But in a sense I reversed the flow of history. I did something that an immigrant shouldn't do. Immigrants in the United States should say, "Thank God I'm an American. It's the most wonderful thing in the world." You don't find many Italian-Americans going back to Sicily.

CSR: Here we've been talking about the melting pot. You resisted the melting pot.

CB: I don't know that I resisted the melting pot. I'm very much a melted American. It's not as if there's some remnant that refused to be assimilated. I'm a totally assimilated American. But it didn't satisfy some other aspect

—I don't know what. I think it's that my parents were unassimilated. It was because of the fact that my parents were never there in the States, really, that I was never there in some aspect. I was ninety-nine per cent there but not that one per cent. The thing is that artistically I was not there.

CSR: There's a passage in *Resident Alien* in which you are in Milwaukee and feel called to come to Canada. You go to Montreal and there's the moment in which you say, "I'm leaving my swampy past all behind me. I'm a new person." The amazing thing, you said, is that it worked. So your Montreal experience sustained you.

CB: Yes. It still does. Everything that I thought would happen did happen. It wasn't wrong for me. It wasn't wrong just for myself to have done what I did. And I think that if I had stayed I would have continued to build on that. Probably what I would have done was to write the novel that I felt I should write, which is the novel of my father's life. Really writing a turn-of-the-century Quebec novel and taking the character up through Prohibition and through his boxing career and his marriages. I would have created a real, rounded, nineteenth-century kind of character. A Dickensian kind of character. Or a Célinesque kind of character, anyway. A lowlife, *demimondaine* character. And I think I would have had the confidence and the audience to do that. Now I don't. So instead of writing that book, I will eventually write the fragmented one that I talked about.

CSR: You think it takes confidence to write certain kinds of novels.

CB: Right. I don't know if I will ever be able to write an aggressive novel, a novel based on the positive delineation of a character, as opposed to a subtractive novel in which I am taking away from the character. That is, if I were to write a story about my father, it would be a very traditional nineteenth-century kind of novel in a twentieth-century voice. It would almost be a Rodin-like creation of a brooding, thick, dense character. Instead I'm going to have to write, it seems to me, some Cubist thing where you're looking at fragments and angles.

Yes. It takes a great deal of confidence to do the other kind of novel. You can do that when you are speaking authoritatively from the centre of a culture, when you are speaking authoritatively from the centre of an experience that you are the master of. I don't really have any place that I'm the master of or any place that I know from beginning to end. My life has always been a matter of beginnings that have no middles — or middles that have no beginnings. So that's why short stories are a far more conducive form for me, why I've done more stories than novels. I can only envy people who have that great vertical command of a place and of material. I don't.

CSR: Can you say a bit more about writing *Resident Alien*?

CB: I wanted to write about a world that was reasonably sunlit and clear and lucid from my mother's point of view and that was tortured and sick at its core from my father's point of view. I wanted to put the two together and show that it was possible in one life to live in both worlds, to have access to those worlds. I felt that as a real statement about how a segment of North America is. And I wanted also to be true to things that had died, things that had passed, things that are no more, like the South that I had known as a child, the Quebec that I had known, and the really twisted Jansenist Catholicism of the pre-René-Lévesque, pre-gentrified Montreal.

I wanted to be faithful to all of those experiences. I wanted to be faithful to a Canada that was still authoritatively British, confident. My sense of English Canada was always its confidence. I never knew a Canada that had an inferiority complex *vis-à-vis* anywhere. Especially the States. People in Canada *pitied* the States. My relatives in Winnipeg — what did they know of the States? They only knew North Dakota. There was no comparison between the lifestyle of my relatives in Winnipeg — the culture they commanded, the sophistication they had — as opposed to people in Grand Forks. So I wanted to be faithful to the fact that it was a Canada of virtue and rectitude and resolution and confidence. I wanted to get all of those things in.

CSR: Is there anything important to you that I've forgotten to ask?

CB: No. I think you're up to date.

Something That Cannot Be Contained: An Interview with Clark Blaise [1998]

Nicholas Johnson

NJ: Clark and I talked about beginning tonight's event as sort of a conversation. Then I will fade into the woodwork as he does a reading later on.

We met earlier this year, in April I believe it was, on an airplane. We happened to be sitting next to each other. I had heard of him, of course, and, not only that, had extolled his virtues as a part of my forty-five-second stand-up routine that I'm compelled to do on the East Coast and West Coast of North America when asked the question, "Iowa, Nick. Why would you want to be in Iowa?" And then I launch into all my Iowa brags, and Clark was always well up on that list. But I had not in fact met him, nor had I, at that point, I'm really embarrassed to confess, read any of his great works.

And after a very stimulating conversation on the plane during which we discussed the similarities and differences of our two fathers, I found in inter-campus mail the next morning an autographed book, this very book here, *I Had a Father*. And I was so taken by this fellow I had met on the plane that I dropped everything and did nothing that morning but read the book and send him an e-mail about how wonderful it was.

I have been intimidated ever since at the prospect of ever writing myself, notwithstanding the inscription to me which was, "Now it's time for you to get on with your own." My wife, Mary Vasey, who teaches at Metro High School here in Cedar Rapids, got me into a writing program this summer in Iowa City. But I'm having difficulty doing the kinds of things that Clark does with such seeming ease.

I thought, first of all, that I would survey some topics that I want to ask questions about, some of which he and I have already talked about at one time or another.

One, and the most obvious I suppose, is the content of the book, the story of his life, the insights about his father, the places where he lived.

A second would be the structure of the book. Members of the audience who have read the book may have been taken, as I was, by the brilliance of his ability to weave from description of person to place to personal insight. Was this something that just comes out when he sits down with his word processor or his pen and paper, as it may be, or is this something he very carefully outlined from the beginning and knew where he was going with?

A third is, as readers of the book will know from it, during his childhood he sometimes was in as many as three schools over the course of one school year, moving from town to town with this father and mother of his. I thought it might be interesting, particularly because he is now writing a piece that is to some degree related to this, to hear his comments about the impact that he believes there is on a child who goes through this kind of moving from school to school and also his comments about other experiences he had as a young person in school.

Another topic would be to talk about the life of a writer: how he first got interested, how does he go about writing every day, what advice would he have for young aspiring writers with regard to the economics of the life of a writer.

Then there's a cluster of issues that have to do with globalization. Clark has been the Director of the University of Iowa's International Writing Program, which has involved now some 112 countries and 1,100 writers from all around the world who come here to eastern Iowa and so enrich our state. So he has had that experience and the travel that has necessarily gone with that. He has travelled the world to find and talk to these people and help fund the program. He is also the husband in an intercultural marriage. Some of you may have had the experience of trying to maintain a relationship with someone from another country or of a different culture. He certainly has a wealth of observations about that which might be interesting to us.

And finally there's the matter of globalization in general. On my latest plane ride, the day before yesterday, from Washington to Chicago, I was sitting next to the Commander of the Great Lakes Naval Training Station who said that in his judgment the number one national defence concern that he had was the general ignorance of the American people about what is going on around the world. The very first thing they have to teach these 50,000 new entrants into the Navy is basic geography, even to know where the oceans are and what the countries are. Here's a man who certainly knows where the oceans are and what the countries are. So I thought that Clark might have some observations about that as well.

We can either begin to go through these topics now or open it up to questions that the audience may have. We might even be courteous enough to let Clark have an opening statement of his own rather than sit here and listen to an old law professor.

CB: Thank you, Nick. You were a Commissioner and I was only a Director. So I yield to your expertise.

All of those topics are touched on very much in what I wrote and the way I wrote it in *I Had a Father*. I stress, first of all, it's not my only book — it's one of about eleven books. So it's not necessarily the way I write.

But it was the way I was writing in 1992 under the influence of this job at Iowa, which was putting me, as I think I said in the book, in New Zealand one day and Argentina the next and Iowa City the third, then off to Finland or somewhere else the next. It was the kind of job that stretched me, but also stretched any concept I had of a coherent and stable self, of a coherent and stable world. I was the comet making a kind of movement between these fixed planets. I would land in Argentina and everyone there was Argentine and Spanish-speaking. Everyone was very much at home in Argentina. I wasn't. Wherever I went, I was always having to read the literature, meet the people, and quickly try to get at least one foot on the ground. And listen to the writers, especially, and talk to the various writers, and then, of course, try to raise money for the IWP.

All of that was part of my job, and would have been part of anyone's job who was in that position, but as a writer it adds a particular kind of flavour to what you're writing. It really does make you ask, "Who are you? Where did you come from?" Because that's the first thing you're asked: "Where are you from?" I say, "Well, I was born in North Dakota. But I'm not from North Dakota."

My parents wanted me to be born in the U.S. in 1940 because Canada was at war and the U.S. wasn't and there was a lot of fear in 1940 that Britain would fall under the Battle of Britain. Britain was at that moment very, very tenuously free. Parts of Britain were already occupied by the Nazis. The Channel Islands, for example. And Newfoundland, the big island off the East Coast of Canada, was a British colony. It was not a part of Canada at that time. The fear was that it would become German. And that the two little French islands off Newfoundland, which are French dependencies, would become German with the fall of France. Quebec, the big buffer between all that, was in fact quite sympathetic to the Nazis — just as Spain and Ireland and Portugal were, even though they were neutral.

Quebec refused to fight a so-called English war, so the Canadian draft was suspended as far as Quebec was concerned. Very few French Canadians fought in World War Two. You simply didn't do it. Even Pierre Trudeau, who became the Prime Minister of Canada later, said, "I regret that I was part of that world view, that I, too, sat out the war." My father would never have fought in that war — it was an English war. The perception in Quebec was that it was an English war. And you had a number of pro-fascist groups in Quebec that were supporting some sort of idea of a Catholic ruralism — very right-wing, very authoritarian. Unions were illegal. Protestants were virtually illegal. Jews were not allowed to vote. It was a real right-wing state, Quebec.

This meant that Ontario — with the Ottawa River in a sense being the dividing line between Ontario and Quebec — was going to be the front line of the war if you were a Canadian nationalist as my mother was. So they thought the best thing to do was to have me born at least in the country that my parents believed would never go to war. And the U.S. was out for another two years. So I was born in Fargo.

I do have a section in the book, as the audience will recall if they have had a chance to read it, about the moment that I in fact consider to be almost central to my life. And that is the moment in New Delhi in 1977 when I was attending a party. I was at a Canadian agricultural attaché's party. He was a friend of my family from Winnipeg. And I met a man, an older man. And he said, "Actually I'm an American. I feel guilty being at a Canadian party, but I'm almost a Canadian because I'm from North Dakota." And I said, "Well, hey, I'm almost an American. I was born in North Dakota, too." I was a Canadian citizen at that time. Then I asked him where in North Dakota he was born. And he said, "Fargo." And I said, "So was I!" And he said, "What hospital?" And I mentioned the hospital. "What doctor?" And I mentioned the doctor. And he said, "Would you like to meet the woman who delivered you?" And that was his wife, the doctor's delivery room nurse.

And I've thought many times that in 1977 I was thirty-seven years old. And if you look at your life as a kind of rocket going off and falling down to earth in a kind of parabola shape, that is probably the top, that is probably it. Double thirty-seven and you get seventy-four, a healthy life. Probably I would not succeed in going further out than that. Something was calling me back to my origins — what more than the nurse who actually held me at birth? — and it was a mystical thing to me.

Mysticism is not central to my concerns. But it's there, it's another organizing principle in my work — coincidence and the various kinds of patterns that begin to emerge in your life. Most of the people here have lived long enough to have seen the patterns. You are not surprised by anything anymore. When I was thirty-seven, I could still be surprised. I was astonished by meeting this woman.

Now I say, "Of course." I'm not as surprised. That is, events that happen seem to be analogies to earlier events. They don't seem to be in and of themselves fresh and new even when I'm in fresh new places, like here. Haven't I said this before, haven't I done this before? Yes. Will there be something that can actually shock me? I just felt that things had settled in after that experience, more or less things settled into a pattern.

I expect that the world is growing denser and denser and denser with coincidence. Patterns are coming closer and closer, are getting more and more finely textured. So by the end the bright little scheme of interrelated activities in my life will probably be able to be held in one hand. Everyone will be there. Everyone I ever contacted will all know one another and they will all sort of make their final appearance.

NJ: Do you know the play *Six Degrees of Separation*?

CB: Yes, of course.

NJ: That's sort of the theme there — that if you go far enough you are connected to everybody one way or another.

CB: Yes, that's one thing. Of course we are connected. They have had all those DNA tests to show that we are all related.

NJ: You talk about both mysticism and coincidence. Coincidence suggests something that doesn't have any particular force or reason behind it. Do you think there is some hand that is guiding your life to these events or do you think they really are random? Are you agnostic on this?

CB: I think that coincidence is coincidental. That is, there probably is not coincidence. If you sit down and do the mathematics of it, there is a high degree of probability that you will be in a particular place at a particular time meeting a particular kind of person, being responsive, giving the right signals, the right body language, the right eye contact, so that you will somehow make contact with someone who is significant to you. Even though you don't know it. And that person will in fact read you in the same way.

But I think the mysticism part of it goes back to classic mysticism, where the mystical vision is that the world is inside you. It's not that you are being directed as a puppet by some higher force. It's rather the unification of whatever is inside you with the sense of whatever is outside you. That's what mysticism is usually about. You look at a stone, or you look at a flower, or you look at a bird on the wing, and suddenly you see all. Everything makes sense in that one moment. That's the mystical moment I'm talking about.

Whatever set of autobiographical peculiarities led me from North Dakota to Florida to Pittsburgh to Quebec and gave me the life that I have, along with marrying an Indian woman and going and living in India for different periods of time — all of those particular things are special to me and to no one else. But they all radiate in patterns for people who have never left a small town or a small city or a region or a country.

I've talked about this with hundreds of writers who specialize in coincidence. This is a common experience that we all have. I think, in fact, a fiction writer cannot write fiction unless he believes in these things. First of all, you have to have the arrogance to believe that if I set down in a book experiences that are only peculiar to me, people are going to be interested. What arrogance that is. What chutzpah that is. How can other people believe that my life is going to relate to theirs in any way? You have to have some degree of confidence, some degree of luck, that is going to make the bridge.

I said at the beginning of *I Had a Father* that autobiography is the triumph of consciousness over experience. And I think that's what I was trying to do in the book — to elevate not the experience I've had, but the consciousness behind the experience. So that I've tried to say, "OK, I may have been in New Zealand and Argentina and Iowa City in one week and maybe you haven't. But that's not the important thing. The important thing is the connections I can draw from it, the consciousness that it brings to me.

Fiction, however, it seems to me, is the elevation of experience over consciousness. I mean if the character is too conscious, then it's going to ruin it as fiction. I mean if he already knows he can draw a parallel or some sort of conclusion from everything, then he's a boring character.

NJ: But your book *I Had a Father*, because it's an autobiography, does the reverse.

CB: Yes. It's a book about consciousness. I was trying to play on consciousness, not on experience. I could have written about "I was born" — you know, starting at the beginning and taking you through the narrative of a lifetime. I could have done that. But that seemed to me to be a betrayal of the kind of life that I had led.

Anyone who wants to start an autobiography by saying "I was born" means that he has already separated himself from his experience. Because you were not conscious when you were born. To go back and try to claim that as an experience is invalid in some way. It seems to me that autobiography functions best when it is written out of a moment in which you realize you cannot go on further until you assess or reconnect with the past. And so it starts not at the beginning, as a biography would. If you were writing a biography of Dickens, yes, you would probably start with "His parents were hardworking, blah, blah, blah." But if you are writing your own autobiography you are saying, "Here I am, a guy in his fifties, whose father died twelve years ago, who suddenly is seeing his father everywhere."

He is smelling his father's cigarettes in an apartment where he is living in Atlanta. That's how it starts, right? It's the ring of the cigarette burns on the bathtub. And suddenly I remember my father even though he has been dead a long time. It was that. And I realized that I was living a life very much like my father's. I was living apart from my wife who was in Iowa City. I was teaching for a semester at Emory University in Atlanta, where I was put up in this institutional housing. I had never been to Atlanta as an adult. I had been a kindergarten student there — but that was a different Atlanta, that was an Atlanta that was segregated. And I realized that I was leading a life like my father's and that my life had degenerated, if you wish, into a series of semester gigs. I could work a semester here, I could work six weeks there, I'll take this, I'll take that, anything to support the family. I was becoming like my father, though I don't smoke. And that was the thing that triggered it.

Why was my father speaking to me then? Why did I hear him, why did I see myself in him? It's an *imposture*, as you say in French, to think of myself as like my father. You saw the cover of the book — we are not similar. He was a prizefighter and a very different sort of person. But nevertheless the patterns were clear about what I was doing.

So that's what seems to me is the formula for a real autobiography: that I have to write this book and that it is in the writing of this book that I will come to a conclusion. I will find the answer as I write, as I pull it out of thin air. And I will not rely on experience. I mean I'm not Colin Powell, who is going to sit down and write a so-called autobiography out of copious notes and press clippings of a documented life. I don't have a documented life. I'm an anonymous person. No one is going to read the book because it's by me. If they are going to read the book, it's because they are going to be caught somehow by the web of circumstances or the style or something in the book. I'm not John Irving writing his autobiography. It's that situation that is, I hope, universal to people at a certain age — that I can't go on until I account for who I am right now and why something is bugging me.

NJ: But a lot of what connects with a reader, at least with me, is just the sheer joy of reading this book, your way with words, your eye, the things you've observed that you comment on, that you relate one to another. This is another aspect of the book that, to me at least, stands apart from the particular story you're telling. Maybe it's because Mary now has me in this class where I'm supposed to be writing description, which I'm having great difficulty with, that I'm so intimidated by your capacity to do it. But I just think that's a joyful experience. And isn't that a part of what writing is about?

CB: Yes. The pleasure of it is certainly there.

But I'm aware, just as I get older, that I've lost an awful lot of the sheer observational talent that I once had. When I started writing in my early twenties, I was under the beat, under the throb if you wish, of Faulkner.

He was my writer because I was writing about the Deep South of my childhood. And I could smell it, I could hear it — those voices, those characters, those defective people that were part of my childhood experience in rural north Florida, which is not anything like the Florida that people visit, I mean it's still not visited except by fires these days. That world spoke to me in kind of clotted words like Faulkner's. It was thick in my blood. I could write like Faulkner in my youth. But I can't do that anymore.

A long time ago when I lived in India in the early seventies I was writing a book with my wife called *Days and Nights in Calcutta*. It's about living for a year in a joint family in Calcutta, my wife's family, and being responsible, as I told it to myself, for the outsider's view. I was going to give an outsider a sense of what it's like to live in Calcutta and my wife was going to give her side, what it was like returning into the family. She had access to things that I didn't have and presumably I had access to things she didn't have.

It was at that time I got to know the great Indian film maker Satyajit Ray. He had made any number of great films. Getting to know Ray was the most liberating moment of my life. I met an artist who was a complete man of his art and his culture. He was an artist, a writer, a film maker, and a musician, and he remained engaged in every aspect of the world. To me he was the greatest single man I'd ever met. Seeing him as the archetype of the artist in society. Not just the Third World artist, but *the* artist. To him wherever he was living was the First World. He may have been living in Calcutta, but he was playing Mozart on the piano, and he was reading French and German and English, and he was doing art work, and he was making great movies.

Seeing how he as an artist worked in the world and how he was a man of total lucidity.

In other words, there was light, there was lucidness, that he aspired to. He did not want to get involved in tortured and sensuous things. It's very easy to do that in India. I mean the world of India is just omnipresent, it's just in your face the whole time, you can't escape it. But he gave you a measured distance, a very uncluttered vision of India. And it was at that time I saw — it has been my burden now for twenty-five years — that lucidity or consciousness was the thing I wanted to write about, not the tortured and jumbled life that I had led. That was one big turning point in my life. I owe that to Ray.

NJ: You say at the beginning of the epilogue that you had given up on this book in despair for three years and then you came back to it and finished it. What was the despair about, what was the problem, and what brought you back to this book?

CB: Well, a part of it was the sheer idiocy of the publishing world.

I was asked to write an autobiography by an editor I admired very much, kind of a legendary old drunk of an editor. And I started writing it for him. He was an old hockey player. He had been the only American hockey player in the NHL in the early 1940s. And then he was fired for being an old drunk. Reprobate that he was, he was fired.

And that company assigned me to someone from the office, a woman who knew nothing about Canada, knew nothing about hockey, knew nothing about French Canadians, and who was pregnant and couldn't even come into the office. She was sitting at home to protect her foetus. And she said, "Tell me, what are some of the things you've written?" This was like starting all over again, after I had already turned in fifty or sixty pages and was really into it. It took another year and a half for my agent to break that contract and get me into a new house with a new editor that we mutually approved of.

So that was one part of the problem.

The other thing was that the late eighties were not a good time for me. I was writing constantly and not publishing at all. The stories were not falling into print. And I was losing confidence in myself. The idea of writing about my father was something I had done briefly in my book *Resident Alien* several years earlier. I thought that I had exhausted it, that there was nothing more I wanted to say about it. And I was so involved in the IWP, so involved in the Iowa job, that it was what I wanted to write about. I didn't see how it had anything to do with my father, how it had anything to do with my autobiography. So wedding the two became difficult, but was something I wanted to do despite that. And it took me a while to find a voice for it.

NJ: So you had to find the right voice for all of this seemingly unconnected material and also, as I said earlier, you had to choose a structure that would allow you to weave all of those memories and insights together.

CB: I was trying to make the form of the book imitate the sputtering of my own consciousness and the ways in which it comes to self-knowledge. It does follow an associative linkage, so that I am associating memory and ongoing activity and trying to make sense of the chaos that was thrust upon me. I had a chaotic life up to a certain age. And I thought I had achieved release from that chaos. I thought I had taken control of that chaos once I left home. But I realized as I was writing this book that in fact, no, I've probably had more moves since marriage — I've been married thirty-five years —

than I had before it. I've probably imposed more chaos on my family than I had as a child.

In other words, the persistence has gone on. And that was a sobering notion — that in fact I still thrive on taking my seat on an airplane and sitting down and waiting for the next chapter, knowing that I'm going to be a certain number of hours without a telephone that can reach me, without any expectations, knowing it's going to be restful and it's going to end up in a new place without any responsibilities on my part. I may have to learn a few words to get around. That, I realized, was a kind of thrill.

So I was trying to give free rein in that book to the pain and the confusion and the chaos, as well as to the growing sense that there is something inside me that is feeding on it or demanding it or wanting more of it or trying to understand it. Where does this — I called it at one time "border consciousness" — come from, where if you are on one side of the border you constantly want to be on the other, where if you are on one side of the border you are a defender of the other side? That I was more American than the Canadians, I was more Canadian than the Americans, more English than the French, more French than the English. I was all of these things at various times in my life.

I think a lot of it had to do with all the moving I did at a sensitive adolescent boy's age. From about the time I was ten to the time I was thirteen was when this reached a crescendo of chaos, just at the time your hormones are kicking in, just at the time when all of your adolescent confusions are starting to hit. And that was the time, starting in central Florida and moving to Winnipeg and back, that ended in the Cincinnati ghetto. I was a twelve-year-old fat white boy in a ghetto school. And not only was I attacked frequently but I was assaulted. I nearly died from an attack. Then I was beaten by the teacher.

Suddenly, after all this, I was put into Jewish schools because that was the only way you could be protected. The only white community around consisted of Jews. So my mother put me into a Torah. I was studying my letters for my virtual bar mitzvah. If I had stayed, I don't know what the rabbi would have done. But he was happy to have me there. That influenced a lot of my life, actually. It was the only community I'd ever had.

My father was in the furniture business. It was sort of top-heavy. The ownership and the general managers were largely Jewish, but the salesmen were largely Catholic guys like my father: Irish, Italian, French-Canadian, whatever they might have been. So you had kind of a non-speaking relationship, at least you did in the fifties, between the guys like my father, who were out on the road getting drunk every night, getting laid every night, doing all sorts of naughty things every night in a different town, and the owners, who I realized much later had been sort of re-routed in their lives by the Depression. They were immigrants' children themselves usually, who would have been heading to law school or medical school, would have done the professional thing, but the Depression in the thirties re-routed them into business.

But they had behind them the interest in art, the interest in culture. And they saw my mother as a godsend. "How did you ever marry that man?" they would say. And they saw me as fit for their daughters. They saw me as just the right kid, a terrific kid — so that how I survived my teens was in a sense by feeling that I still had that ongoing connection to a community I could talk with and where I had friends and where I could hang out. That was important.

And then when I went to Harvard I studied with Bernard Malamud. He was my real mentor in writing. The great figure in my writing life was Malamud. And that influenced me a lot, too. Then I came to Iowa and studied with Philip Roth. That was a comedown.

NJ: It's now five years since you published *I Had a Father*. Would you handle anything differently if you were writing the book now?

CB: That's an interesting question. I don't think I would want to return to that book to change anything too significant. There are things I could add. There are things you could continue the narrative on.

I ended it at the Rodney King episode in Los Angeles. That was to me a very significant kind of postmodernism where the actual film footage — the very thing you think would indict the officers — becomes the thing under postmodern scrutiny that gets them off. That's part of the book. You would have thought, twenty years ago, if you had a film of a man being beaten, "Open and shut case." Now you can cut the film in so many ways and slow it down and comment on it frame by frame until finally you've reduced it to a *Road Runner* cartoon in which there is no consequence for that kind of brutality, there is no antecedent. And that's how I was writing my book. I was going without consequence or antecedent.

Probably I would add a number of other things. The world keeps throwing up examples of the same things. But that's just patterns, you know. O.J. Simpson becomes a pattern, Rwanda becomes a pattern, India going nuclear becomes a pattern. These are all things you could say are implied in the book but not really talked about.

I've been writing about a lot of things, so I've been busy in other ways.

NJ: I would like you to say a little more about the International Writing Program, about what you think the benefits are for Iowa, for the university, for the writers who are brought here. How would you go about explaining it if you were subjected to a management information reporting system with the new fourteen-year-old MBAs from Harvard who seem to be running everything?

CB: I left that.

NJ: How would you document the success? How would you know whether the money put into this was accomplishing what it was set out to accomplish or not?

CB: First, I should say that the IWP was founded by Paul Engle, Cedar Rapidian, in 1967. This was after he left the Writers' Workshop. He and his wife started the IWP.

And I would not have given it much of a chance, I think, if I had been thinking about it. I was living in Montreal then and I wasn't thinking about it. If I had thought about it, it would have looked incredibly idealistic. That you were going to bring established authors.

The Writers' Workshop brings infant writers — that is, very talented youngsters, generally, who have not published yet and who are hoping to learn in two years all the techniques and all that is going to carry them. That's what I did. That's why I left Harvard to come to Iowa. And that's how I met my wife.

NJ: In the Writers' Workshop.

CB: In the Writers' Workshop. We were very, very thankful for it. There was no IWP then.

But the idea of bringing established authors — that is, people who are in their seventies down to their late twenties, who have published, in some cases, a hundred books, but in most cases at least five or six, who have won national prizes in their own countries, and who are writing in languages not English — to Iowa, not New York, not Los Angeles, and putting them in a cinder-block eight-floor dormitory in which they share a kitchen and a bathroom, can't smoke or drink, and have to observe quiet and decorum, is doomed to failure, one might think.

And yet, for the very reasons that I have mentioned, it has been a success. Because it's Iowa, it has been a success. They come here because this is an America that no one from their country has ever seen. Everyone in reasonably affluent countries has gone to New York or Los Angeles, San Francisco, Washington. No one has ever gone to Iowa. No one would choose to go to Iowa, frankly. But this is a city, they soon learn, where the bank throws a reception for them. What writer has ever been welcomed at a bank, you know? First National Bank throws this wonderful reception.

This is a town that writing built. It has a bookstore, Prairie Lights, that gives them all sorts of freebies. And there are more writers coming through, more writers per square inch, than probably anywhere outside of Calcutta in my experience. It's an incredible collection of people. Writing did make Iowa City and the university in many ways. And the town is aware of that.

The town shows a great deal of respect, the people show a great deal of respect, for the IWP writer. Very few writers are accustomed to respect. Maybe Nobel Prize winners get it, but most writers toil in oblivion. So they know that when they give a reading there's going to be an audience. They know that when they give a talk there's going to be an audience. And it's going to be a well-informed audience. These are things they have never had.

They don't live munificently. We give them $35 a day while they are in Iowa for those three months in the fall, but they find that it's more than enough. They're amused at that because they remember going to New York and spending $500 on a weekend. And suddenly they're told $35 a day. They feel they're going to be frying hotdogs in the park or something, but they adjust very quickly. And they find that the community of writers who are all living on the same floor, thirty-five writers using at least ten or fifteen languages, all living together, they're in it together, they're in Iowa City together.

And they start making translation projects — they translate each other's work. Beyond our attempts to translate their work, you have Albanians translating from Hebrew, you have Poles translating from Afrikaans, you have all sorts of other strange things going on that are based purely on personal affinities.

So there is a lot of stuff that happens and I am merely, was merely, the remote Director. I get to know them very well. I introduce them at talks and at their readings, I am on panels with them, and I do interviews with them. But I can't control their daily or nightly life, of course, so it's a matter of setting a tone and hoping that they are all people such as yourself.

Writers universally, no matter what their background, have the same love of mischief, they enjoy the same kinds of humour, they have generally the same kind of scepticisms about the world and about authority. They are a brotherhood, a sisterhood, that is universal though it takes different forms. Muslims are going to take different forms from Buddhists, different forms from Jews or Christians. French are going to be different from English. There are enmities that exist between countries that you can't overcome in some cases. I'm thinking particularly of relations between Israelis and their neighbours. Those have nearly always failed.

NJ: You've described the importance of coming to Iowa for other writers. But what has coming here meant to you?

CB: Iowa gave me my life. That is, I came here as a student in the Writers' Workshop, got my degree here, met my wife here, had our first child here; both our sons are graduates of Iowa City high schools, our older son is a graduate of the University of Iowa; and it gave me my most satisfying and most prominent job. So I could say that without Iowa I don't know what my life would have been like. I would probably have been an academic out of Harvard or something. But I'm also moved by Iowa — that people are coming out on a ninety-degree night for this, for example. But of course it's cool in here, it's nice.

Iowa has created a literary atmosphere. Iowa cares about the things I care about. When I go to other communities, I see that this is not a universal trait — just as our writers in the IWP find out that this is not universal. They go to larger cities to give a talk and they don't get anything like the reception that they get in Iowa City. And they realize they may call it Minneapolis, but it's not Iowa City. They may call it Chicago, but it's not Iowa City. And I have that same feeling, too. I'm going off to Berkeley, to San Francisco, to be with my wife, to take the commuting out of this marriage and to have more time just for my own writing. If I could have done it here, if she would have come here, I wouldn't have left. And I will continue to come back. I've lived in Montreal longer than any other place, but Iowa City is second.

NJ: Would you mind saying a little about what it has meant to maintain a long-distance marriage for the entire time that you've been the Director of the IWP here and your wife has been a professor at Berkeley?

CB: I'm about to experience the joys of cohabitation. We have been leading very interesting lives alone and reporting back to the other, but in some cases not really being able to share it all. Yes, I have been seen as a person alone and she has been seen as a person alone — which means a lot of people hit on you, especially on her. So you are having to reinvent almost daily the bond that brought you together and keeps you together. It's a virtual kind of connectedness in a sense because you are not there to boil the water for coffee, you are not there to do all those little things, so you are having to keep the other person virtually present at the opposite side of the table and you are reinventing that person almost all the time. I find myself thinking of what it's like to be an Indian woman in North America who doesn't drive, who was raised for much better things than I was ever able to give her. She was raised to be servanted to and she has had to do all this totally by herself. And I was not born or raised to be married to an Indian woman. It was not in my stars, let's say, I don't think.

So the wonder of it all has never left me; the wonder of it has never left. I've never settled into an idea that this is a familiar person and we share all this together. We don't share a damn thing. There's nothing in her past and nothing in my past that would bring us together. There's only this ongoing momentary present.

NJ: Do you try to talk every day on the telephone?

CB: We do. And we do far more than once a day. We have horrendous phone bills.

NJ: I always had sort of a twenty-four-hour rule when trying to maintain relations with people.

CB: Oh, yes.

The Iowa job was such that I was always able to be out in California in the spring. It was four months in Iowa every fall, during which time I was totally occupied with the program. Then the next four months I was based in California, but that's when I would be out in the world recruiting and raising money. Then in the summer she would come out to Iowa while I was starting the next year, so we were together more than that.

NJ: At the outset I mentioned wanting to ask you about the life of a writer, about the advice that you would give to young writers, advice perhaps about how not to get distracted by other concerns, other pressures.

CB: That's a big, big, big question. The writers who are good, who are true to writing, to the artistic vision, to the vision of their work, will, it seems to me, transcend national and religious and all other abstract pressures upon them, or abstract loyalties even. And those who are lesser will in fact write through them, will use those as the filters — not just the filters, but the trench which they filter everything through, which they pour everything into. And their work becomes tedious, it lacks character, it lacks depth.

But how do you teach people? You can't teach people not to be stupid, not to be fanatical, not to be materialistic. You can't teach that. You can try to give them the example of the finest works around and say, "Isn't this how you want to see your work? Isn't this how you want to be remembered?" And say to them, "The work will endure. You may not be rich in your own lifetime, but wouldn't you like to have the royalties that James Joyce earns now? Wouldn't you like to have the royalties that Faulkner eventually earned — though he didn't touch them in his own lifetime? Those writers who become very, very popular in their own lifetimes tend to fade later on."

It's a question of "Which would you rather have: happiness and wealth now or in a hundred years?" I think it was a French writer who said that writing is like picking a ticket in a lottery. If in ten years your work is remembered, then you have won. If in a hundred years you are still being read, then you are part of immortality.

NJ: But a part of the question is mortality. How much satisfaction is it for a young, budding writer that there may be some money a hundred years from now when the rent is due next Tuesday? What advice do you have for folks who probably aren't going to be remembered a hundred years from now, but would like to be writers now, would like to be actors now, would like to be graphic artists now — that they get some other job that provides the money and do this in their spare time?

CB: In all those fields the lessons are clear. Actors wait tables when they're not being killed by O.J. Simpson. Actors do what they have to do. They work as fitness instructors, they do whitewater rafting, whatever it may be. They put the money aside for acting lessons, singing lessons, or dancing lessons. They live five to an apartment and take whatever job is available.

And the same thing is true of writers. We fortunately can teach. But even those jobs are rare. If you can't teach and you still want to write, you do whatever you have to do that doesn't stop you from writing. That is, if you can find a job at a Kinko's that pays the rent, do it. If you have a spouse who believes in you and will set you up, do that, without guilt, but produce.

And then I think all the arts have this history that the apprenticeship process and the early emergence of the artist is really like a little crocodile coming out of an egg. The big bad birds are waiting before you can even get to the water, the birds are going to pick you apart, even hatching doesn't guarantee a long life.

NJ: What in terms of the daily routine? Do you recommend that a writer write every day?

CB: I think so. It would be unthinkable, for example, if you wanted to be a musician, that you wouldn't be practising all day every day. It would be unthinkable for anyone in any other art not to be working all the time. And I think it would be unthinkable for a writer not to be writing every day.

So much of it is practice. But it's not just practice — you are really trying to reinterpret the world through your art form. If you're a dancer, you're trying to make every movement reflect so much passion, so much agony, so much world history, whatever. If you're a film maker, you're sitting there going through life saying, "Can I do this? Can I make this? How does this look?" If you're a writer, you're doing the same sort of thing. "Can I use this? Can I turn this into something narratively interesting? And what is it that makes it interesting?"

And the descriptions. Yes, the descriptions are terribly important — to make it concrete, to put the reader in this reality and keep the reader in a reality that she doesn't want to be in particularly. She has many other distractions around her and yet you have to keep that person not just amused but informed and instructed and make them say, "Yes, I've been there. This person is speaking to me. This is true." And to do that without being didactic, without being pretentious or bombastic in some way.

NJ: Lots of note-taking throughout the day?

CB: All of that. All of that.

NJ: How would you characterize the responsibilities of the writer and the responsibilities of the reader?

CB: It is incumbent on the reader and even more incumbent on the writer to make experiences into metaphors. Even though you see it as a metaphor, I didn't write it as a metaphor. I'm aware that it is metaphorical — but I didn't say, "I need a metaphor for my boxes." This is what I mean about practice. Going through life like this so that it becomes so much second nature, so that anything a professional writer writes about out of experience has a metaphorical dimension to it. It just automatically does. It's like a Dominican shortstop who just knows to glide to the ball. He has practised it so many times that he's not going to be caught out of position. The same thing with a writer.

A journalist will say a box is something that contains books. But a writer says a box contains memories, right? You can make it journalistically a dull portrayal — I shouldn't say dull, you can make it journalistically an accurate portrayal — of nothing more than a piece of cardboard that contains objects. And if you're writing in the newspaper, that's what it has to be. It would be considered a violation of journalistic ethics to make it anything else.

But for a fiction writer, or for an artist in general, everything, every square inch of the canvas, is metaphorical. Watch it all. For a writer it's all metaphor. It's all standing for something else. Something larger. Something that cannot be contained. If you were to try to describe it, you would come up with an abstraction. So you are always looking for these concrete things that give you that abstraction.

NJ: Well, I have a lot more questions here and would be happy to keep going. Normally when I begin to speak it takes a semester for me to stop. But I thought this might be a good point to hear some questions from the audience. And I should remind you, Clark, that you do have a story with you to read to us that no one has ever heard. It's called "Sitting Shiva with Cousin Bennie." I'm sure the audience will enjoy that.

CB: Yes. We have just about time to do that.

Crossings and Transformations:
An Interview with Clark Blaise
[2000]

A l l a n   W e i s s

AW: I was wondering if we could begin just by talking about your very peripatetic biography. You were born in Fargo ...

CB: ... North Dakota, of Canadian parents, one French and one English, in 1940. At that time Canada was at war and America was not. My mother was very concerned about protecting this precious bundle that was really an accident in her life and certainly an accident in my father's life. I was a very sickly child. She wanted to give me the best chance of survival and there were questions about that. The Battle of Britain was going on at that time. Quebec, which was where they had met and married and where my father was from, was clearly more sympathetic to the Axis in many ways than to Britain. And there was the possibility that Newfoundland and all would become a kind of Channel Island. You know, taken over by the Germans or whatever it may be. There were already U-boats patrolling the Gulf of St. Lawrence. One could imagine, say, the Ottawa River as one of the battlegrounds for an expansive Germany against a passive North America. Canada was the only North American country enlisted against Germany at that time.

And so coming to the United States my father got a job in the Sears store in Fargo. That's how they were able to finance the waiting out of my birth. And then they went back to Winnipeg, where my mother was from, to show me off to the grandparents. My grandfather — and he was a doctor — allegedly felt the bumps on my head and said, "Don't worry, Annie, this boy will never be a boxer." And that was very prophetic, very true. But that sort of started the peripatetic quality of my life.

I was genetically implanted with Canada from my earliest memories. In fact, most summers I was sent back to Winnipeg to spend time with my cousins and my grandparents, because my own family life was too hectic. We were moving every six months to different parts of the United States. The only stability I knew was provided by Canada, by that very rooted family that my mother had come from and that is still there — she's buried among them in Winnipeg. That's the place where I went to school. Whenever things got too crazy at home, I would be sent to the grandparents or to my aunt and they would put me in school in Winnipeg.

Those were the educational advantages that I had as a child, because every time I would come back to the States I would be significantly ahead of any classmates that I had and so I was always being advanced. When I would come to the States I would be advanced two or three grades, but when I would go back to Canada I would be retarded a couple of grades. I ended up graduating about a year and a half ahead of my classmates in Pittsburgh. It was there I was doing my junior-high and high-school years.

AW: That must have had a number of disadvantages for you in terms of wanting to feel that you were part of a class or part of a group. Did it isolate you?

CB: I'm sure it did. I'm not really able to reclaim those memories now about how excluded I felt or how self-

conscious I felt. I certainly was aware when I was going
to school in Canada. I was aware because of my accent
being improper by the standards of Winnipeg, which
was very Scottish at that time. I was well aware that I
couldn't keep up. I would get breathless trying to keep
up with my cousins' speech patterns. I would have to
stop and catch my breath. And they were always making fun of my slow ... Southern ... way ... of talking. I
guess I had that. I didn't think I did.

When I was in the Deep South as a younger child, I
certainly was aware of the fact I wasn't of that place, I
wasn't of those people, and I didn't come from there,
although like any child I desperately wanted to belong.
My mother was there to tell me that I didn't and that I
shouldn't aspire to being a Cracker. My father was himself more of a classic immigrant, in a sense; my mother
was always resistant to the immigrant clan. They both
died still Canadian citizens and never were Americans.
My mother was very resistant to the idea of America,
whereas my father would go along with whatever it took
and usually tried to mask his French-Canadianness by
calling himself French.

My father made up an elaborate tale of himself coming from Paris. It was supportable in the sense that we
did in fact bring over his older brother, who was in
France — I've written about him; he was a small-scale
bantam rooster of a person. And since he was actually
from France it gave my father even greater credibility,
because he could claim in fact a great many nephews,
and cousins on my part, who had never seen the New
World, and really were French.

AW: So you came by your sense of borders quite hon-
estly, because you were crossing them so frequently.

CB: I think borders, and the frail containments that

they promise, always held a fascination for me. The ability to leap out of them has always been an exciting notion for me. It's almost like treasure maps — they tell you where something is buried and what elaborate ruse you have to go through to get to it. If you have to show documentation, if you have to sneak across it. Certainly in my childhood when we were doing it all by car, when I would see those signs saying so-and-so state line or welcome to the new state or whatever it may be — and in the South, of course, states were very important, state divisions were very important — I would thrill to that. And when I would see the bison, let's say, on the Manitoba highway signboards, that was and still is an ongoing kind of thrill to me. Or the crown on the Ontario ones or the fleur-de-lis on the Quebec ones. Those are all signs that I am no longer who I was in some way. They tell me that geography influences fate and destiny, which I think it does to a very large extent.

Then I had the possibility of transformation. It was handed to me by the fact that I was now travelling through North Dakota rather than Minnesota. I would suddenly see myself as a different person. Even when I would see the cardinal points on the compass — North, South, East, West — they all held potential magic for me. So that if I saw a sign saying Route 19 South, even though it might have been in Pennsylvania, I would see the word "South" and I would start thinking of swamps and palm trees and heat and all those things. And then I would see "West" and even if it was just a suburban direction marker, I was already into the covered wagons going across the prairie. "East" and I would see some sort of lobsterman out with his traps.

AW: So that fluid identity was actually a source of excitement rather than concern or fear for you.

CB: I think so. We had managed to mess up wherever we were so badly that we had to leave. My father would get us into a lot of trouble. And I would get myself into a lot of trouble simply because, being the kind of kid I was in those sorts of rural schools, it was very hard to be anything other than a target for ridicule or a target for abuse. So I was always happy to leave. And as soon as a new town was announced, I would have the maps out and would look for those little tell-tale squiggles on the map that would say, oh, there are hills there, and immediately they became mountains in my mind. If there was a little wrinkling on the map that showed there was even an elevation of six hundred feet above sea level, I was already transforming it to Mount Fuji or something in my mind. Because when you had a Florida childhood, when everything was flat, anything that offered relief — literally "relief" — was appealing.

AW: So many of your stories are about children — sons — and their relationships with their fathers. It's clear that — and you've even said this frequently — your stories are quite self-consciously autobiographical.

CB: Well, they were up to a certain point in my life. But like all writers you finally exhaust the store of built-in stories that were given to you, that you had no control over, that left deep impressions and you just had to let them out, you just had to release the pressure. But about 1985 or so, I think, about fifteen years ago, that ended. The stories that were given to me were more or less exhausted. And the books that have been written since then — let's say the stories that are in *Resident Alien*, the stories that are in *Man and His World*, the stories that are in *If I Were Me*, and the stories that I'm doing right now — are all entirely imagined. They are based more on my observations as a world traveller in jobs that I've recently had, or on my accumulated years of seeing how places and people interact. I've been able to fashion a new kind of story for myself. The need to certify or to validate my stories through my personal experience is no longer there. In fact, I would shy away, I think, from writing something that was ultimately autobiographical right now. I don't feel any need to do so.

AW: I did notice that the stories in *Man and His World* leaned more towards magic realism — towards challenging conventional realism.

CB: Well, I would hope so. That book is very loosely structured along the idea of the father. I mean, it starts with "A Tour around My Father" and ends with "The Love God." And the character of Leo runs throughout that book. It's loose; it's not intended as anything other than a very mild version of things I've written much earlier that were explicitly autobiographical, explicitly about my father and me. This one is about a father-son fascination, but the son is no longer destroyed. Well, in "The Love God" he is destroyed by his father, but the connection is still there. But I'm now happier exploring the varieties of that conflict rather than the conflict itself.

I want to say that in the last few weeks I've been proofreading the Southern stories that make up a new volume that is coming out with The Porcupine's Quill. It has been kind of a strange experience for me doing that, because those are stories that in some cases were written over forty years ago, when I was an undergraduate. I'm seeing things that were written when I had the sensual memories of the South intact, which I no longer have. So I was brought up short many times as I was reading by how intimate those experiences of the South had been for me at one time. And I realized something else that's a little disquieting, which may become part of a longer work that I'm involved in right now — that the effect of so much travel in my childhood and my adolescence and continuing right on up through my young manhood and even into middle age has been to create non-communicating layers of experience and personalities.

I see the Southern kid that I was — fat, victimized, sluggish, intelligent surely but not capable of transcending his physical shell, and with parents intact — set into this primitive region of the United States before any kind of law touched it or before any kind of transformation came about. And then, because the next volume I'm putting together is my Pittsburgh stories, which is my adolescent self — this is where I was during junior high and high school — I look back at that and there I was among the high-school intellectuals, the bright boys, but the bright inhibited boys who would much rather tinker with radios and go to the museums and the planetariums than engage in any kind of adolescent skulduggery, any kind of adolescent dating. There was no dating, so the sexual urges were all thwarted or suppressed and put into play, into the intellect. But that boy in Pittsburgh and that boy in Florida, though both me in a sense, do not communicate. Along with that, my whole Montreal and Canadian side came into play. And that, too, does not communicate with my Pittsburgh self or my Southern self.

Then in more recent years my international side was released by the job that I had here with the International Writing Program, in which the sexuality was rampant, the sexuality was everywhere. The confident, world-class intellect who travels the world and experiences all of its pain and pleasure is presumably me as is presumably the Montreal self as is presumably the Pittsburgh self as is presumably the Southern self. But all of them seem to be in some strange way cut off from one another.

So I can't write, for example, a Southern story now because that self has disappeared. I can't put my sixty-year-old self into my ten-year-old body. And I can't write a Pittsburgh story. Well, I have been writing some Pittsburgh stories, but I realize that the two new Pittsburgh stories that will be in this next volume are in fact adolescent memories that have been brought up-to-date by a contemporary teller. I still have to write a couple of new Montreal stories and I feel as though I should because each book is meant to include new and selected stories. But what can I write about, since the Montreal that exists now, post-referendum Montreal, is no longer the Montreal that I knew?

What I lack is that Alice Munro or Peggy Atwood sense of having been in one place all of one's life. I think of Peggy's novel *The Blind Assassin* where you have eighty-plus years of Toronto life. She can project forward twenty years and she can project backward forty or fifty or sixty years from her own timeline because she is so confidently at ease with that setting. I can't do that. I have been effectively cut off, almost like an exile in time, a temporal exile, from each of these places that I spent significant parts of my life in.

AW: Geography, then, is very much tied to identity. Where you are is that self at that point in time. Geography and identity and time all seem closely connected to each other at any given point, but there's a lack of continuity.

CB: Right, right. Perhaps it's inevitable that I would have been attracted to Sir Sandford Fleming as the topic of my next book, *Time Lord*, which is about the

Canadian who was the leading nineteenth-century theorist on standard time and the man credited with having given us a way of demarking the world through time zones and all the rest of it. And as soon as I discovered that he was a fifty-seven-year-old Canadian at the time of the adoption of standard time and I was a fifty-seven-year-old self-styled Canadian here in Iowa City when I read about it, I immediately dropped everything I was writing at the time and took up the two-and-a-half years of research that led to the creation of *Time Lord*.

To me it's in many ways a novel and to me it's in many ways my story. Of course it has got all the trappings and the bibliography and the index of a scholarly work, and I'm not in it except at the last, but I am, I think, struck by something that he was struck by. Between his Canadian self and his Scottish self, between his sort of dreamy romantic self and his practical railroad-building self, there were discontinuities that I too feel.

AW: I wondered if the diversity of experience that you've had permitted a special level or an unusual level of artistic freedom. That may not be the case if you find that you can't really put yourself in the mind of somebody at a different time and a different place anymore.

CB: It may be. I think it probably has a lot to do with my preference for the short story over the novel. Certainly the novel would imply that you have a greater confidence, a greater range of stability, temporal or psychological or whatever it may be, than you have with the short story, which is really a study in destruction and rebuilding. In a collection of a dozen stories there are a dozen small deaths and a dozen rebirths, really, in which like a child with a sand castle or some Lego construction the artist breaks it down and builds a new one. And that's what a collection of stories does. And while they may all be the work of a single child or the work of a single artist, they are also demonstrable muscle-flexings, or whatever you want to call them, where an artist gets impatient perhaps with the time he is wasting on these characters and wants to go on to something new. I think that's probably where the freedom is, if you are not happy with this or if you're not committed to it over the long haul.

AW: Right.

CB: I've had relatively little to do with novels. Right now I am working on one. It is set in the nineteenth century, in Quebec and in upper New England among the Franco-Americans. That is a region and a people I feel I do have some historical connection with, largely maybe because I had a father from there and also because I have simply continued to read in their diaries and letters and histories. I've taken whatever I can either from personal experience or from conferences or from friendships I've had with rediscovered family members in New Hampshire and in Quebec. Putting that all together, plus of course having spent these years researching in the middle and late nineteenth century, has given me enough confidence to the point where I can handle the historical elements.

AW: Getting back to the possible contributions of your experiences to your writing, without getting to that question that I know you've resisted in the past about *whether* one can teach writing. You've spent so many years doing just that.

CB: Close to forty.

AW: Right. People who teach creative writing often say that it's stimulating primarily because of the way that they are able to interact with their students. I was wondering if you've found that teaching writing stimulates your creativity.

CB: There were times when it may have, especially in the early years when I was teaching at Sir George Williams and Concordia. I started the graduate writing program there because I wanted to have a community of writers and I felt strongly, coming out of graduate school here at Iowa, the benefits of that to everybody — benefits to an English Department to have writers around, benefits to writers to be in a community. But I also wanted to find my way into my chosen community of Montreal. And the only way I could do that was with what I had, which was teaching, my talent for teaching or my experience in teaching. That time I would say was probably the best time I've had as a teacher, where I really did feel that I was transcending the role of teacher. Yes, I was a teacher and I was an administrator, I was giving of myself, but I was also learning about the region that I had chosen at that time to make my home — permanently, I thought.

Some other times that I've taught, it has been, frankly, for a paycheque. I was not engaged by the students, I was not engaged by the setting, I was not engaged by anything other than the need to put bread on the table. And there I really did feel I was dulling my tools. I was wasting my time just as much as the students were wasting their time. So I've become a lot more selective about how much I teach and what I teach. When I was here at Iowa as the Director of the International Writing Program, I didn't teach at all. That was nearly ten years of administration and fundraising and travel and giving introductions and taking people around and doing all sorts of impresario-like work. But I was really not teaching and that was very beneficial. I enjoyed not teaching.

Now, at Berkeley, I'm teaching only one course, an undergraduate workshop. And I miss the fact that these are not serious writers. These are smart kids, but they're kids, they're undergraduates. I realize that nearly all my teaching has been on a graduate level, in which the students are really apprentice writers in their final stage of apprenticeship. They know that's what they want to be and they have made the prior commitment to learning everything they can learn and absorbing everything they can absorb, whereas a busy undergraduate at Berkeley in microbiology or something is not ever going to be a writer. He or she is going to be, thank God, a person with a certain sympathy for and understanding of literature, maybe with a fond memory of the time when they took a writing course, but their career path has been carved out for them, and it's not towards writing.

And so I'm leaving Berkeley in a few weeks and will be a member of the graduate writing program at a local arts college in San Francisco — the California College of Arts and Crafts, which has a graduate program in writing and is very ancient and established and well thought of — a sort of Bauhaus by the Bay, as they call it. What I'm looking forward to there is that all the graduate students in all the art forms that they teach, like film and fashion and sculpture and painting, are allowed to sit in on any other workshop, so that I will have graduate workshop students in writing who may in fact be fashion designers, too. That strikes me as an interesting mix. I've never done that. I'll do it for a semester. If I like it, I'll continue. If not, I'll be perfectly willing to move on into full-time freelance work.

AW: You mentioned a community of writers and certainly what you've been able to enjoy here at Iowa, and also when you were with The Montreal Story Tellers,

has been a group of writers with whom you could discuss the craft, with whom you could theorize, and so
on. Would it be fair to say that those two main groups
that you've been associated with shaped your vision of
what the short story is?

CB: Probably not fair to say that. Community is important.
And among all the people in all the various arts that I
know, I think writers — fiction writers, I'm not talking
about poets — are among the least competitive of souls
and do seek community, especially in North America.

I think maybe in Europe you can see a sense that
there has never been an established writing faculty and
practice of teaching writing in the universities. Writing
is still looked upon as an outlaw activity by the God-
given few and they guard their turf and they guard their
vision and they guard their time jealously. They are able
to survive much better, I think, than North American
writers, who really don't have much of a market — or
much income, except for what the universities pay them.

But I think fiction writers here in North America
enjoy one another's company. I've seen enough of the
other art forms to know how rare that is. Musicians and
painters and sculptors and poets and playwrights are
more like dogs in a dog pound, fighting over a bone or
whatever it may be. But I think fiction writers really
choose to connect with other writers. Many times I
have received letters in the mail or phone calls from
writers I don't know saying, "I'm in town, I like your
work, I'm hoping we can get together." That strikes me
as a wonderful thing that's part of the writing world.

I don't know what shaped my sense of what the short
story is. You would certainly have to go back to the
reading I did, the reading that I underwent, the sort of
self-education that I put myself through with certain

guides. Malamud being a very strong influence. My original writing teacher, Paul Bennett at Denison, being another. People who guided my reading. But I was just this avid sponge. And I was certainly reading far more novels than short stories. I just wanted to inhabit the space that was opened up by those works. It was almost a complete sensual experience. In those years — I'm talking about my late teens and early twenties — I would pick up a new book and, even from holding the book before I opened it, I would be in kind of a trance. And either the music would start playing in the background from the first paragraph or it wouldn't. But generally it did. Those were books that just immediately sank into my brain.

Nowadays I read less than I did then, though I still read a lot, but there's no music. It would be easy to say, "Oh, the books I'm reading now are not as good as the books I read then." They are probably even better, but I'm no longer the same person, I'm no longer able to absorb them with that same avidity or that same innocence that's necessary.

I think by the time I was in The Montreal Story Tellers I was probably still at the tail end of that period in my life when if I heard of a new writer I went out immediately and made sure that he was no longer a new writer. I knew of Hugh Hood's work when I was in Iowa because Dave Godfrey and I were classmates at Iowa and Dave reviewed *Flying a Red Kite* for *The Canadian Forum*. And after he had done his review he came over with a copy of *Flying a Red Kite* and declared, "Canadian literature is now born." So there we were, graduate students here in Iowa forty years ago, thirty-eight years ago, or so, reading *Flying a Red Kite*. I was known as a Canadian then, even here before I went to Canada.

So I knew Hugh's work. John Metcalf's *The Lady Who Sold Furniture* and *Going Down Slow* I'd read in Montreal as soon as I'd gotten there, looking for other things in Montreal to read. I didn't know John but I'd read his work. I'd certainly read Ray Smith's "Cape Breton Is the Thought-Control Centre of Canada." I'd read that when it came out in *The Tamarack Review* and the book as soon as House of Anansi brought that out, since I knew all the people at Anansi. I was reading everything that Anansi brought out because Dave Godfrey was running it at that time. I would go down to Toronto, or I would see Dave in Montreal, and I would collect all the new books.

So it was just simply my sense of seeing people of my own time and place and of my own age — Hugh was a little bit older — doing the things I did and caring as passionately about them as I did. I had always thought I was the most passionate and the most concerned and the most dedicated, but I found wherever I went there were people equally dedicated and I would always seek them out.

AW: You mentioned earlier the consciousness that you had as a child of voice, of accent, of how that creates for others a sense of who you are. And in earlier discussions of The Montreal Story Tellers I believe that you commented that the oral nature of the act of going in front of people and reading them a story rather than simply having them read it themselves might have influenced the role of voice and the emphasis on voice that you exhibit.

CB: Also, we marketed ourselves, if you wish, as being of that time and place. What we would choose to write about was going to be very much the Montreal the way those kids in the audience knew it. And we would use the language of the streets, if we had to. We would certainly be true to being Montrealers of the late sixties and early seventies. And of course Hugh was the most gifted at that, I think, and the most prolific at that.

But the idea of taking the short story form out of the anthology, where it had resided with Hugh Garner and G.K. Chesterton and even Morley Callaghan, people like that who were taught in the Catholic school system, and saying, "We can understand why you're bored by that. We represent something new and something fresh and something here and now and living." That was the important thing, it seemed to me — that however you did it, whatever voice you used or whatever devices, the real thing that you were after was that shock of the new, that shock of recognition, and you were aiming not for the approval or the respect of the audience so much as that shock of recognition.

AW: And that's key to your use of telling detail.

CB: Yes.

AW: What you call "texture."

CB: Yes.

AW: Bringing the things of reality sharply into focus in the work.

CB: Yes, yes.

AW: And creating that response of recognition. I was interested — given the emphasis you have on the visual as well as on the aural — that at one point you saw yourself as an artist. It was the visual arts that you actually started off working in and they continue to be an important part of your work.

CB: Yes. In fact, I have a chapter in *Time Lord* on Caillebotte, the French painter of the 1870s, whom I look on as one of the touchstones of the time. Even his very large painting that you can see in Chicago at the Art Institute of Chicago, called in English *Paris Street, Rainy*

Day — I think it's a magical piece of work. But yes, I'm still a child of the visual arts and I go to museums religiously wherever I am. When I say "religiously," I mean "adoringly" — with a view to regularity but also towards adoration. I think of painters as possessing a gift that I would like to have had. But there are many artists' groups that I have the same awe of. I have the same awe of acting, when I see what actors can do with lines, and delivery, and singing. If I'd been given a great voice, I would probably have contemplated that — I listen to the voices, too.

AW: When you're trying to bring the details of life into fiction and portray the contingency of life through a disjointed form as you often have in the most recent stories but even in your earlier ones as well — stories that are divided up into thirteen sections, stories that transcend a given point in time but you might have parallel narrations going on, earlier and later — how do you work at imposing form on experience that is so diverse and contingent? How, in other words, do you strike a balance between portraying chaos and imposing form to create a story rather than just a direct portrait of life?

CB: That's a huge question, worthy of a book of criticism, because I think it's in fact, is it not, the lesson of the last half of the twentieth century: How do we impose form over chaos? We have a strong sense of the chaotic nature of our own being, as well as the chaotic nature of society and history. Society seems a very thin membrane stretched over chaos, stretched over disparate "veto blocks" — people who can cancel out your presence like that [snapping his fingers].

You look at all the competing forces that go into the make-up of a work of art or an individual personality or a society and say: How do you arrive at form? Well, here in the United States you impose form by invoking the Constitution, something in some ways irrelevant to our lives and in other ways central to our lives. But it's over two hundred years old. It's like a novel in form, you know — there's a beginning, middle, and end, there's consequence and antecedent, there's still respect for authority and law and all the rest of it, even though we realize that people when they're left to their own devices are probably lawless.

Now in the short story, or in fiction, one way you try to stretch this membrane over disparate experience is through voice. I think it's obvious that so much of what we desire to have in a short story is in fact a representation of chaos and a representation of the irrational. You can do that in a short story because it's like a one-hour session with a shrink: you're not there to listen to the cure, you're there to get the facts, you're there to get the story, and you want to have just enough recognition coming out of that chaos that someone knows something is wrong. If it's not the author, then it's the character. Something within the story tells us that this is an intensification of reality.

So I would say that what modernism has taught us — modernism meaning going back into Fleming's time, the 1880s — is that rational inquiry into the nature of society and the nature of history and the nature of faith and the nature of the human mind, which was all undertaken with Victorian confidence that it was going to lead us to an even greater confirmation of God's plan, whatever it may be, of a knowable universe, led us in fact into a quagmire of irrationality. So the rationalists who led us into the unconscious couldn't find their way back out. And it became far more appealing for the painters and for the musicians and for the writers to valorize the irrational.

I almost feel that anyone who pretended to know what was going on, any artist or any art form or any genre that pretended knowledge, was pretentious and pompous and a joke. That attitude was launched almost immediately with the turn of the century but it derived from the failed rational enterprise of the earlier part of the late nineteenth century. So we were left with the notion that society is a seething cauldron and the human psyche is warring instincts. And we haven't really gotten out of that, it seems to me. Even the universe, which seems methodically placed, is a seething cauldron of quantum bits. It's a plasma. It's not fixed. So why shouldn't the arts, why shouldn't we, have a form to reflect that?

And I think the short story has become that form. We don't expect out of the short story the kinds of resolutions we expect out of the novel. Not that all novels resolve themselves, but I think if you live long enough with a novel, you presumably see enough of the world through that novel, see enough of the characters in that novel, that you would feel cheated if you didn't have some sort of resolution, not of the world's problems but of the conflicts in that book. Whereas I think in a short story the whole paradigmatic form of rising action, climax, dénouement has been pretty well subverted by generations of masters who now give us voice as sort of the alternative to form.

I think we distrust form. A perfect form is distrusted. The only thing we trust is voice. And even voice, we know, is in fact risky to trust. There are so many charlatans out there. But we feel confident that we can understand and interpret the mistakes in a voice, whereas I think the comfort of structure is something that is taken out of our hands as readers, so we tend to distrust it. You know what I mean — if we feel the artist is following a conventional path of construction, we say: "No, no, no, I want solar panels, I don't want natural gas. No, no, no, I want a den off this room. I want my kitchen here." In other words, we don't want to follow what convention has laid out for us. I think that the short story, being more modular in a sense, has more moveable parts to it. You can still call it a story even if it looks like a poem or if it looks like a play. But novels, I think, are a little more rigid.

AW: So in many ways we've abandoned dramatic structure, but you still maintain some other forms of structure in your work — for example, duality. We've seen your relationship to borders in many different ways. We can see dualities operating throughout your work in terms of past/present, different places, different identities, it might even be different names for the same character. Do you see duality as a major structural principle in your work?

CB: Not as a structural principle. I simply see duality as part of the shape-changing, chameleon-like nature of reality. We can't trust appearances. We can't trust even our own experience at times. So I don't see it as a structural element so much as I see it as simply an honest reflection of complexity. I mean, I can handle duality, but really it's a polymorphous thing. It's not a duality, it's a triality or pentality, whatever you want. Just as I was saying, in terms of my Southern, my Pittsburgh, my Montreal, and my international selves: Where am I? What or who am I? I don't know.

Maybe everyone has that feeling and mine is just more dramatically laid out because it has geographical underpinnings. Maybe someone who was born and raised and is still living in Toronto feels all of the same pressures. To what do I ascribe my identity? Is it religious, is it gendered, is it communal, is it linguistic, is it geographical? I've made a fetish perhaps of my differences, whereas others have not been forced into fetishizing their differences and then are able to parade at least a seemingly unitary nature.

AW: Is it more a quality of contemporary life? Is it more universal than that? Is it something that we face in our post-whatever period?

CB: I think definitely there is a greater awareness of the fragmented world, of the world in fragments, but also the fragments that are inside ourselves. And we now have new allegiances. So that instead of saying that my allegiance is to my state or my county or my village, you can now say, no, I see myself aligned with gay and lesbian activists around the world, or I see myself reflected in some other way. So that what at the turn of the century might have been a liberating notion in seeing yourself in the brotherhood of labour, that we are in the union, which brought people of diverse backgrounds into a single cause, was perhaps an early example of what is now a universal given.

AW: So is there something to fall back on after all? Is there the art itself? Some have seen your work as primarily about artists. I'm thinking about Robert Lecker in particular. He sees your work as fundamentally about art itself.

CB: Well, it would be very hard for me to imagine writing something that is not reflexive in some way, that isn't aware of the fact that it is undertaking a work of art, that it is using art to explore something else, but nevertheless is aware that it is doing that. Whether that means the work is about that is something else. It seems to me that's a tool towards full disclosure. It's a way of reassuring the reader that you're not trying to hide anything, which is a way of saying it's a more ultimate trickery. It's like the magician deliberately working in short sleeves so that you know he has nothing up his sleeve. It just means he has to put it somewhere else. That's how I feel about it.

I would shy away from overtly wanting to write about an artist as the subject matter. But I have no problem indicating that the person is a writer or is an artist of some other sort because to me that only means he's concerned about what tools he has at his disposal and how he's going to use them. I can't talk about, say, a mid-life crisis among roofers and plumbers because I don't have the tools. I can talk about a mid-life crisis for someone who is an intellectual, someone who is an artist, which is probably no different. But that doesn't mean I'm talking about art. I'm talking about a mid-life crisis and using art.

I would love to be able to have that range of experience, as Richard Ford might. One of his characters is a travelling salesman who is seized by a vision of his guilt-ridden self when he is on the road in Wyoming, or something, at a bar, picking up a woman. That's not my world. But I understand, I think, what he's getting at. We shouldn't confuse ends and means here.

AW: One of the dualities that has most interested me in your work is the duality of the surface order and the chaos that underlies it. I'm thinking in terms of stories like "Words for the Winter," the way in which vermin seem to represent, particularly in an urban setting, the natural chaos that seems to permeate the subsurface. And it's certainly the case in stories like "Grids and

Doglegs," where people are trying to impose an order on chaos and it doesn't quite work.

CB: Well, that's carried over from my Southern childhood — from Silver Springs, where you go out in those glass-bottom boats and look down through the clear waters and you see the turtles and the fish. That gave me an early and permanent sense of something going on all the time just out of your range of vision. And if anyone doesn't take into account that there are worms in your feet or cockroaches under your rug or leeches in your lake, if you don't take that into account, then you're just a bloody fool and you'll not only be foolish, you might die from it — you'll certainly suffer from it.

I look upon that really as just more or less my Pascalian nature. This is almost a religious view, not necessarily Manichean, but certainly a view that there is the world of reality and also the world we prefer to live in, which is like a dream — "I who live in dreams have suffered something real." There is a reality and there is a dream that we prefer to live in and for the most part we don't want to be wakened or disturbed from our dream state. But it's a dream of perfect harmony, a dream of a perfect world, a dream that there is meaning and love and that the good are rewarded and the wicked are punished. And that has just not been my sense, I think largely because I had that early training in nature red in tooth and claw and my body was one of the sites of that struggle.

AW: The city in your work, all the way through to recent stories but particularly in "How I Became a Jew," set in Cincinnati, and various stories set in Pittsburgh and Montreal, is very much a place where various ethnic groups, various races, come together and you find yourself caught in this tribal world, where you have to find your way through and figure out which community you're going to belong to, which community you are expected to belong to, which community you ultimately do belong to. Do you see the city as the site of that kind of conflict?

CB: Yes, I see the city as the fragmentation of the unified world and the attempt to construct a new world. You come to the city prepared to discard an earlier identity and to pick up a new one. That's exactly how I see cities. The cities are the site, if you wish, of the violence of the death of an old identity and the rebirth of a new one.

But that's the way it has been for at least two hundred years. The documentations we now have of Vienna and Berlin and Paris and New York over the last two hundred years attest to the fact that the only progress in humanity — the only social progress, psychological progress, intellectual progress we make — is because of the ability of the city to destroy traditional identity and to force something new and sudden upon you. That's what happened in all those sites and in the great despairing works that came out of that experience.

You have to have a critical mass of people who are undergoing the same trauma who then band together and find a new preferred identity for themselves. Usually that identity is in the sciences or in the arts — it transcends ethnicity, religion, and all the rest of it. That's why in the European model Jews and Christians were able to forge at least some degree of harmony, working towards a common new identity. That's why men and women could, once women were able to walk away from their prescribed roles and become forces in and of themselves. Gay and straight, in modern cities, finding coherence beyond their sexual roles. These are important moments. The city to me is the central place where all this happens.

AW: And then there are the stories about travelling to India, from "Going to India" through to "Man and His World." What does India become symbolically as well as psychologically?

CB: India I've used as really the sexual sparkplug, if you wish, the sexual dynamo. It's where characters go and are maddened, sexually maddened, by India. It's I hope a little bit hotter than Forster did it, but perhaps it comes out of the same impulse. These characters go to India as professors and they end up becoming fools, totally naked, totally destroyed by their lust. I wrote about it in *Lusts*. I wrote about it certainly in stories like "Sweetness and Light" and "Doggystan." It's sexuality. This is the one place where I cut loose on that score. How it bears upon my own marriage I don't know. It's very strange.

I'm well aware of the fact that it's dangerous in these times to write that way. You know, it's seen as colonialist and misogynist and all sorts of terrible, terrible things like that. You can't worry about that, you can only write what seems to be probable. India offers the distance and the provocation for these characters. And it's not as though they come out of it as swaggering conquerors. They are transformed far more than India is transformed.

AW: They are conquered by India.

CB: Yes.

AW: And as with so many of your stories, geography becomes a catalyst for exposing the self, revealing the self, creating a new self.

CB: India has been the source of my most violent imaginative leaps: man and dog in "Doggystan," for example, or the layers of man and monkey in "Sweetness and Light" and man and the mother and the daughter in "Man and His World." It's as though India has offered a place for my imagination, in that spirit, to have free rein. And I've let it have free rein. I'm tired of the stories set in India by Western writers that play on other stereotypes of India. Maybe I'm playing on a stereotype of India, too, but I really have no interest in the colonialized India, the Raj and all that. I'm not interested in the colonial interaction. And I have no interest in the spiritualized India, the Vedantic India. I'm not interested in any of that sort of stuff. But I do know Indian literature written by Indians for Indians, not for Western consumption, and how sexual it is, so that I feel my work is closer to the Indian model of how it renders its own self than how Western people, especially politically correct Western people, have portrayed it.

AW: So what are you working on in the short story these days?

CB: I have a short story right now that I was hoping to finish and read here at the conference. But then I saw that I had only twenty minutes allotted and it's too long for that. It's set in Pittsburgh. And it's really based on *Romeo and Juliet*. In fact, there's a lot of *Romeo and Juliet* in it. It's about a sixteen-year-old boy who out of loneliness asks his parents for a foreign exchange student in the house. It's supposed to be a German boy who comes, but instead they send an Indian girl. So he who is living this life of a repressed high-school intellectual in Pittsburgh in the mid-fifties suddenly has this smouldering sexpot put into his life. I am quite consciously paralleling *Romeo and Juliet* — there are lines from it. That finishes my Pittsburgh stories.

AW: And that story is called ...

CB: "The Waffle Maker." The story just before it, another new story, is called "Sitting Shivah with Cousin Benny." It's about a cousin Benny in Pittsburgh from the Jewish side of the family on the other side of town who is the musical genius in the family. My character who is narrating is the literary side of the family. And the two have always sort of envied one another. Benny, who was the prodigy and had all sorts of early success, ends up being a diplomat in various parts of the world. The story heads to Moscow, where Benny and his girlfriend stage a little cabaret. The cabaret is called *Perestroika Is an Old Hotel in Sverdlovsk and Kurt Vonnegut, Jr., Is a Bellhop Inside It.* What cousin Benny ends up doing is becoming a song-and-dance man in Moscow with Yelena Vaingurt, who is his girlfriend. So that's the shivah that he's sitting — for the old Benny.

Other stories ... I feel I have to do a new Montreal story. And I don't know anything about it except that it starts with someone running across someone else on a street in New York and saying, "Hey, aren't you, weren't you, so-and-so?" It has two Montreal exiles meeting in New York who didn't know each other all that well though they do recognize one another. But I don't know what it's going to be about.

AW: So these are for the new series of stories being brought out?

CB: For the Pittsburgh and the Montreal volumes. And then I have to do a number of new international stories. Those I can do easily. But really what I'm doing is the novel. So this is a sideline.

AW: Well, I'm certainly looking forward to seeing the new series of stories come out — and then the novel after that.

CB: And *Time Lord*, too. That's my hope for a prosperous retirement.

AW: Thank you very much for your time.

CB: Thank you.

A Long Way from Autobiography: An Interview with Clark Blaise [2011]

Catherine Bush

BUSH: It's a great pleasure to be here this afternoon with you, Clark, at the International Festival of Authors in Toronto. We'll be talking today about your most recent book, *The Meagre Tarmac*. But as I was saying back-stage, Clark, I'm interested in the movement of your work, over the course of your literary career, between autobiography and fiction. This trajectory culminates in *The Meagre Tarmac*, a collection of linked stories that on the surface doesn't appear autobiographical at all. But I'm also interested in the way you have created, or have, a hybrid identity as a writer: someone born in the U.S., who has lived in the U.S., but who has also lived in Canada and self-identifies as a Canadian.

CB: We were French-Canadian and English-Canadian. My mother was from Winnipeg; my father was from Lac-Mégantic in rural Quebec. They were very mis-matched. My mother was an artist and a very well-edu-cated person. She had done all of her work in Europe. My father was illiterate, quite literally. He left a monas-tery at six or seven. He was the eighteenth and expected to be the last child in his family, though another one came along later. And, as was the custom in those years, the youngest boy was given to the church. Well, he was a very inappropriate gift for any church. He went in at four and left at six or seven. That was the end of his schooling. Then the family moved to Lewiston, Maine, where he got a job at the age of eight or nine at a shoe factory. And then they moved to Manchester, New Hampshire. These were all French-Canadian enclaves in those years. And in Manchester he worked in the Amoskeag mills as a bobbin boy, as they were called, for twenty-five cents a day. That was my background, coming from the suburbs of Pittsburgh to Denison University in Ohio.

Somehow or other I always had it in the back of my mind that I wanted to be a writer. But I came from such unpromising origins that I didn't know what to write about. It took until the last half of the first course I ever took in writing, when I was a sophomore in college, before all that "Write what you know" business finally caught on to me. And what I knew was that when I was a very young kid — from the age of six, when we entered the U.S. from Montreal, until the age of ten — we lived mainly in a very backward part of central Florida. It's now called Disney World, but when we lived there it was really primitive. It was unchanged since the Civil War, more or less. Very Faulknerian in every possible way.

So I wrote a story about that. And it shocked everybody at my little school in Ohio, because they thought of me as a suburban Pittsburgh kid and here I was writing about these people who were the children of moss pickers — far lower than tenant farmers. They lived an itinerant life, from cypress tree to cypress tree. They took the hook and brought the moss down from the trees in order to stuff pillows and stuff furniture. And suddenly I got this kind of blowback or feedback from my fellow students that was sort of awe-inspiring for me. I had been a fairly indifferent student. And suddenly everyone said, "What else are you going to write?" So I wrote another story.

After finishing my B.A. at Denison, I went to Harvard for a summer and studied with Bernard Malamud. And *he* was impressed by what I wrote. He said, "What do you want to do with your life?" And I said, "Well, I want to write." Then he said, "How are you going to do that?" Because by that time my parents were divorced and I was totally free or totally unpaid-for. So I said, "Well, I guess I'll go to Iowa." Because Iowa was the only school that gave a master's degree in Writing at that time. And he said, "I can get you into Iowa." So he did. And I did.

By that time I was starting to say, well, this Southern stuff is not really my material. I'll run out of it, sooner rather than later, because I'd left the South for Winnipeg in 1950. I'd only had four years down there. And the South I was talking about, even then, by 1962-63, that South had disappeared with Civil Rights laws and all the rest.

My parents were Northerners in the South. And not only that, they were Canadians in the South. And not only that, they were French and English in the South. So each of those stages of autobiography was like peeling the onion. Each opened up new possibilities.

By that time I had finished at Iowa, had gotten my MFA. My thesis was called "Thibidault et fils," about my father and me. Then in 1966 my wife, Bharati, and I moved to Montreal and I started writing totally as a French person. I wrote in English but as a Franco-American or as a Québécois.

Since then I've been trying to explore these various autobiographical avenues in my life. I married, as you well know, an India-born author. And so I tried to incorporate

India in my work, which is a far cry from Montreal or the Pittsburgh suburbs or the Deep South. But I managed to link them up one way or another. And that satisfied me or satisfied readers for about twenty years — developing this kind of autobiographical voice which, even if it hadn't ever happened to me, I tried to make it sound as though it had, I tried to make it credible as autobiography.

BUSH: Can we talk just a little more about that impulse, as we move towards discussing *The Meagre Tarmac*? I'm interested, for instance, in a book like *Resident Alien*, which dates from the mid-eighties, but you're using autobiography explicitly there. What's interesting about that book is that it has both sections that are autobiographical essays, these frame essays, and fiction in it. You describe it as "an autobiography in tales and essay[s], though it contains some of the most thoroughly invented stories I have ever written." I'm curious about how the book came to have that shape, that roping together of explicit autobiography and fiction.

CB: Well, I have to plead guilty to a little bit of plagiarism there, a little bit of theft.

BUSH: All writers steal — but tell us more!

CB: I was thinking of Naipaul's book, *In a Free State*, where he also sandwiches stories between journal essays. And I was struck by that possibility. Not that I was in any way beholden to it, but it was something that struck me as being a way, maybe, of ridding myself of my autobiography. That I would simply state, openly and nakedly, in essay form, "This is what happened to me," and then try to match those essays with stories that took off from them but were totally invented. There were four stories in that book — well, three stories and one sort of novella. The first story was very much autobiographical. It took place in the South. It was my last Southern story, more or less. Then the next one was set in Pittsburgh. And the one after that was set in Montreal. And the novella was set in Montreal. The character becomes progressively French. By the end, he's back in Montreal as a French author.

After that, I really did rid myself of my autobiography. The next book, *Man and His World*, was in fact totally invented. I mean, the next fictional book. I did one or two nonfiction books in between. And thereafter, leading up to *The Meagre Tarmac*, I haven't really been indebted to my own life.

The reason why I started writing autobiographically was I just felt that I had been given a unique world: the Canadians in the South, the French and the English. All of that stuff resonated with me if with no one else and I felt I had to make it resonate for other people. My particular quest was to make people aware, first of all, that there were such things as French Canadians, Franco-Americans, whatever they may be, because that was not a well-known thing in the U.S. and I was living in the U.S.

And I also wanted ... You alluded to this earlier: I self-identify as a Canadian, with Canadian parentage. But I'm the only American in my family — everyone else is in Canada. My parents wanted me to be born in the United States because it was 1940 and Canada was at war and the U.S. wasn't. Quebec was not about to join the British cause. In fact, it seemed possible that Quebec might join the Nazi cause. The Quebec reality was decidedly anti-British, whereas the U.S. wasn't. And my mother was in her late thirties, and I was the first child, and she didn't want to lose me. So there were a lot of reasons for them getting out of Quebec.

Mémère, my father's mother, who was living with my mother and father, died in September 1939, the worst month of the worst year in the twentieth century. She died and that freed my parents, who were looking after her, to be able to move. This may sound strange, but my father knew as a French Canadian, he knew as a Québécois, actually the word "Québécois" didn't exist then, he knew as a French Canadian, as *un habitant, un Canadien*, he knew that he had no future in Quebec.

I wanted to share, I suppose, how the shadow of French Canada — in its worst years, the Duplessis years and the early part of the twentieth century — lived atop my father's head, or inside his heart, all during my lifetime with him, and how it twisted him and produced his hatreds and his shame and his embarrassment. And maybe his pride. I don't know.

BUSH: Turning to *The Meagre Tarmac*, your new collection ... The stories here take us, at least superficially, a long way from autobiography. They are narrated mainly by first-person narrators, all of whom are South Asian, most male, but at least a couple female.

CB: Four are female.

BUSH: Four are female. And one is a thirteen-year-old girl. Some might say there's something transgressive here, though certainly you're writing about a world you're familiar with through your marriage to the Indian-American writer, Bharati Mukherjee. So I wondered if you could talk about the impulse behind these stories.

CB: In a certain way, this was a book that you always hope will happen to you. I really felt that these characters were like actors that were off-stage waiting for their cue to come on. Writers often talk about just copying down what their characters are saying — or just feeling as though the characters are there and you are a witness to it, you are trying to get it down as fast as possible. This is what happened to me with this book.

All of these characters seemed to have come prepared with a backstory. They were from different parts of India. They came to different parts of North America. They had different careers. But they all seemed coherent to me, the women and the men, the Bengalis, the Maharashtrians, the Karnatikans, the Parsis, the Christians, whatever. They were all in the book, and they seemed to be all in my head, but they had intact personalities and identities. I never felt I had to build them, or had to create them, taking a rib and clay and making a person out of that. These people were already there. I guess they had probably been there for a long time, but I had lacked the confidence to enter their world. I had written *about* India a lot, two full books and many many many stories, but always as an outsider, always as a declared tourist or whatever it might be. This time, they were the ones who were speaking.

BUSH: So did you hear their voices?

CB: Oh, yes. As I say, I was simply copying. I guess it was time — after fifty years of marriage it should be — for them to take over. I'm doing another book right now of linked stories about people who are Franco-American and the same thing is happening. The characters all seem to be pre-formed. It goes back two hundred years and up to the present day.

BUSH: I'm curious if the nature of these characters in *The Meagre Tarmac* affected the shape or the structure of the individual stories, too. Could you talk a bit about that?

CB: There's a larger arc to the whole book: that these are people who came very well-prepared to succeed in America, or Canada, in the early 1970s, when finally the quota system that favoured Europeans was suspended and well-equipped, well-educated people from all over the world could come to North America. They took full advantage of it and they prospered for the most part. They were taught to invest wisely, to study hard, to live frugally, and good things would happen.

Now, that would all be true if they had stayed in India, where their parents would have selected a husband or a wife for them. But these people came as graduate students, without marrying, and had to go through that battle of finding a wife or finding a husband when they had no training in dating or anything else like that. One of the characters says something like, "We never had the Archie-and-Veronica high-school experience. We never made out in the backs of cars, we didn't know about sports, we didn't know about songs and movies. We knew all the important things that universities can teach you, but we didn't know any of the trivial things."

This is a culture that is based so much on trivia, on being able to exchange tales and exchange references. And these people didn't have the references. They had the big things, but they didn't have the little things. And that eats them up in some ways. The characters here have not made wise decisions, sexually or maritally or whatever you want to call it.

The other arc in the whole book is that once you've reached, say, the age of sixty or something, you have to start making plans about death, making plans about who you are and where you want to be. And a lot of these people don't want to die in America. They want to go back to India. But the India they want to go back to is the India they had in their minds when they left. And that India has disappeared. That India is in fact deader than anything sixty years ago, forty years ago, thirty years ago in America. I mean, India has changed more.

The third thing is that there used to be a saying among Indian immigrants, "Twelve and out." Meaning that when your child turns twelve, you better go back to India or else you'll lose — especially her, but him too. You will never have the comforts of a child in your home. In India the son is supposed to marry and then bring his family back to his father's house. You always have the large family with you. You have your grandchildren. But that doesn't happen anymore. If the child is over twelve in America, he's not going to be that kind of child.

BUSH: One of the most vivid voices in the collection is certainly the young thirteen-year-old girl.

CB: Pramila.

BUSH: She's being threatened with going back to India. It looks like she is going to be forced back. What's interesting, again at a formal level, in a collection of linked stories, is that for the first two stories we are within her family, we hear her voice and get very invested with her as a character, and then we never hear from her again, which is part of the nature of the form of a collection of linked stories, which gives you some overlap but then leaves certain characters for others.

CB: You have a little bit of her in the third story, which is from her mother's point of view. Everyone fears her. I mean, she's a genius. She's going to be entering Stanford at the age of thirteen — the youngest person that Stanford has ever admitted — as a mathematical genius. But she's also having an affair with her ice-skating coach, a Russian. She's sort of the Lolita figure in the book, except she's brilliant. She tries to see the world totally in mathematical terms — this is algebra, this is geometry, this is trigonometry, this is calculus — and she treats people that way. She says to her brother, who is a tennis player and not a genius, "I can give you an algorithm for beating the Stanford ace." And she gives him an algorithm, but he can't even read the algorithm. She's that kind of person. She is a genius and she is bold and she is edgy. She's also conniving. And she is scornful of her family. But her father is the one who has destroyed this family. His arrogance. His pride.

The mother has been quiet in the first two stories of the book. We think of her just as someone who stands over there, frown on her face. And then we find out her passions in the third story. So the mother and the daughter are a lot more alike than you might think.

BUSH: Again, the decision to create this as a series of linked short stories — as opposed to something more novelistic — seems very important. I guess I'm interested in the particular attractions of the short story form for you.

CB: Oh, they are enormous. I find novels — this is going to sound arrogant — I find novels too easy to write. You just sort of sit there and fiddle around and after three hundred pages you can say, OK, it's over.

BUSH: [Laughter.] Oh, I wish it were so for all of us.

CB: [Laughter.] Well, I mean, I've done it. But the short story demands that there is a consequence for just about every word that you put in the story. And everything is under such pressure. To me, it's like a cloud chamber in physics. You see collisions happen and then they fade. But you know that at any given moment it might erupt again, because you have this confined space.

To me, in writing a story, you have to account for what a person does, what a person thinks, and what a person says. So you have exteriority and you have interiority. And you have to have a transition that allows you to go from what a person has just done to what a person *thinks* about what he has just done. But you can't slow it down in order to have their thoughts. Their thoughts are also part of the dramatic action.

It's a demanding form. I have a friend, Lee Abbott, who has done about twenty volumes of stories — I've only done ten — and I asked him, "When are you going to write a novel?" He's sixty years old. It's getting time. And he said, "I never had an idea I couldn't handle in twenty pages." And I guess that's sort of my view. If I have an idea that is going to take more than twenty pages, then I'll make it into nonfiction.

BUSH: That's an interesting distinction: If it's going to take more than twenty pages, it will become nonfiction. I think there's certainly a way that these stories do encompass lives within them. They have that kind of wholeness.

CB: I suppose the message I would extract from all this is that to me the short story is an expansive form and the novel is a contractive form.

BUSH: Contractive — how so?

CB: The novel says the least it can get away with saying about a much larger span of time or number of characters or whatever it may be.

With the short story, if you go into writing it with the idea that it's a miniaturist form, you're going to minimize all of these rich interactions I've been talking about. You're going to say, oh, I can't do this, I can't do that, because I have to keep within twelve pages. But if you are really thinking it through, you know that within those twelve pages you have to account for everything that happens within that one scene or the two scenes or whatever it may be.

My favourite story of all time is Thomas Mann's "Disorder and Early Sorrow," in which you are really talking about the destruction of the entire German middle class, and the Weimar Republic, in the German inflation after World War One — a trillion marks to buy an egg. Here is this family that never leaves their dinner table in that whole story. Yet what Mann is relating is the death of a civilization. You know that just outside the Nazis are beginning to stir.

It's of course a brilliant story. But that, it seems to me, is what the short story can do. It can suggest by analogy and by all sorts of other modes a very much larger story than it seems to be.

Dancing Over a Sentence:
An Interview with Clark Blaise
[2013]

Brian Bartlett

BB: From your fiction workshop those nights in your living room in Montreal in 1975-76, to my office here at Saint Mary's University this afternoon in Halifax in 2013 — it has been a long road, Clark. I was thinking back to almost forty years ago now, and it seemed our first encounter was at that Concordia workshop in September 1975. Then my mind went back a bit further, when you'd read as a member of The Montreal Story Tellers on the UNB campus a year or two earlier. One reason I later wanted to move to Montreal from Fredericton, other than the lure of that city, was to do the M.A. under your guidance, and some of that desire came through strong impressions made by reading your first story collection, *A North American Education*. One of the few memories I still have of the UNB reading is that you read the beginning of the title story, quite a big chunk of it, maybe up until the end of the circus scene.

It all began: "Eleven years after the death of Napoleon, in the presidency of Andrew Jackson, my grandfather, Boniface Thibidault, was born." And I remember thinking, "Sounds like the beginning of a novel." The first paragraph went on in that vein, encompassing wide stretches of history, decades upon decades. And it struck me with a sense of revelation, as a young reader, that the first page or two of a short story could offer that kind of sweep, something akin to nineteenth-century novels. But then, within paragraphs, your story moved into the minute detail that we think of as so much the art of the short-story writer — the horseless carriage churning through the mud, and, eventually, that wad of bubblegum offered to the stripper Princess Hi-Yalla. Everything from Napoleon's death to that bubblegum — it amazed me that this could be done within the first few paragraphs of a short story.

The short story, then, the short story … In the graduate class you said once, and I do believe you had a glint in your eye when you said it, and were speaking hyperbolically: "Anybody can write a novel. But the short story, *ah, the short story.*"

CB: [Laughter.] I probably did say that. Right, right. The novel seems a far more forgiving form, in that if you have the patience and at that time the typewriter ribbon, you can probably churn out a novel. I realize, of course, I'm foreshortening a lot of the ordeal that goes into it, the work that goes into it, the planning and the plotting. But it does seem to me that the short story more or less calls upon a certain kind of writer to write it, whereas the novel doesn't send out any necessary signals — it's open for business at any time. The short story is not, though, I don't think.

BB: So, how would you describe that kind of writer?

CB: Well, I think it's someone who wants to expand upon a moment, who wants to see all the connections that are possible within a fairly short span. I've often written that short stories are an expansive form and novels are a condensing form. That novels leave out so much in a twenty- or thirty-year span. The short story cannot afford to leave out anything in a much shorter span. So I think there are people who simply look through one end of the telescope and people who look through the other end.

BB: Is there a kind of horizontal/vertical difference? Thinking of your first academic field, geology: Does the short story have a vertical, subterranean, sedimentary quality?

CB: Stratigraphy, it's called. From "strata." That's how you learn about things in geology, and paleontology, and things like that — by going through the onion and peeling off the various strata. Yes, I would think there's something to that. Of course there are so many kinds of short stories now. I'm talking largely about the classical short story as it has come down from Chekhov and Joyce and all the rest. But now we have a very broad and wide-open kind of short story. You read short stories that are sort of modelled on Ikea furniture, self-assembled. You know, tab A into slot B, it's that kind of writing. And you can import any number of contemporary commercial, or political, or sports, or certainly telecommunication languages and come out with a short story. It doesn't have to be a lady with a lapdog.

BB: And then, as you've noted in regard to Munro, we get the development of stories in which ideas about singularity of effect, all those things Poe insisted upon, have largely fallen by the wayside — or at least been drastically modified. In Munro's later stories, it's often hard to forecast how the focus will change from page to page, and there's a great fluidity of consciousness and time.

CB: And there are so many false closures in a Munro story. You think you're heading towards this particular conclusion, and you find out that it's just on the wayside. And an entirely different conclusion is being drawn.

BB: That technique appears in some memorable films, too. You're expecting a certain conclusion, the film seems to be building up to one — then you're relieved when there's not yet a winding-down or a winding-up. The script, the director, and the characters take you somewhere else, to yet another place.

CB: It's not always the *O.K. Corral* exactly.

BB: Another memory of Montreal, from September 1975. The first class was on campus, then after that we met in your living room ... and thank you for all those bottles of wine, and all those *hors d'oeuvres*. [Laughter.] You probably don't remember, but I missed the second class because it was the first one in your house, and you'd given us the Westmount address, on de Maisonneuve, corner of Clarke Avenue — C-l-a-r-k-e, wasn't it?

CB: Right, as opposed to Clark, further east.

BB: Well, I went to C-l-a-r-k and de Maisonneuve, between St. Urbain and St. Laurent. Totally lost, new to the city, didn't know what was going on, your place wasn't there — here I'm going to *Clark* Blaise's class on Clarke Avenue, but I get the wrong Clark(e). Yet in retrospect, sometime in the next few years, I thought how utterly appropriate the confusion had been. Because we have Blais/Blaise, and Clark/Clarke, and it's easy to connect them to all the twin names in your fiction: Thibidault/T.B. Doe, Boisvert/Greenwood, Carrier/Porter.

Back to your fiction workshop: in your essay called "Mentors," in *Selected Essays*, you give very high praise to — and provide very affectionate memories of — Bernard Malamud. You've identified him as perhaps the greatest inspiration and model for you as a fiction writer. You say that he taught by "tolerance" and "conviction." You describe him as not flamboyant, but as "calm, even serene," and say that "as a reader, as a teacher, and as a writer, he takes *delight*; there is no other way of putting it." And then you speak about how you could see "his eyes, his mouth, his brow, suddenly dance over a sentence, or a word, or an idea." And I just wanted to say your description of Malamud reminded me of your own approach to teaching in that workshop.

CB: Well, I'm honoured, at least.

BB: Here's another memory, about a workshopped story by someone who has remained our friend, Peter Behrens. In one scene he was describing a police or an ambulance siren, the way its sound moves up and down in volume. And he used the phrase "thready wail" — do you remember that?

CB: Yes.

BB: That's the sort of thing that poets notice, and poets in prose: "thready wail." I recalled it when I read your description of Malamud's features dancing "over a sentence, or a word, or an idea." What I took away from that class was your response to "thready wail."

CB: How inefficient. I mean, two words from a whole semester!

BB: [Laughter.] No, I meant that one night, that one class, not the *course*.

CB: Speaking of Peter Behrens, I remember something he did that I tried to point out to the class — he so perfectly described the heat that comes from an old car's heater. You know, on a cold, cold Canadian night, when you had the heat coming in from the manifold and you had to open up the two little doors. And I said that it's more worthwhile to be able to describe the heat coming off a heater than it is to describe anything else in the story. That *that* was the thing that gave me the assurance that this was a writer who paid attention, who noted things.

BB: Another thing that has stuck in my memory: I'd written a story that included the word "multifarious-ness" — somehow that word came up in the conscious-ness of a teenage narrator. And I distinctly remember you saying, "Good old multifariousness."

CB: [Laughter.]

BB: [Laughter.] Which strikes me as an appropriate word to see your work through, because there's so much that is multifarious about it, in terms of geography and point of view, and the fragmented sense of self, and short-fiction structures, and so on.

CB: You know, I'm also remembering, when you say that, Malamud's description of the short story, which was "the multifarious adventures of the human heart."

BB: It's funny, I hadn't made that connection, but just this week I remember reading that word in your mem-ories of him.

CB: So "Good old multifariousness" probably was ...

BB: Yes, you may have been silently thinking of Malamud, then.

CB: Right.

BB: Now, in *Selected Essays*, one of your essays ends with a tantalizing memory of a novel you'd begun before you went to Iowa, then continued working on at Iowa, called *The French and Jewish War*, about your parents, mostly set in Canada. And that memoir ends dramatically, with a scene of you in Iowa City rereading pages from that novel, vomiting, and then going outside to a near-by garbage can and ripping the manuscript into shreds.

CB: It was about 130 pages or so at that time. Well, you know, it was necessary to do it. Out of the ashes of that came the stories in *A North American Education*, "The Thibidault Stories," like "A North American Education," "The Salesman's Son Grows Older," all those stories that had to do with a Southern childhood with a French-Canadian/English-Canadian parentage. That was the novel, but I was upgrading it to Pittsburgh, and my parents' divorce, and my father's relationship with a very dubious, shady woman. And so I think the parts just didn't mesh at that time.

BB: But you make your dissatisfaction with the novel sound so visceral.

CB: It was visceral.

BB: Was it filled with disgust at what you'd written, or disappointment...?

CB: I think I was regurgitating a lot of the disgust that had happened when my parents divorced, and when my father was sucked into this relationship — or, give him credit, he probably wasn't sucked into it, he probably initiated it. I'm sure he initiated it.

BB: So, there was maybe too much of that draft that was insufficiently distanced, or wallowing...?

CB: Too personal, too autobiographical. The stories that are in *A North American Education* that arose from that are often thought of as very autobiographical stories, but they were not really in a sense *to me* as autobiographical. I think I had somehow been able to shield them or ironize them in some way, to where I didn't feel at all exposed to anything in those stories.

BB: Yes, they very often are couched as memories, with the distance of years looking back. They are third-person, past-tense. They would be very different if they were first-person, present-tense stories.

Some critics have referred to a "rootlessness" at the heart of your vision and in your characters' lives. While I can see that being valid with, say, *If I Were Me* or *Man and His World*, I've wondered if "many-rootedness" might be a more useful metaphor for talking about the

lives of your region-crossing, border-crossing characters in North America. Do "roots" have to be singular,
in other words, or can one "put down roots" temporar-
ily in several or many places? With their attentiveness
to place, your characters dig into the loam of Florida,
Pittsburgh, Montreal, and other places. Some of them
seem to put down roots wherever they are, and the
roots remain, even if the plant is torn up and your characters hit the road for other places. Even in *Days and
Nights in Calcutta*, you dramatize efforts to put down
roots. Maybe this is several questions at once — but how
do you respond to the difference between "rootlessness"
and "many-rootedness"?

CB: Rootlessness has a sordid history, thinking back to
the anti-Semitism of "rootless cosmopolites." Even in
this continent of celebrated rootlessness and diversity,
virtue seems to reside in some sort of deliberate im-
mobility. I've always tried to put down some kind of
second- or third-generation root, knowing full well that
the only root that continually nurtures is probably the
first one. I think my truest root is probably Pittsburgh
of the 1950s. Nothing there was problematical: I fit right
in. Everywhere else, the Deep South or Montreal, Iowa
or California, came too late or was fraught with obvious
impediments to my total absorption. But all my life,
wherever I've found myself, I've found reasons to call it
"home" even if there hasn't been a satisfactory *click!* to
tell me that I'm truly rooted in a place that was meant
for me. I think I've used the "shallow-rooted" metaphor
in one of my books, though I don't know which one. It
would probably be in *Resident Alien* or *I Had a Father*.
You know, one of those easily uprooted tropical trees
whose root-system is shallow, but extensive.

BB: On another topic altogether, I want to mention how

helpful your two essays "To Begin, To Begin" and "On Ending Stories" have been over the years. I've almost always used those in fiction-writing classes and literature classes on the short story — not necessarily using the essays, but giving credit — summarizing aloud, for instance, different sorts of ways that stories can end. One thing I've found so helpful is that for many students, who are used to thematic criticism, those essays redirect their attention to structure, pacing, imagery, phrasing, all the things that — more than a set of themes — give a story its uniqueness.

CB: Endings are important because they're the *last* thing that you can say. It's the last chance you have to hold the reader's ear. I also use the other one of those essays, "The Cast and the Mold," sometimes when I'm teaching to try and get students to see what is the mold of this story, you know, just what is the largest idea that the story is contained within?

BB: Right, the words on the page make up the cast, but what they suggest — the mold — is something with limits that aren't so easy to define.

In terms of endings, this week it struck me that one example of what you call a "trapdoor" ending might be the final sentence of your Carrier story "North": "She took my hand in both of hers and swung my arm like the clapper of the biggest bell in the world." The sudden simile there gives a sense of leaping off into something unexpected, rhetorically, like the example you gave at the end of Cheever's "The Country Husband," where the language and imagery reach into something fantastic, far from domesticity — Hannibal crossing the Alps.

CB: I had in mind there also the Catholicism ... that Carrier had made a certain amount of peace with the Catholicism or the essential Frenchness of Montreal.

BB: An unexpected ending that dazzled me even more is from a more recent story, "Life Could Be a Dream (Sh-boom, Sh-boom)," the second-last story in *Montreal Stories*. The last paragraph of that tells of a couple at their, what, fortieth high-school reunion, clasping hands — there's the image of the ants. Suddenly there are those ants. And bones. Grotesquely the couple are disintegrating into nothing but bones, they're dead.

CB: They're dead, yes.

BB: It's a shocking, really shocking ending and yet feels so right.

CB: Well, so right for a fortieth reunion. [Laughter.] It's like that old D.H. Lawrence title, *Look! We Have Come Through!*

BB: A different sort of ending, which *sounds* more conclusive, is that of "At the Lake," from your second collection, *Tribal Justice*, which simply goes: "I haven't been back since." By the way, that's a story I've taught in nature-writing courses, partly from an ecological point of view, you can understand why. Your fiction seems ripe for consideration from within the whole tide of ecocritical approaches to literature, which has grown enormously in the past couple of decades. In your writing there's so much about human interrelations, families, and contrasting cultures, but there's also sometimes a strong sense of the non-human, or the animal, creeping in. The Florida stories, with the lush ...

CB: Well, that's unavoidable.

BB: The alligators ...

CB: ... and snakes, and birds ...

BB: ... and the giant turtles, and the buzzards. And at the beginning of *Lunar Attractions*, it's there ...

CB: The alligator, yes.

BB: Nature suddenly ... grabs on. And your new story,

"The Kerouac Who Never Was," we have the archetypal, the moose ...

CB: That's for you, Brian.

BB: [Laughter.] The moose-in-literature tradition — Thoreau describes encountering them in *The Maine Woods*, one of Alden Nowlan's best-known poems is "The Bull Moose," and there's the great Elizabeth Bishop poem "The Moose," with its bus trip from Nova Scotia into New Brunswick. Bishop's moose is a mysteriously benign cow-moose, a "curious creature," but in your story violence arises — a collision with a moose decapitates a driver. And that's a reality of Atlantic Canada. A few years ago my mother spent a week in the hospital sharing a room with a woman who had recently become quadriplegic after her car hit a moose. That woman's accident is one of several that caused the New Brunswick government to build the moose fence you would have seen last week on your drive between Moncton and Fredericton.

But to return to the last sentence of your story "At the Lake," "I haven't been back since": when I first read that ending I took it literally. I simply thought it meant that once the narrator has been coated in leeches from the lake, his pristine dream — his kind of National Film Board dream of the Canadian icon, the summer cottage — crumbles, and he's never able to go back to the lake. So I was recently intrigued to find, in "Words for the Winter," from your first collection, *A North American Education*, though I don't know if it was written earlier ...

CB: Yes, it was.

BB: So, in "Words for the Winter" — it's the same character, right, it's the same narrator? Who is married to Erika?

CB: More or less. I should think so, yes.

BB: The same name, Erika, is used for the wife in both stories. In "Words for the Winter," you have an urban infestation of mice — but at one point your narrator says, "The lake has taught us to live with black flies and leeches." So then I thought, well, in terms of the chronology, maybe when the narrator in "At the Lake" says, "I haven't been back since," he means, "I haven't been back to that naïve state of mind, to a belief in the escape to the realm of nature as all tranquility, health, support." He and Erika have learned to "live with" the black flies and the leeches. Is there something like that going on in the intersection between the two stories?

CB: That's very interesting. Those are stories I wrote forty years ago, so I'm really not on top of what my motivations were, or what my thoughts were, at the time. But I like your idea very much. Seven types of ambiguity? Well, you know, a thousand types of ambiguity are possible in interpreting languages, and I think if you had an actor reading those lines, he could probably extract from it exactly that meaning. The way he would pronounce the word "back" or "since" would give you the sense immediately that we're not talking about just the road from Montreal up to Lac Bibitte, we're talking about a mental journey back. Also, that he's having to learn to live with voyeurs in the alleyway and with raw eyes inside the pigs' skulls.

BB: Oh, so you think of the story you've just alluded to, "Eyes," as overlapping with the two we were just talking about?

CB: Yes, there are a lot of things that he's having to learn to live with, coming to a new country.

BB: Now, that's interesting, because I'd never thought of "Eyes" as having the same central character as "At the Lake" or "Words for the Winter." Maybe because "Eyes" is your only second-person story. Your only one, isn't it?

CB: Yes, I think so.

BB: Another interesting connection between a couple of stories: in "Translation," we're told, "Porter, still confused, had mumbled, 'Montreal can break your heart.'" In the earlier story "Among the Dead," a different narrator says, "Despite its reputation, its tourist bureaus, most of the island of Montreal will break your heart." So the two characters are heard speaking the same line. And with different stories of yours there are other moments of crossover, which, in a sense, question the stability of self or the idea of characters as closed entities. There's a fluidity among your narrators and characters. In your "Autobiographical Essay" you've talked about the many selves you've invented — so, why not have different characters use the same line?

CB: Well, there are parts of Montreal that will break your heart. Let's face it, there are endless tracts of Montreal that are soul-deadening in ways that even American suburbs are not, or American inner cities are not. I've lived in some of them — outer NDG and places like that. You feel as though they have been untouched by any architectural intelligence.

BB: And even worse, the industrial wasteland far east. Doesn't Hugh Hood have a story about it in *Around the Mountain*? I remember cycling through it once, feeling like I was travelling through something post-apocalyptic. No residences, no restaurants, no trees — in my memory at least, like some blasted lunar landscape with no more than a few sterile-looking structures of industrial civilization around.

CB: I think I talked about bleak landscapes in "Translation," about the Catholic retirement home in Laval. Big yellow scab on the horizon.

BB: As you can tell, in the past week I've been thinking a lot about the varieties of your story endings. "South," for instance, comes to a close with a one-sentence paragraph: "Mother, why couldn't we love you enough?" — which reminds me of the ending of the epilogue of *I Had A Father*, simply the exclamation, "Father!" Teaching poetry, I've often talked about how the emergence of address or apostrophe can be very special and intense, because something that has been talked *about* — it's an object — suddenly becomes a subject, it's spoken *to*.

And yet the exclamation "Father!" is ambiguous — like the ending of Melville's "Bartleby, the Scrivener": "Ah Bartleby! Ah humanity!" I've never quite been able to figure out whether or not there's an element of address when the lawyer, Melville's narrator, exclaims, "Ah Bartleby!" Is he just commenting on Bartleby, or is he also addressing him from this side of the grave? And is "Ah humanity!" also addressed, in part, to us, the readers? Your single-paragraph "Father!" is haunting in similar ways.

CB: It's also about the pumpkin seeds that have grown. That thing that was thrown out has come back to germinate. And the "Mother, why couldn't we love you enough?" of course is, or at least I was hoping was, the unstated, sort of felt but unstated, undertone of that whole story. But I wanted to emphasize it.

I felt, for example, in thinking of Alice Munro's "Walker Brothers Cowboy," her first story in the first book — that's a line that she could have used. The father gets all the attention, but the mother is the one who is sitting there in the heat making her dress for school. The mother doesn't get the ice cream. It's that kind of thing, the unappreciated person, that I wanted to emphasize.

BB: The ending of "South" is clearly an address, because

it's "Mother, why couldn't we" — but the ending of *I Had a Father*, did you think of that as an address, an apostrophe, "Father!"?

CB: No, I thought of it as a manifestation. The transmogrification, if you wish, of those random seeds spoke to him at that moment as "Father!" Because it's from the same general area that the father had come from, upper New Hampshire in this case. People try to throw something out, try to throw something overboard, in a sense, and it comes back and mocks them, in a certain way, and says "I'm not going away." And that's really what *I Had a Father* is about. It's that the father doesn't go away, even though he's dead. The book starts off with him, with the little cigarette burns on the porcelain, which was like the father leaving things behind. So that it goes from the cigarette burns on the porcelain to the germinating pumpkin seeds. The father is somehow an eternal ... You know, he's eternally there.

BB: Whenever I read that ending, I also hear it as almost like a raw cry, as a "Father! Father!" As a plea or a cry to him, not just a comment on him.

CB: Well, you know, the book has been trying to understand him. So that what might have been a complete rejection of the father at the beginning — that he destroyed the family, and he was a destructive force in many ways — by the end, after all the research and after all the understanding of what he went through, he has been reinstated in some way in my consciousness.

BB: When *I Had a Father* was published in 1993, the Canadian edition included a blurb by Russell Banks that said in part: "I've long admired Clark Blaise's fiction, but I think that with *I Had a Father* he's written his best book."

CB: Well, Russell is a good friend, an old friend, from

New Hampshire. And Russ is the only American writer — Russ has said this before — he's the only American writer who has ever met my father. We were in New Hampshire together — my father was by that time living in Manchester. And Russell was living in Dover, where the University of New Hampshire is — he was teaching at the University of New Hampshire. Either he came down to Manchester or else I had my father with me and we went up to see him. So, anyway, Russell is the only one who has ever met my father, the mythical guy. So it's understandable that he would feel that way about the book.

BB: In the afterword to the book, you write that you began it "nearly three years ago and suspended it in despair." Was that in relation to not knowing if the book worked, or a lot to do with the material of the book, or something of both?

CB: Well, some despair also having to do with the literary world. It was commissioned by one editor, who was in fact quite a well-known American editor, who had married a Blais. He was the first American to play in the NHL — during World War Two, of course. I didn't know, but he was always tracking me. So when he had an opportunity as the editor-in-chief of that company, he immediately went for me — he came to me and said, "Would you write an autobiography?" He said, "I think you've got an autobiography in you." And so I started, but then he was fired. My agent and I had to find an entirely new editor and I was introduced to the new editor and it was someone who didn't have the slightest idea who I was or anything else like that. And I said to my agent, "This isn't going to work." So she had to find a new publisher. It was about two years before we found someone who would take on a book about a man who had no currency in the world by a writer who had very little currency in the world. So all huzzahs to Nancy Miller and Addison-Wesley.

BB: In *Selected Essays*, another tantalizing thing you say, in the "Autobiographical Annex" that goes up to 2006, is: "I have added a couple of chapters to *I Had a Father*, though it still requires a publisher to rescue it from oblivion." That was 2006, quite a few years ago. Has there been any headway made on that?

CB: No, they're still there. One virtual part of it was published by *Brick*. It's in *Selected Essays* — "A Delayed Disclosure."

BB: Oh, that was an addition to *I Had a Father*.

Now, I'm going to be a bit of a devil's advocate here. One passage from *I Had a Father* reads, "Because my father had no friends, valued no friendships or commitments, denied his family, expressed no nostalgia, held nothing sacred, I have become a man of revisitations, sentiment, heritage, obligation, and letters. I've let nothing, and no one, go, from high school, college, or thirty cities afterward." So it's like the pack rat has for a father the antithesis of the pack rat. The question I would like to ask about that passage is: If the father is the great mystery and the great unknown, which seems to be a running theme in your work, how can all of those absolutes about him be used? You know, he had no friends, he valued no friendships, held nothing sacred.

CB: He had cronies, I think I said later on. He didn't have friends, he had cronies. That is, he had fellow furniture salesmen with whom he drank and chased skirts and went on weekend benders. But they were not friends, and they abandoned him as soon as he showed some variance from that. I think all of those categorical statements are true. I asked him once about his friends and he said his only friend was Charlie Gagnon from Manchester. Charlie — and he didn't even pronounce it Gagnon. Charlie Gag-nun. He pronounced it in the American fashion that he had known in Manchester — or Meanchestah. And that was the only friend he ever cited. He had other cronies. But they were not people he wanted to expose me to or to expose my mother to. They were rough customers. Like my father was. My father could put on a veneer, whereas the others really didn't even bother. He knew a lot of boxers, too. He had been a boxer, so he was attracted to the ring, and to guys — when I shook their hands I could tell. If I couldn't fit my hand around theirs, I realized they had been boxers — because they were anvil-fisted.

BB: And whereas your father was very distanced from you, your mother was more accessible.

CB: Oh, absolutely. And she loved to tell tales, to tell stories.

BB: She was vocal.

CB: Educated. Sophisticated.

BB: Some of the details about your mother that have appeared in your essays include her going to Germany in 1930 for an art education, and listening to lectures at the Bauhaus. You describe her as a bohemian atheist, but a small-town Canadian still, an anti-imperialist, but also anti-Catholic. She went to theosophist meetings and read tea-leaves, she revered George Bernard Shaw — a lot of this sounds quite fascinating.

CB: Yes, I re-encountered her in *The Stone Diaries*.

BB: In the Carol Shields novel? And did you say somewhere that she could have been a character in a Mavis Gallant story?

CB: In an Alice Munro story.

BB: Do you think there's an *I Had a Mother* in you?

CB: Oh, that's what I was starting to write when I got distracted into *Time Lord*. What started *Time Lord* is that I was writing about my mother and I said, "Our lives are like time zones" — meaning that they contain cities and prairies and forests and tundras and jungles and all the rest of it, like a time zone that goes around the world. And then I looked at "time zone" and said, that's odd, because ... When did time have zones? And I went to my encyclopedia — I was living and working in Iowa at the time, directing the International Writing Program — and it said time zones came in with a Canadian engineer, Sir Sandford Fleming, who devised standard time for the world. And I practically sent in my resignation letter that day. I did within that semester. I said that this is a book I have to write.

BB: It sounds like *Time Lord* was something that sort of fell into your lap, a big surprise. Suddenly it was there, it was a detour from another project.

CB: The next morning I called The Hutchison House in Peterborough, where Fleming first lived when he came to Canada, and they immediately sent me copies of what they had of his papers, of his various journals, and I read them. And I was on my way to Peterborough two weeks later, talked to the people there, and they said, "No, you really must go to the National Archives. That's where all of his papers are." So I immediately went to Ottawa, rented an apartment for about five or six months, went to the Archives every day, read through the 145 boxes of letters and papers, and started writing the book.

I still haven't written the book about my mother. I toy with the idea — but it was easier in effect to find the necessary documentation on my father than it would be to uncover the hoards of material that refer to my mother.

BB: Because there's so much more of it.

CB: None of it exists. I mean, none of it was saved. I said, when she went into a nursing home with Alzheimer's disease, it was like a shelf of Canadian history was eliminated, because I don't think there was ever another Canadian woman who went through ... who lived the life she did. She saw the Nazis marching down the streets. And the school that she was in was closed almost the day after the Nazis took over. And she went to Prague to work for another two years, until friends there said, "You should get out. You have a Canadian passport, you can get out. And you might want to take me with you."

BB: In his introduction to *Montreal Stories*, Peter Behrens refers to your "deliberate and daring instability of form (is this memoir or fiction?)" and says that your "1970s work anticipates writers like W.G. Sebald." I was wondering if you've read Sebald much, if you see a kinship there.

CB: That would be a reach. But, yes, I do see a kinship. I think we were after some of the same things. I didn't dare integrate photos and overt histories, and the intertextuality and all that Sebald did. Others have talked to me about that too, not just Peter. Sebald and me? Well, I leave that alone. Or let's say they're inflected in the same direction.

BB: Peter was talking about the structural thing, the instability of form or genre, or the overlapping of genres.

CB: Yes, right. "What is this thing?"

BB: And the sense of haunting, certainly. The past-haunted quality of the work.

CB: Sebald had a true haunting from the past. I have personal ... What would be the right word? Inconveniences. [Laughter.]

BB: One last passage from *I Had a Father*. You wrote, "Life without my parents' unspoken, unacted erotic violence is literally unimaginable to me ... which guarantees I'll always be a son and not a husband or a father in everything I write. Life after their divorce seems lacking in pain and moral authority." Now, you wrote that twenty years ago or so, didn't you?

CB: More than that.

BB: Does that still hold or has that changed somewhat?

CB: I think it still holds in the sense that when I write I generally do write as a son. Well, I'm writing a nonfiction book right now where I, of course, write from the point of view of a father and husband, but mainly father in this case, because the illness I'm researching is genetic. But I think the first book that I could claim to have adult narrators was probably *Man and His World*. When I think about it almost all the characters there are adult.

BB: And they're not defining themselves primarily as sons.

CB: Right, right. And that was 1992, I think.

BB: In *I Had a Father*, you speak of "my own sense of incompleteness" and "myself and my prior selves being born," of yourself as "a meta-self at times, a construct of pieces adding up to a self" and possessing a "chameleon-nature." And in your "Autobiographical Essay," you refer to "my Self, those dozens of fictional self-portraits I've executed through the years." It's hard not to think of those passages in relation to the subtitle of *I Had a Father — A Post-Modern Autobiography*. That experimental memoir isn't just postmodern in the sense of its structure and its non-linear, unchronological backing and forthing, or its fragmentariness, but also in its presentation of self — or selves.

CB: I thought, you could pick it up at any place and read

it, like we used to go into the movies in the middle of a movie, and just sort of sit there and wait until "this is the part where we came in," and then you get up and leave.

BB: Your writing about being chameleonic made me think of some Buddhist conceptions of self, which in fact have been compared to postmodernist conceptions — and vice versa. Not so much that the self doesn't exist, as that there's no *independent self.* A self is always dependent, reliant — it's immersed in culture and history and genetics, in both nature and nurture. It's never fenced in, so there's always shifting and transitioning. Much of your work shows how the fences aren't there.

CB: If you read Margaret Atwood's review of *The Meagre Tarmac* that was in *The New York Review of Books*, she talks about when we were together at Sir George Williams, back in the old days. She said how I easily occupied many, many personalities, and I was reading every language, reading every book, and trying to ... and sort of becoming ... She thought that I was an entertaining person, that there was kind of a sliding scale of identities.

BB: Hard to pin down.

CB: She was on to that, too.

BB: Another interesting case involving identity is found in your story "The Belle of Shediac," which concludes *Montreal Stories*.

CB: Ah, yes. Very few people know that story.

BB: Oh, I love that story. Here the narrator is a writer who ends up becoming a translator not because he particularly wills it, but because it just sort of happens to him. And there's the fictional Québécois novelist who almost becomes the narrator's reason for existence, because of the novelist-translator bond, that novelist who escapes Quebec forever during the period of strife in the province — his name is Lacroix. With the allusion to the kidnapping and execution of British diplomat James Cross by the FLQ, some kind of bilingual word-play is going on. Would any readers outside Canada have picked up on that?

CB: Wendy Lesser, the editor of *The Threepenny Review*, where that story first appeared, certainly would have gotten most of the context. She's one of the great intellectuals. She's seemingly the inheritor of Susan Sontag. But even *she* would probably not have known about James Cross. We know the magazine, because it's published in Berkeley. Bharati had published a story, one of the stories in *The Middleman*, in *The Threepenny Review*. It's a very well-respected magazine. And, in fact, it was one of Bharati's best stories, one of the most anthologized of her stories. "Saints," it's called. So I was just trying to keep the family business going in *The Threepenny Review*. I don't think any other American magazine would have had any interest in publishing "The Belle of Shediac."

BB: Too bad Shediac isn't on your Maritime tour, so you could have gone and read "The Belle of Shediac" there.

CB: I passed the exit for it. I was amused.

BB: It would have gotten quite a rise out of the Shediac audience, when the woman who is assumed to be this exotic from Europe turns out to be from the Maritimes.

CB: Well, she is — these are all quite real people. "The Belle of Shediac" was, in fact, *LOOK Magazine*'s 1946 cover girl. Even earlier, at sixteen or seventeen, I think, she was starring with Laurence Olivier in the West End and also starring on Broadway. Her name was Suzanne Cloutier. She was born in Ottawa, married Peter Ustinov, and died in Montreal.

BB: Oh, so some oldsters in Shediac would know the connection.

CB: Yes.

BB: Earlier you mentioned your story "Eyes," with the boiled pigs and their blue eyes and all that. One thing that appealed to me early on in your work was how it can be read as poetry — so many passages in which it isn't a narrative arc, or even characterization, but imagery — crystalline, visceral imagery — that creates the greatest power in the prose. And the pumpkins in *I Had a Father*, as you mentioned, that paragraph about pumpkins, which you don't need to explain, it's just there, followed by the exclamation "Father!" In your "Autobiographical Essay" you quote a passage from *Resident Alien* in which you referred to yourself as "wedded like a reborn Wordsworth to the epic of my own becoming." I wish I'd had time in the last week to reread *Lusts*, your novel that has a female poet as a central figure. But you could say overall, in your fiction and memoirs, there aren't a lot of references to poetry — clearly, fiction dominates your world. Still, I was curious to see that when you were in Iowa in the early sixties, some of my favourite living poets now, decades later, Charles Wright, Mark Strand, and James Tate, were all there ...

CB: And Marvin Bell. Yes. And Don Justice, Donald Justice. We're all friends.

BB: Being a huge fan of theirs, I have to ask: Did you remain in touch with them?

CB: Oh, yes. When Jim Tate was writer-in-residence at Emory and we were in Iowa City, neither Bharati nor I had a job. We were just hanging on because we wanted to see our sons graduate from their high school in Iowa City, which was a good school. And suddenly one day we got a phone call from Emory for Bharati. Jim Tate had just finished his term as writer-in-residence and had recommended Bharati as his replacement. That meant everything as a change because it brought in an income and she immediately went down there and wrote *Darkness*. Within three or four months, all the stories just came pouring out of her. And then they invited me down to be writer-in-residence the next year and then to be the Director of their summer programs for the next few years. So because of Jim Tate we had, suddenly, this Atlanta connection that no one had ever thought of. Mark Strand I've seen innumerable times over the years. We taught together in Mexico, about five years ago. Chuck Wright I haven't seen as often, but whenever I do it's very close, very warm. Of course Marvin Bell and I get along very well. He was the pitcher on our softball team.

Anyone who has lived as long as I have in Iowa City has seen all of the poets coming through every night, all of the poets in America or in the world. Also, when I was Director of the writing program at Concordia, we had a very active Canadian and American poetry series. So, among the poets, Carolyn Forché is a very close friend. Louise Glück. John Ashbery is a friend, because my cousin is his haircutter. My cousin — from the French side of the family — has a salon in Greenwich Village. My ongoing connection with poets runs pretty deep. I was looking at your poetry anthologies here — and this one about movies. I know just about every poet in them. Michael Van Walleghen, people like that.

BB: So, do you see the presence of all those poets as having subtle influences upon your work?

CB: No. No, the only one that did died of AIDS — Joe DeRoche, from Nashua, New Hampshire, and French-Canadian. At Iowa, we had a very close connection about our French backgrounds. But that was about it.

BB: Was it about ten years you were doing the International Writing Program?

CB: Yes. From 1989 to 1998.

BB: Were you teaching in that time, or were you largely a sort of talent scout?

CB: No, I was fundraising, then being the housemaster to thirty-five authors from all over the world.

BB: But that wasn't so much workshop leading or teaching.

CB: No, because they were established authors. They weren't writing *in English* necessarily. Some were, but most of them wrote in their own languages.

BB: Did you miss the teaching during that period?

CB: I have always taught. During the summers I was teaching summer courses. But the second semester was when I had to go out and raise the money, so I was all over the world for ten years. I was out recruiting writers and then going to various arts agencies and granting agencies that could pay for them to come.

BB: Now was it a difficult transition to begin writing on a laptop on airplanes, as you mentioned in *I Had a Father*, or was that just something brought on by necessity that you easily moved into?

CB: It was brought on by necessity. I never had much of a problem one way or another that way. I could write anywhere.

BB: So, do you think there's a lot more of the history of Iowa's International Writing Program that's yet to be written?

CB: Oh, yes. It's an evolving thing. Chris Merrill is now running it. And the university has, I think, corrected a lot of the errors that it was making with me. He no longer has to go out and raise money. The university is paying for it or the State Department is paying for it. I had State Department support for about fifteen of the writers, but I had to find support for twenty others. He doesn't have to do that. So he has been able to expand the program, its outreach. He has been a good force.

BB: You must have been so pleased a decade ago or so, when The Porcupine's Quill started publishing the beautifully printed *Selected Stories* volumes — on fine paper, with coloured endpapers, and so on. But more importantly, as Alex MacLeod has written, they reconfigured your stories in new ways.

CB: That was me doing that, by the way. That was me who suggested it.

BB: But those books didn't have American publication, as integral volumes, did they? It breaks my heart that those were never published in the U.S.

CB: They're beautiful works — that is, the publishing work is beautiful. And there could have been, should have been some reason for publishing American editions. But it was never even attempted. I didn't have an agent at the time. So ... And now it's too late.

BB: You have an agent now?

CB: I have an agent now. Didn't have one then.

BB: Do you think that the new book of stories you're writing, about Franco-Americans in New England, is more likely to find an American audience?

CB: I think it is.

BB: So, you don't think the title you're considering for this collection, *Entre-Nous*, is going to be a hard sell in the States?

CB: The other title I was thinking of was *French in America*, because I have a cache of letters, postcards that my relatives wrote back to my other relatives in Manchester, New Hampshire, back in the thirties, when they were on a French tour in France. And I realized that what they were talking about was not being Franco-American, not being French-Canadian, but being French in America. I mean they wanted to short-circuit the idea that they were twice transplanted. So they felt themselves directly French, despite the little excursion into Canada for three hundred years. So *French in America* is a possible title.

BB: The nonfiction work you've started on now, about genetic diseases, is that going to be a similar project to *Time Lord* in terms of the scope of research?

CB: Yes. Learning about genetics these days is really taking on a bucking bronco, because it's changing every week. Even if I'd gone through biology and I had a genetics degree, it would have been useless today — even if I'd gotten it five years ago. All I can hope to do is be able to roughly translate into English the discoveries in these scientific papers, which are very, very densely written in genetic codes and all the rest of it.

I don't pretend to know what's going on, but I have friends who can help me. I have a lot of friends who run labs — in muscular dystrophy especially. At Stanford, just thirty miles down the road from where we live in San Francisco, there's the inherited disease centre, so they have a lot of stuff. And I know Harold Varmus, a past Director of the National Institutes of Health, very well. And Harold can get me into any lab I want to get into.

There are things like that which are helpful. More than helpful. I mean, they are necessary. I wrote a forty-page proposal for the book, plus the essay from *Selected Essays*, "A Delayed Disclosure." So the editors who have read it are all quite enthusiastic — none of them has made a bid, because they say, "We know he can do memoir, he does that very well. We have to see how well he can do the science." So I have to write another thirty or forty pages purely on the science. And I haven't done that yet.

BB: It will be a different book from *Time Lord*, with the personal dimension.

CB: Yes, it will have the personal dimension. It's memoir and science. I'll have to interview people who run labs, and workers in genetic pharmacies — big pharma, little pharma.

BB: So, is this going to be years of legwork?

CB: They wouldn't allow years, no. If they put money into it, they're going to want results. If today I got word that someone has come across with enough money to do this, I would have to give up doing my Franco-American book. But until then I'll keep going on my *Entre-Nous*.

BB: Clark, to ask a tricky question: Are there books of yours you value more than others?

CB: I would say that the significant books to me, the ones I would really go back to if I were a Blaise scholar — I would say *Days and Nights in Calcutta*, and *The Sorrow and the Terror*, and maybe *I Had a Father*, and maybe *Time Lord*, but certainly *Man and His World*. Because I felt in *Man and His World* I had broken out of the mold of autobiographical storytelling, and I was reaching for really improbable and wild structures and contents. And *The Meagre Tarmac*, yes, again it was a breakthrough in a certain way — that I was able to put together what has been forty-nine years of close observation and close experience, though I had never thought of entering their world through their point of view. I've written about India a lot, but it has always been as an outsider. Those were to me the significant, breakthrough books.

Each of the books I've mentioned surprised me — they opened me up. The stories in *A North American Education*, *Tribal Justice*, didn't open me up. They were already in me and it was just a matter of getting them out. But, you know, throwing myself into the joint family for a year in Calcutta ... that demanded an awful lot of adjustment and an awful lot of, well, atonement, for going into it with Western ideas and Western preconceptions.

Certainly *The Sorrow and the Terror* was, again, totally investigative. Some people have written to me saying that it is the best way of understanding 9/11, and it's the best way of understanding the Lockerbie tragedy, that these are both directly taken from what we discovered in writing that book. Especially Lockerbie — a radio transmitter exactly like Reyat had made a year earlier in B.C. And the Khalistani cells are very much like the Al-Qaeda cells ... only much, much smaller. You just see how the terrorists, which is what they were, can maintain a perfectly conventional Canadian exterior, friendly, open, laughing, and also plotting to kill. And we were able, when we interviewed members of those cells — this is before they were identified — we were able to figure out who was really an RCMP plant, even though he was a full member. And he did turn out to be a plant. We spotted him right away and apparently his colleagues didn't.

This was a giant leap, because it gave me a very hard attitude towards this sort of terrorism, and towards other kinds of terrorism. This got me into a lot of trouble in Ireland a couple of years ago, when I said the IRA, to me, was just a matter of power, vanity, and money among the leadership. And that's the way it was among the Sikhs, the way it was among, to me, all sorts of terrorists. Like Al-Qaeda. Especially when they start going into third and fourth generations of the terrorism business and it's their family franchise. But *The Sorrow and the Terror* gave me an operating philosophy about terrorism.

The criticisms of *Time Lord* that are out there are,

you know, that I'm essentially a literature professor, not a biographer — I take that at its word, it's true. But what it gave to me was an idea of the interrelatedness between technology and the arts that came about in the Victorian era. Because the Victorian era was the great era of technology, the implementation of all the discoveries of the Romantic era, of Humphry Davy and all those people. The Victorians were Prince Albert creating the Great Exhibition, and creating all the technical universities, Glasgow and London and Manchester, that replaced, in some ways, certainly augmented, what Oxford and Cambridge were for the gentleman, and led to Britain's greatest decade, the 1850s, ending with Darwin. Thereafter the long decline. Because all the other European countries started doubling and tripling their investment in the universities.

Well. Those are the ideas that I would leave you with. You know, in a career there are highs and lows, or there are highs and plateaus. And those were the highs to me, working on those books. I think this French book is also going to be one of those, because it's a stretch for me. I didn't grow up Franco-American. My father was ashamed of his origins, and hated Catholicism with a kind of Spanish Civil War hatred — "We castrate them, then we string them up," you know, the priests. And he was far more anti-Catholic than my mother was. My mother was sort of intellectually anti-Catholic. My father was viscerally anti-Catholic, because something happened to him when he was given away to the church. He was the *donné*, the youngest son. So I was not raised in French. I had a consciousness, of course, of what I was, and every now and then we would visit my aunts, his sisters, in Manchester. They never learned to speak English — it was that dense a ghetto. And I picked up

curse words and numbers and things like that, but that
was about it. My father didn't want to teach me French.

BB: The main character in your new stories is younger
than you, right? About ten years younger — born in the
early fifties, not at the beginning of the forties as you
were?

CB: And his brother, Paulie, the gifted one, of course
has the muscular dystrophy. And drops out of school.

BB: That's a very dramatic moment in "The Kerouac
Who Never Was" when Paulie grips the baton but can't
let go of it because his muscles have seized up.

CB: Bart noticed that when he was on the Saratoga
Springs track team.

BB: Yes, I remember you writing about that in "A Delayed
Disclosure" — Bart having to pull his bunched fingers
apart, one by one. So, exactly what is the background
of your main character in *Entre-Nous*?

CB: I've made him thoroughly French-American, and
Catholic, and French — speaking French and with
French-speaking parents. So this is a reach for me. And
later he goes off to Europe at the age of fourteen, at the
invitation of Betsy Robitaille.

BB: Is the book going to cover a period up to the seventies?

CB: I think it's going to cover more than that.

BB: So it will see him well into adulthood, then.

CB: Oh, yes. Because the big arc is the break-up of those
communities, the assimilation of those communities.
This is at the very tail end, even in the sixties it's the
very tail end, of the Winooskis etc. All the towns in New
England, all the larger cities in New England, had a
French suburb — not a "suburb" but a French part that
was all mill workers, tenements. By the seventies they
were all gone.

BB: It sounds like you've got a lot of exciting work to look ahead to.

CB: Well, yes — but you know the years are running out, the sands of time are running down, and my energy level is less. There's that, and there's just the need to look after my family. I've gotten them into a fix, in a sense, and I can't get them out of it. That's my tragedy — or the tragedy of our families.

In the Beginning:
An Interview with Clark Blaise
[1992]

J.R. (Tim) Struthers

TS: The importance of understanding history is a point made subtly yet forcefully in the concluding sentence of your early Southern story "The Fabulous Eddie Brewster" — the truly revelatory type of final line that gives you new information and insight, takes you right back into the story, makes you see the story completely differently. At the end of that story, the narrator states: "After their divorce several years ago, my mother went back to Canada and now teaches history in Regina." That's an important choice on different levels. Yet some people, considering the idea of going back to Canada and teaching history in Regina, might regard that somewhat in the way we interpret the word "Saskatchewan" when it is introduced in Mavis Gallant's story "Speck's Idea" collected in *Overhead in a Balloon*. That is, some people might regard that final line of yours rather ironically.

"The Fabulous Eddie Brewster" is a story about the ways in which the title character, the narrator's father's older brother, born Etienne Broussard, now calling himself Eddie Brewster, is willing to accommodate himself, about what he is prepared to give up in terms of ideals to do that. And in the final line of the story we are given a vision, a look into the future, which for the narrator

135

is now a very important part of his past, at which point the mother is seen as finally having refused to accommodate herself to her husband's schemes. And we may also remember that Regina is the home of the drafting of The Regina Manifesto. Is all of that working in this story's final line — and more?

CB: Well, my mother was a CCFer. Whether she would have thought of Regina as the home of The Regina Manifesto or anything else like that, I don't know. But she was a lifelong socialist.

First of all, I was trying to distance myself just a little bit from Winnipeg, which I had used before and which I could have legitimately used again but I wanted to find an equivalent for it. Ontario clearly doesn't strike the right note. You have to have something that is starker than Ontario and less built up with Royalist and other kinds of Tory sentiments. So I wanted to have something that was prairie, that had a prairie radical streak to it, and that's why I chose Regina, Saskatchewan, because there was no starker opposition on this continent than Saskatchewan and Florida.

I was not using Saskatchewan in the sense of Mavis's saying "Saskatchewan" like a slap in the face to European culture. It is the equivalent of my mother's vision. Saskatchewan, with all of its harshness and its ruggedness and its unpromising unappealing aspect and its socialism and its progressivism in general, its sort of Tommy Douglas-ism though I don't want to be unfair to him, its practically religious socialism, its smug quality, its very, very strongly self-confident socialism, not a tentative Fabian branch of socialism since it has all the thundering righteousness behind it — that was what I was trying to get. I wanted to get my mother's stiffness in that way.

TS: These are attributes which your father, because of his personality, his upbringing in Quebec, his apparently terribly punitive childhood initiation into the Roman Catholic church, would have opposed.

CB: Right. So that I meant to be a little bit ironical. My mother was not as stiff as that character in that story. There is a slight difference between Manitoba and Saskatchewan. There was a kind of harshness and ferocity to some of the reformism that was abroad in the land in those years that I associated more with Saskatchewan on the Left, Alberta on the Right, than I did with Manitoba.

TS: And as you've explained in the memoir essay "Tenants of Unhousement" published in 1982 in *The Iowa Review*, when your mother was a young woman she left her family in Manitoba to go to Europe to study art and design.

CB: Right.

TS: There's your parents' history and then of course there's your own history and how that shaped you as a writer. I would like to read a couple of comments that you make about William Faulkner in the opening segment of autobiography in *Resident Alien*. You say: "In the beginning, then, I thought of myself purely as a Southern writer on the basis of five potent years in my life — ages six through ten — spent in the swamplands and hamlets of north-central Florida. Faulkner was my guide: his language, his evocation of doom, of age, of the implacable determinants of race, class, and history. My small world fit perfectly in the Yoknapatawpha legend...." And a little later you say: "I understood those favourite words of Faulkner, and I used them myself: *deep, beyond, further*. It was Faulkner, to his glory, the divine and sometimes tangled rhetorician, who had the faith and the tact to title a story simply and forever, "Was." It is a title for a collective experience of story-telling." In this context — that is, in the context of the formative influence on you of the American South, the world of William Faulkner — I would like to ask you about two other early Southern stories, "Relief" and "Notes Beyond a History."

CB: They're both very old stories.

TS: And they're both Buck's Cove stories.

CB: That place has been filled in now. When I went back a few months ago to do a reading at the University of Central Florida in Orlando, I walked along the shores of that lake with the professor who had invited me, Anna Lillios, trying to point out to her the various land-marks. She also had read those stories.

TS: You call it Lake Oshacola in those stories.

CB: It's Lake Griffin in reality. Lake Harris and Lake Griffin are the two lakes that are around Leesburg, Florida. I went to the old cove where the boat landing was and it has all been filled in. It's cottages now.

In my forthcoming book, *I Had a Father*, I'm simply making the discovery that while my father was raised among illiterates without running water or electricity on the edge of a tranquil lake, Lac Mégantic, in Quebec, I too was raised at about the same age among illiterates on the edge of a tranquil lake, although it wasn't all that tranquil, in central Florida. At age six or seven he left Canada for Lewiston, Maine, then later for Manchester, New Hampshire; at age ten, I left central Florida for Canada, for Winnipeg. So there are some strange analogies to be drawn.

In writing this newer book, I went back to Lac Mégantic and now it looks like a peaceful cottage-strewn little pond on some giant's greens as I've said, I think, of Lake

Oshacola or Lake Griffin in one of the stories that you want to talk about — "Notes Beyond a History." Driving around Lac Mégantic and looking at the little cabins of the *petit bourgeoisie* of the region, you would never think that it had ever known squalor, death, suffering, on the scale that my grandparents went through.

And the same thing would be true of this lake in Florida now. Disney World is nearby and tourists run the place and the little cabins are comfortable and well-maintained with flowers and bougainvillea growing and you would never think that it had the alligators, the snakes, the pestilence, the death, the squalor that I knew.

TS: "Relief" is a hurricane story. It's a story, to me, that invokes one of the great dualities: art and nature — or, as you refer to this pairing in the title of an early Pittsburgh story, "Grids and Doglegs." The young boy in "Relief" goes to school one day and his teacher says she has heard on the radio that a hurricane is coming. Later, as he narrates the story, he reflects how that very morning in school he had been reading a story about "a frontier family cut off by a blizzard and their near-starvation before relief had come."

One of the ways in which I think of stories is as a dialogue with the dead — to echo the title of James Joyce's novella, "The Dead," at the end of *Dubliners* — the dead who are very much present and in that sense living with us. But I also think of stories as a dialogue with other writing, sometimes even with specific earlier stories. Hemingway, for example, had different storm or hurricane stories — "The Three-Day Blow," "After the Storm."

I was wondering if you had any particular story or type of story in mind when you introduced this detail of the boy's reading assignment that morning about "a frontier family cut off by a blizzard and their near-star-vation before relief had come."

CB: It was a story about southern Nebraska, as I recall. It was a standard anthology piece. I think the story was by Ruth Suckow.

TS: Ruth Suckow. A couple of her stories appeared in John T. Frederick's 1924 anthology, *Stories from* The Midland, which contained selections from Frederick's magazine, *The Midland*, founded in 1915. Also included in that anthology were a couple of stories by Walter J. Muilenburg, one of the favourite authors of Southwestern Ontario writer Raymond Knister, as well as Knister's own story "Mist-Green Oats." Interestingly, the magazine came out of Iowa City, home of the University of Iowa where you did your MFA in the early 1960s and where you became Director of the International Writing Program in 1989. I'm sure that Frederick's anthology was the inspiration for Knister's 1928 anthology, *Canadian Short Stories*, the first work of its kind in the history of Canadian literature. But to return to your story "Relief" …

CB: Part of what I was doing in that story was remembering the anger that I felt, as a Southern schoolboy, being forced to read this stuff about the North. Not because as a Southerner I didn't want to read Northern stories. It was because I felt they were taunting us. Snow was such a powerful concept. Snow was such a sign of grace. So if they were throwing stories about mountains or stories about cities or stories about snow into our laps, they were telling us this is something you can't have, you're not good enough to have this experience. That was my feeling at the time. I felt a great anger and a great envy towards those kids being cut off by a snow-storm because I knew if we were cut off it was going to be by water, by flood.

That story is really about a physical phenomenon called a seiche, which happens over large bodies of inland water when a hurricane passes over. What happens is the eye of the hurricane is at very, very low pressure and so the low pressure forms a kind of vacuum over the water and actually sucks a dome of water, a visible dome of water, up into the eye of the storm. That's why the story begins with the great retreat of the water away from the cove, so that the kids who are fishing there are seeing things that they have never seen before as the water is released and the mud appears and old sunken boats and fish and other creatures of the water gasp to the surface.

There's a sense of an enveloping and approaching terror — first from the physical world of a seiche, and then, as the storm passes, that dome of water is released and all of it comes rushing back in like an inland tidal wave creating the unnaturalness of fish deposited many miles into the forest, of fish on your lawn, the unnaturalness that even causes the snakes and the alligators to seek refuge, and then, added to that, the social dislocation which causes Whites and Blacks — in those times, in the Deep South, of segregation — to be forced into the same world of almost dismemberment, of social dismemberment. At the end of that story, whether one gets it or not, I intended that the White boy was actually attacked in the night by his own father when the father heard a noise and thought the boy was a Black.

The vision I was trying to get across here was that the natural and the unnatural divisions of the world — you know, water should not retreat, fish should not be in the woods, alligators should not be out of their nests — are in fact reflected by, or enhanced by, the unnatural barriers that are being broken down in the social and racial world so much so that a father would attack his own child in order to preserve what he thinks of as the natural order of things.

I should say that those early Southern stories you're talking about come from the period in which I was exploiting the one clear advantage I had as a young writer. That I had seen and lived in and inhabited and in fact owned a world that was unique to my time and place. That is, writing — as I was as an undergraduate at Denison University or in the very first year that I was at Iowa — so that none of my classmates had the least experience of what I had seen.

I had not yet seen my way into Canada, or seen my way into French Canada, the French-English situation, or anything else like that. I had only seen into the most superficial level of my distinction or of my uniqueness, and that was as a Southerner. And I wasn't even writing in those stories as a Northerner transplanted to the South. And I wasn't writing as a Canadian transplanted to America to the South or as a French and English Canadian transplanted to America to the South. I was writing as a Southerner from the South.

So long as I wrote about those childhood experiences, I could be authentic. But if I wanted to broaden the context to bring in anything else at all, it wouldn't be authentic. I couldn't pretend to be a Southern adult, which I was not. Nor did I have possession, really, in my mind, of the transformation of the South from a rural segregated world of pestilence and ignorance to a reasonably modern world. I couldn't write about that. I certainly couldn't write about the transformation of Florida into a tourist haven or a retirement village. Those stories were written with confidence and a kind of defiance and a kind of local colour enthusiasm to show what I knew that other people didn't know.

TS: By writing implicitly about the notion of story in "Relief," you elevate it beyond being a story about nature. It becomes a story about the intersection of nature and art. This is signalled by the emphasis you give — metafictively — to the act of reading by referring to the boy studying the story about the frontier family caught in a blizzard. You also mentioned in an interview by Barry Cameron that the opening of "Relief" is indebted to a Faulkner story.

CB: "That Evening Sun." It was totally unconscious. It was unforced. It was only later that I realized the connection. The incantations, the rhythms, and the duality — that was then, this is now; that was then, this is now; that was then, this is now — that sort of thing is so Faulknerian. I was simply showing that my own world resembled his. My own world paralleled Faulkner's so clearly that it was an unconscious lifting. Years later I understood where it was coming from and I wanted to identify it.

TS: My introduction to Faulkner, after an initial reading of *The Sound and the Fury*, came with his story cycle *Go Down, Moses*. I was wondering if you could say something about your response to that book.

CB: Well, sure. The idea that a book of stories can be as carefully integrated and calibrated as a novel and that these stories are, as Joyce said, chapters in "the moral history" of a society — not its paralysis as in *Dubliners* but its decline and in fact damnation leading to the discovery in "The Bear" of the source of the damnation, slavery — is, I think, a powerful, powerful lure for any of us.

TS: The other Buck's Cove story that I want to ask you

about — and doesn't a character named Uncle Buck figure in the opening story, "Was," in *Go Down, Moses*? — is "Notes Beyond a History." In this story you have two boys instead of one boy as in "Relief": the unnamed protagonist/narrator and his brother, Tom. The protagonist/narrator becomes a historian and a teacher and writes a history of the fictional town of Hartley, Florida — though, as he says, he's not as successful a historian as he might have been if as a youngster in Florida he hadn't experienced the extraordinary river journey with his brother on which they discover a hidden population of Creole people who aren't listed in any of the official histories. And Tom, who appears to have been traumatized by that event, becomes a builder of rockets for the exploration of outer space. The protagonist/narrator muses that both of their vocations seemed determined by their childhood journey.

I was wondering if you would talk about the impact on the two boys of their archetypal journey, about the distinctions that you establish between the historian and the scientist, and finally about how this particular story moves, as its title proposes, beyond history to art. I'm interested in the ways in which the vision of an artist includes, yet differs from, the perspectives of a historian and a scientist.

CB: My structuring of that story was a little bit more elaborate than anything I had attempted before and probably it's strained because of its structures. I don't normally work in terms of those kinds of overt dualities, the two brothers, the two professions, whatever they may be.

Clearly when I say "Notes Beyond a History" I am referring to art — that is, the only thing that is beyond history here would be science on the one hand or art on the other. My narrator is not an artist; therefore, he is, by his own account, a kind of failed historian because he is in possession of a body of knowledge that he cannot nail down historically. There are no documents for these people, no documents to explain them. According to history they did not exist, they were never there. So he has seen something that never existed. According to his discipline, according to his world view, they never existed. So in other words they were a vision, they were a visionary reality. They are rather like the drawings done by the late husband of old Theodora Rourke, the woman who lives next door, who seems to have *lived* beyond a history. She seems to have been there from time immemorial. She is a racial survivor.

The only thing that is autobiographical in that story is the fact that when I was a child of seven or eight we *did* have a woman next door to us in Leesburg called Big Mama, Big Mama English, who was a hundred years old in 1947, in fact had been a teenager when the Civil War was on. She was totally White. There was no mixed blood in her. And she used to love to tell us stories. I was the one, of course, who absorbed these stories. I would go over there every night and listen to Big Mama telling stories about central Florida in the 1850s, 1860s. I never lost that sense of a world beyond the one I knew. The point is that I have seen it embodied.

She was the repository of stories that my mother was — but even better stories and older stories. And she was also the repository of stories that my father never told me, which would have been equally powerful and strange and odd except he never told them. She was my mother and my father, in a sense, in the stories that she could tell. The stories she told, of course, were very, very Southern stories. Maybe they were coloured by subsequent revisions and *Gone With the Wind* kind of nostalgia. But in any event they were powerful stories. Had I had a cassette recorder or had we known about things like this or had she ever been identified by some WPA person, she could in fact have given William Styron and every other American writer a version of reality that, again, I alone was privileged to have ever heard. I alone, among people who have lived to write about it, am the only person who has those stories.

This story is a little bit about the mixed inheritance, if you wish, of having had that experience. It's a primordial experience such as the early explorers had when they first landed in Santo Domingo and saw natives, or Marco Polo had when he first came to China. It's wondrous and it's horrifying and they try to kill you so that you will not carry the story back.

The narrator survived — he has the story. But he doesn't have any audience for it. He doesn't have any believers and he can't prove that these people ever existed. That, to me, is art. The only thing you can do is try to make people see it and he doesn't have the tools for making people see it. He only has the confusion or he only has the pain of finding his discipline not up to his own experience — which is of course the opposite of what a historian should be. A historian has no experience, he has only the facts, and he creates a picture from the facts. What if you have been given the picture and there are no facts? That's the art.

TS: What does the story that the narrator can't tell — but that he, paradoxically, does tell in the telling of this story — represent?

CB: Well, it has been twenty years since I've read it, and even more years since I wrote it, but I think what he's trying to say is that we cannot go forward successfully until we can understand the nature of our past, this collective past. In other words, we can pave it over, we can confection it with trees and shrubbery, we can invite Disney to come in, we can build pizza places and franchise malls, and we can send men to the moon — we can invent all these powerful tools of denial — but very deep in our soul is the knowledge that populations have been exterminated, populations have been denied, history has been unable to account for some of the monumental blunders or some of the monumental wonders in the world. The narrator of that story wants powerfully to be able to account for them but he can't, he needs help or he can't, and the country he is seeing is collapsing into foolishness, whatever he says at the end, the last words are something like that, "crumbling into foolishness."

TS: "And made Tom, eyes skyward in St. Louis, indifferent to it all — the broad facts and the sidelights — and everything else around us crumbling into foolishness." A concluding statement that echoes the narrator's opening statement in that same paragraph: "A passage I once marked from a story of Henry James reads, '... the radiance of this broad fact had quenched the possible sidelights of reflection....'" Can you, by any chance, remember the source of that quotation from James?

CB: I think I read the story in a selection of James's stories called *The Madonna of the Future*, but I can't remember the title of the story at the moment.

TS: I'll see if I can track it down and I'll add any details that I discover.

Yes. I found it. The quotation is from the story "At Isella," first published by James in 1871 and subsequently printed in 1962 in the Signet Classics volume of his work entitled *The Madonna of the Future and Other Early Stories*.

But to return to "Notes Beyond a History" ...

CB: I think the narrator of that story feels like a lot of, say, conservative historians would feel — that until you can get a true accounting, everything that we've built upon this uncompleted and unseen history is rotten at the base. He's enjoying a kind of physical comfort, air conditioning and all the rest of it, that he never thought would come to his little area, but he knows what lies underneath.

And I do share this with that character. Just as I felt in the case of the old lady in my old home town of Leesburg, Florida, whom I met recently when I went back to see my old house and found her living there, I know what lies underneath that house, I know what lies underneath her backyard, I remember when there was a stone wall there where the snakes would come out and sun themselves in the afternoon and where the birds would come and try to pick them out of the crevices at night. I saw all that. She denies it. I saw it.

There's blood. There's a lot of death and there's a lot of blood. Across the street from where her little house is, where my old little house is, is now a walled-in retirement village. But on that very ground is where we had cleared a baseball field and where my jaw was broken as I describe in the novella "Snow People." That's right across the street. All of these things happened within fifty feet of where I was standing. And it's all denied now. It has Palm Meadow Court Retirement Village or something. It has old geezers from Buffalo, with their canes, walking around. And while you can't say that this is all a mistake, no, no, no, go back, I do powerfully want to mark these things with a little plaque.

TS: The final early story that I want to ask you about — not, in this case, a Southern story, but one set somewhat further north in the United States — is "The Sei-zure." The story is only thirteen or fourteen pages long but it is very richly textured. It has the kind of density and scope that one might expect of a novella. You've written a number of novellas — "Snow People" in *A North American Education*, "The March" in *Tribal Justice*, and "Translation" in *Resident Alien*. And it seems to me that the wide range of characters included in "The Seizure" allowed you to investigate a large number of issues.

The amplitude, not to mention the intensity, that I'm speaking about is strongly conveyed in the very first paragraph of the story. There the narrator remarks — and this is in first-person plural, which is interesting and which may owe something to Faulkner's story "That Evening Sun" or to his story "A Rose for Emily" — that "We are talking of southern Ohio, southwestern Penn-sylvania, that segregated blade of West Virginia that inserts itself between the East and the Middle West. Where are we? North? East? Midwest? You cannot say. What exactly are these people? A college boy on Christ-mas holidays, working reluctantly at his father's store; a giant Black man in a green uniform, standing over his boss, hammer in hand, a look so hurt and menacing on his face that — let us say — a state trooper suddenly bursting into the store would fire first and be pardoned later;" — semi-colon, a Faulknerian *progreso*, there, it seems to me.

Continuing on, however, there are two specific scenes in this story that I want to look at with you. But before turning to those, I would like to ask how you think titles work.

CB: Well, I've never thought very much about that. I think titles work in some ways like endings — that is, they either emphasize the material that's about to come, as endings emphasize the material that has just come, or else they are deliberately skewed in such a way as to open up or to suggest a dimension that is not touched on. The title and the last lines are to me very similar in how they point. Either they point directly at the thematics or they avert their gaze from it.

TS: Mavis Gallant has said, in an interview by Geoff Hancock, that "the title is the envelope."

CB: It certainly can be. I've never, frankly, had trouble with titles. At least I don't think I have. Sometimes I write a story because I have the title first. The title has opened up all of the possibilities of the story to me immediately. Or sometimes the title has arisen directly from the texture of the story. I can't remember it ever happening that I said, "Well, I've finished the story. Let's go back through it and try to find a title for it." I've never had that experience.

TS: Though you did use a different title for "The Fabulous Eddie Brewster" when it was first published in *The Tamarack Review*.

CB: That was because Bob Weaver wanted me to change it. It was published in *Tamarack* as "The Mayor." I said fine, OK, I'll give you this title.

TS: If I were asked to provide a metaphor for what I think a title does, I would say that a title is a lens.

But let's consider a couple of scenes in "The Seizure" that I think are especially important. One is when the college boy, Justin, or Judd, is travelling out into the hills with his father's employee, the Black man, Delman, to repossess — that is, to seize — the unpaid-for furniture. The other is at the end of the story. In the earlier scene, Judd is described as being caught up with literature, with painting ...

CB: The literature he's caught up with is largely that of

Céline, the *petit-commerçant* world of really hard confrontational capitalism which is highly sexual and highly psychological and class-ridden — "racial," in American
terms.

TS: And I would say that here again, as in the instance
of the detail about Regina, it's possible for a reader,
guided too much by other characters' reactions to this
boy who is interested in the arts, to misread and to mis-
understand what he's searching for and how he's using
art.

Here, as Judd is riding out into the country reading
Céline and looking around, he says, "'God, this is foreign…. It's like a painting, you know?'" That can be read
in different ways. At first you might think of it as completely ironic, as a suggestion that he's being naïve, but
by the end of the story you realize that art has taught
him something very important and he wants to make
a connection between art and life.

What they pass as they head out into the country
— you were speaking of wanting to mark things with a
little plaque — is a State Historical Marker which, again,
doesn't tell a story. Judd and the Black driver are passing by a store which has this State Historical Marker
and Judd asks, "'What's the marker for?'" Then we read,
"Delman knew it well but said only, 'You don't like to
lose a single edifying experience do you?'" — which is
where I picked up on the sense that Judd's love of art is
meant to be seen at least in part ironically.

The narrator explains that this site "marked the
deepest northern penetration of Confederate troops,
where a raiding party and some local copperheads
linked up in 1862 for their own special reasons and
raided this hole of a then-Black hamlet called Enoch.
They burned it down because by 1862 it was one hundred

per cent Black and free although just a handful had their legal papers. After gutting the town they took some people back over the river into Virginia and Kentucky while the local citizens contented themselves with rape and murder and scattering the rest of the Blacks into the hills. Those were Delman's people...." Generations later, as the narrator explains, "basketball and the War intervened," by which time "the Polacks had come and taken over whatever was left. And with the Polacks the whole thing hadn't changed in forty years." The narrator then concludes, ironically, that "Of course the Historical Marker didn't say a thing about Blacks and Polacks. It read: FIRST ENGAGEMENT WITH CONFEDERATE FORCES ON UNION SOIL, Burning of Enoch, 1862."

In addition to giving us insight into Delman's background — and this is an example of what I meant when I said how richly textured this story seems to me, how many different people's stories are being related here — this passage makes an important statement about history. And through the insertion of this background story, the passage also implies something about literature itself that Judd doesn't know. There's an interesting device here, in terms of technique, a stepping beyond what Judd knew at that time, a kind of imposition on top of what he understood.

CB: Right. There's a kind of omniscient tone. In the part that you read earlier about "Where are we? ... What exactly are these people?" there is certainly a voice of history trying to set the stage for this story. And when I was writing the story, I certainly wanted to get out beyond the travails of the college student coming back to work at his father's miserable store — to see it rather as part of an eternal struggle. This is a very Faulknerian story, this is Quentin Compson coming back from Harvard and trying to deal with his brother, the thug, Jason — it's that kind of story. And it needs a mediating voice. It needs a larger voice than this boy's because this boy is foolish. I mean he's reading Céline in the midst of West Virginia. He's involved in a foolish enterprise and he's ripe for humiliation and he's going to be humiliated.

He doesn't have the force, the power, the sheer masculine power of his father or of Szafransky or of anyone else and he is easily intimidated by the real-life counterpart to the world that he's reading about. The Céline world is what he can handle. The language of the Céline world is what he is trying to use to transcend the squalor of the Szafransky household and his own guilt and his impotence and his inadequacy. But he can't handle Szafransky or Szafransky's wife or Delman or his father or ...

TS: ... his father's mistress ...

CB: ... his father's mistress ...

TS: ... who is so vicious to Judd's mother, making nasty phone calls to her.

CB: Right. All of these things are happening around him which are equally powerful to a Céline story, but he's unable to understand or to handle any of them.

So the irony of the story is directed in a sense against him even though he is the most sympathetic and understandable force in the story. Like, I think, Faulkner with Quentin, I feel a kind of disdain for this character. I think that he, like the historian in "Notes Beyond a History," is doomed: doomed not to understand the nature of his own life, in this case because he is being confronted with an experience that is even stronger than the literature that he is trying to read — just as the historian is confronted with a situation stronger than his own historical facilities. Those stories derive from that Faulknerian time in my life.

TS: Did you have a particular Céline work in mind?

CB: Yes. *Mort à Crédit. Death on the Installment Plan.*

TS: At the end of the story, in the final scene of the story — this is the other scene I wanted to discuss with you — the Black man, Delman, asks, "'What's that you're reading?'" and the college boy, Justin, or Judd, is given an impassioned soliloquy.

CB: That's his seizure, it seems to me.

TS: Do you see a strong element of irony working through that soliloquy? Or do you see Judd as being given a little more authority through being allowed that soliloquy?

CB: Art gives you some authority. History gives you some authority. It's not as though you're totally blind. But also it's the kind of authority that Joyce gave Gabriel Conroy at the end of "The Dead." Yes, he is by far the most awake and alert of the people, but his alertness only makes him more acutely vulnerable to what is going on around him. It's a defective virtue. So that, yes, art opens your eyes, but at the same time it also breaks your heart. And I think that's what is happening here.

Texture and Voice:
An Interview with Clark Blaise
[1973]

John Metcalf

JM: What are your working methods? How much rewriting do you do?

CB: I'm a reluctant first-draftsman, a wretched second-draftsman, and it's only when the shape and the tone of the story are really ascendant that I start to become warm to the story. Then I can go through draft after draft, growing more and more neurotic as I go, and begin to see every little typographical and grammatical nicety as part of the voice, every comma as essential as every paragraph.

JM: You studied at the Iowa Writers' Workshop. What did you learn there?

CB: Well, none of what I've just been saying comes from having attended the Writers' Workshop, or Malamud's class at Harvard before that — I'm predisposed to short stories and to kinds of stories that borrow a lot from poetry and I have the work habits of someone with that predisposition. Iowa I don't think teaches anything but a sense of obligation to craft and community and standards and articulateness about aims.

JM: Are creative writing courses a good idea?

CB: I don't want to get involved too much in the "Can you really teach writing?" trap except to say that it's the most valuable thing a literature student can do. And if you're the kind of writer I've been describing, it's not a harmful or wasteful way to earn a living.

JM: How do you accommodate yourself to life as writer and as academic? Does the teaching of technique make you too conscious as a writer? Or is that romanticism?

CB: I learn a lot from teaching and there are numerous instances in my own writing of direct inspiration. I enjoy teaching writing and I especially enjoy teaching literature — *my* favourite authors — from the point of view of the writer's concern. I'm less fond of lecture sections of standard authors for indifferent arts and science students who are frankly baffled or bored or contemptuous of a digressive lecturer and of the slow approach to a book through its associations, its "world," and its minute details.

JM: Can you give me the chronology of the stories in *A North American Education*?

CB: Yes. The stories were written more or less as follows: "Continent of Strangers" 1963-65. "A Class of New Canadians" 1967. "Eyes" in 1968. "Words for the Winter" 1971. "Extractions and Contractions" 1968. "Going to India" 1970. And the Thibidault stories 1968-71, with "Snow People" completed in the winter of 1971.

JM: I remember your telling me that the Thibidault stories were reworked from what was to have been a novel. Why did it abort and what was involved in the reworking?

CB: Those stories were part of a novel which was not taken on by three different agents and not well received by Jerry Newman — an impeccable guide — and politely refused by a friendly independent editor who was really anxious to publish me. All of this I take to be pretty conclusive.

The parts of the novel that I worked into the stories

— they were published, except for "Snow People," in 1970 and 1971 in *Florida Quarterly*, *The Tamarack Review*, and *Shenandoah* — were the "remembered" parts of the novel. The "present action" of the book never really built on its "textured" foundation. I botched it and I'm on my way now for a year in India to write a book that will show me I can do it now — or never.

In rewriting the fragments of the novel into stories, I concentrated on the handling of *time*, trying to make for each of them a self-contained temporality that was lacking in the larger context of the novel. That accounts for the playing with time in three of those stories — the historical/episodic in the title story, the woven back-to-front quality in "The Salesman's Son Grows Older," and the rather more elliptical nature of "Snow People."

JM: Why do you label "Snow People" as a "novella"? The length and form of it don't seem to me to differ substantially from some of the stories.

CB: Well, first of all because it was cut by twenty pages — the transition was written on the galleys, taking about eight lines, which shows how a good editor can benefit a still-developing writer. So the notion of "Snow People" as a denser and longer piece stuck in my mind, the thing that must be read in the book if you're to get as many of the tones of "North America" and "Education" as I could put in.

JM: Landscape and cityscape appear in your work as a *moral* landscape. Any comment?

CB: I think I've been raised in two places where there is a continuity between the moral and the physical — the Deep South and Montreal. I think all writers I've read in Montreal, French and English, and all writers from the Deep South have essentially been writing "the moral history" of their place and have found the incongruities and contradictions too great and too absorbing to go beyond. If I had lived all my life in Pittsburgh — where I spent my high-school years — or in some comparable Canadian city or suburb, I would never have seen the moral dimension in the physical, or the very real passion in even the passively perceived. Flannery O'Connor has written on that — "the roots of the eye are in the heart" — and it's true.

My subject matter is — and has been for five years — Montreal. One of the books I'm taking with me to Calcutta for the year is Muriel Spark's *The Mandelbaum Gate* because I want a sharp rendering of a tripartite city and Spark's Jerusalem is at least perfectly done. All works written in Montreal are finally laments or celebrations. Montreal was the Dublin of North America for the majority of its citizens. And the number of cities in the world of which this can be said are few — Paris, New York, London, and certainly Calcutta.

Of *regions*, the South was one, and so, if I understand the critics, is the Canadian prairie. These are places where setting is not merely an excuse, but where setting is in fact the mystery and the manner.

JM: How do short stories arrive for you? As much of your work is "autobiographical," how do the elements coalesce? How do you transpose and juxtapose events to make a piece of fiction?

CB: It's true that I rely on "autobiography" — whatever that is. I mean, when I am living my own life and dreaming someone else's? Most of my life is lived in dreams, and in my vivid dreams, I am obviously not myself. What I return with from my dreams and finally incorporate into my own reality is a story — or, at worst, a lecture-topic.

JM: Apart from "Continent of Strangers," which I considered the most conventional and the weakest story in

A North American Education, you've moved a long way from any conventional ideas of "plot." Much of your writing is more a "collage" held together by theme but more particularly by *tone.* Can you comment on the voice that speaks in your stories?

CB: I think the real reason I'm fond of "personal" fiction is that two things move me in fiction — texture and voice.

Texture is detail arranged and selected and enhanced. It is the inclusion of detail from several planes of reference: dialogue, fantasy, direct passive observation — "I am a camera," allusion, psychic wound, symbol, straight fact, etc., etc. The sum of all that is *voice.*

So small wonder I'm drawn to writers who are themselves obvious texture-workers. John Hawkes, Malamud — lesser-known story writers like Richard Yates, Tillie Olsen, and Cynthia Ozick. Among the dead masters — Flaubert, Céline, Faulkner. They all have the power to arrest me, really strike me in such a way as to block my approach through similar material.

Texture implies both vitality and unevenness — it probably rules out most satire. I think the job of fiction is to view life through a microscope so that every grain gets its due and no one can confuse salt with sugar. You hear a lot about cinema being the visual medium — this is false. It *degrades* the visual by its inability to focus. It takes the visual for granted. Only the word — for me — is truly visual. I'm reminded of something from Nabokov's *Speak, Memory* where he speaks of the words learned in his childhood always possessing a *colour,* and in later life he sought the proper word with precisely the sensual involvement of a painter seeking a tone. That's what I mean by language as, for me, a visual experience and only secondarily a musical or poetic one. It seems that the expressive gift, when it occurs in language, is frequently visual or aural. Otherwise, presumably, it is legalistic or journalistic, an expediency to communicate data.

By *voice* I am referring to the control, what is commonly referred to when we mention the "world" of a certain author; the limits of probability and chance in his construction, the sanctions he leaves us for our own variations, what we sense of his own final concerns and bafflements. Again, my interest in voice is not one of "character." I see the construction of "character" as an honourable but not necessarily compelling occupation.

When I "see" a story it is always in terms of its images and situation, the tone and texture and discovery that seems immanent in that situation — and very rarely do these intimations demand a thirty-eight-year-old spinster or a college drop-out on an acid trip. I try to work out a voice that will allow for a simultaneity of image and action. Sometimes it is second-person, frequently first-person, commonly present-tense. Sometimes it will have no time-referent beyond the present moment. In my book *A North American Education*, most of the Montreal stories — "Eyes," "Words for the Winter," "Extractions and Contractions," and "Going to India" — follow, at least in part, this pattern. Those are stories of texture and voice — details selected with an eye to their aptness but also to their "vapour trails," their slow dissolve into something more diffuse and nameless.

One learns the traffic congestion in unfamiliar cities from helicopter reports, one notes that dogs outnumber children and that garbage gets deposited in pizza boxes ... it is a matter of texture to select those details and a matter of voice that allows for wider interpretation. Voice allows the reader a confidence that he is in a shaping vision with a tone colouration that is different from that of the actual "character." That's one reason why "autobiographical" is accurate but insufficient; there is no such thing as an "autobiographical voice."

In a story like "Extractions and Contractions," I had to do very little with the events. The events in that story were all based on, or suggested by, a shade of an actual event — heightened in scale with what I felt to be the voice of the experience. But I worked a year with the basic situation: teeth, pregnancy, roaches, buildings going up and down, protest — it was 1968 — before seeing that the best I could do would be to openly insist on the disruptive, non-sequential nature of teasingly similar events. The actual story was written in Amsterdam in the early summer of 1968 and typed up when I got back to Montreal in July. It was revised a few more times that summer and sent out in the fall and immediately accepted by *Tri-Quarterly*. It was the second story that I'd written in and about Montreal, and the first that had an immediately favourable response from my friends George Bowering and Jerry Newman.

I read that story at The University of Western Ontario when I received the President's Medal for a story I'd published in *The Tamarack Review* the year before and there, too, Michael Ondaatje received it enthusiastically. I read it in the States a week later when I was writer-in-residence back where I did my B.A. at Denison University, where I thought I would have to explain nearly everything in it, and a professor in the audience immediately contracted it for an anthology. I read it so many times in the space of the year and came to think of it as so obviously the best thing I'd done that I haven't been able to read a single line of it in the last four years.

I thought the form was original when I hit upon it, but William Gass had published *In the Heart of the Heart of the Country* a few months earlier and I've seen similar "collages" altogether too many times — it has become a trite format.

JM: You handle dialogue well but you seem to avoid it as much as possible. Is this related to your ideas about voice?

CB: Dialogue, for me, has only one purpose and that's to reveal a compulsion that has been hidden from the "eye" or maybe the "I" of the story until its utterance. Dialogue is a terribly inefficient way to set up anything or to impart information. It only works for me as an instance of inadvertence, or pressure released. My aborted novel was crammed with dialogue, it filled the pages effortlessly, but after fifteen pages of dialogue very little had gotten out that wasn't already obvious or — if revealed in speech — suddenly too obvious. So I'm overly sensitive to dialogue. I like it for its obvious *authenticating* quality — but I don't have the ear to sustain a story through dialogue. Though I *do* have more dialogue in a book for Doubleday in 1974 — it's called *Tribal Justice*. Obviously, I'm going to have to find a way of working dialogue back into the kinds of stories I want to write. Otherwise, they will become nothing more than meditations or neurotic internal monologues.

Dialogue is nice also to vary the reader's sense of the author's omniscience — whenever a character speaks, there's an illusion of freedom in the world of the book.

JM: The "plots" of your stories are carried also by an unobtrusive chain of images much in the manner of poems — I read your work *as* poems — and the Montreal stories seem to be moving into a bleak and mysterious world similar to the worlds of Margaret Atwood or John Newlove.

CB: This might be a kind of poetry, especially of the kind associated with Atwood. I used to call it my "aged eagle" stance and Jerry Newman still calls me on it nine times out of ten. But I don't read poetry with any kind of enthusiasm. I attend poetry readings for the old Iowa sense of community and also in the hopes of hearing a "voice" that will stimulate my own thinking.

Poems have a voice, as do paintings, music, and especially film. But only Satyajit Ray and Truffaut and fleetingly Rohmer among world directors today have a voice that I find inherently appealing, or even embarrassing, to my own concerns. I can admire Bergman of course, but he's rather like Joyce or Borges or Nabokov in being outside my greedy cannibalistic needs.

JM: You mentioned some forthcoming work earlier. Can you give me some details?

CB: Doubleday is doing another collection of stories in 1974 — a book called *Tribal Justice*. And Anansi is probably going to do a collection called *Among the Dead* — but that's not final yet. And then I'm doing a nonfiction book for Doubleday with Bharati called *The Bengal Journals*. And I'm also working on a novel, as I said, but the title is too good to reveal.

JM: I think that *A North American Education* is one of the best collections of stories published in Canada. Can you tell me anything of its publishing history? Why an American company, for example?

CB: I submitted a combined manuscript of *A North American Education* and *Tribal Justice* — with some differences — to academic presses in the States. They each took eight months to turn the book down. Then I sent the full manuscript to Clarke, Irwin, which had published four stories of mine in *New Canadian Writing, 1968*. They thought they couldn't afford a book that simply wouldn't earn a profit. A friend advised me to submit the book to McClelland and Stewart. I sent them the book in its present form and I was told that it didn't have "enough meat" and while the stories were good and generally successful, they were rather academic and the reader just didn't come away with a feeling of having had "a literary experience."

So I sent the book to Doubleday on the advice of Malcolm Foster and I was called by my editor-to-be three weeks later with an acceptance. They have been all-supportive and concerned with the *ensemble* of the book from editing to binding to promotion and even though they are very large and I'm very small — Park Avenue conglomerate to débutant Canadian short story writer, to draw out an obvious point — I've been dealt with as a private sort of citizen with dignified "aged eagle" ways and a keen sense of self-promotion.

JM: That's a sad history.

CB: There's something I would like to come back to — the autobiographical thing. I'm content for now — and have been for years — to write from a reasonably settled psychic point of view ... i.e., roughly my own, as I understand it ... and to seek variety not in certain "character-frames" — you know, like the lenses that an eye doctor keeps dropping in those heavy frames during an eye test — but in rendering the texture of a situation in a voice appropriate to it. I have no defence against those critics who have commented on the "ego-involvement" and the "obviously autobiographical" nature of this "first work." I would say that most of *A North American Education* is "a twenty-fifth work" and that the interchangeableness of the various characters is not meant as a particularly well-disguised secret.

In that, I would agree a bit with John Hawkes who said once in an interview that he began writing fiction with the assumption that the true enemies of the novel were theme, plot, and character. I only wish I had begun writing with as clear a sense.

Clear Veneer:
An Interview with Clark Blaise
[1980]

Geoff Hancock

GH: Clark, you're one of the most rootless writers I've ever met. You're always moving around.

CB: Yes, a person gets a taste for movement and it's very hard to adjust to being rooted in one place. I would like to be rooted, I think. I have a nostalgia for it, in a Norman Rockwell sort of way, but I don't think it's going to happen. That doesn't necessarily mean I'm rootless, though. Think of those banyan trees that drop roots down from their branches and just create roots out of thin air. I'll never have the long, long taproot — to exhaust the metaphor — that goes down in one place. I'm kind of a tropical tree with an awful lot of shallow roots and I can easily be blown over. On the other hand, I can survive a lot of changes. I adapt very easily to just about anything around me.

GH: Are Canada and Florida somehow connected for you?

CB: I haven't been back to Florida since I was ten years old and I don't ever intend to see it again. Florida was not so much a landscape as the place of childhood, the place of opening up. If I had spent my childhood somewhere else, I would have had deep attachments to a different place. It turned out fortunately because Florida was physically, morally, and historically an apt place for me:

I exploited it ruthlessly and it exploited me in turn. It was a location — thinking back now to the still-rural, Deep South Florida of the mid- and late-forties — that was made for the hounding out of some central worm-like creature in myself.

Florida was foreign to everything in my nature. It was a brutal confrontation, but it was physically so interesting and physically so unforgettable that it linked up forever a notion of nature, of water, of solitariness, and a kind of harshness that I lost myself in for hours every day.

It was just as harsh as the Canadian prairie, but solar in nature, not lunar. And in Florida you didn't have to worry about dressing for it, so that you literally passed through a wall at seven in the morning and came back at dusk and were out in it all day walking through jungle and water and never felt as though you were in particular danger. Yet you were always seeing things that were dead or dying or that were crawling up from the mud or down from the trees. You saw putrefaction, you saw the tropical world in which all the processes are speeded up and in which the chain of exploitation is just so much more vivid than it is up here.

So I was the beneficiary of that. And later on, much later on, I came to see the social and historical and economic analogues to that kind of nature. The myth was laid down for me pretty early and it was a matter of feeding into the myth with plots and psychologies and characters.

GH: What do you see right now as the state of contemporary fiction both in Canada and in the U.S.A.?

CB: I think the state of the arts there, meaning the States, or here in Canada, is grossly inflated. Reputations are grossly inflated. I don't find very many authors around here or there that I can read with any degree of discovery or excitement or anything other than appreciation of competence.

I think we're in a bad period despite what everyone says about this being a glorious period. I'm fearful.

Recently I read a *New York Times Book Review* article and a *Times Literary Supplement* article about "little magazines" which seemed to glorify a truly disgusting sales- and profit-centred literary reaction. I was appalled at the number of so-called significant authors and editors and agents, and the number of publishers, who agreed with the simple proposition that there is too much writing, that there are too many "first novels" being written, and that the great aching is to "communicate" (awful word), not to create. And that art should be lucid (meaning straight and simple) and narratively strong (meaning, as they say in Hollywood, with a "good storyline") and that the rewards (of the six- and seven-figure variety) will go to people who "perform." And that there's going to be a real gloved fist for people who don't.

I see contempt growing for writing programs and for university courses in which young writers are encouraged to write the "art" novel. They are being sneered at for their pretensions. And professors who teach writing are being called failures because they obviously never made money. Fiction is being cut back in magazines and in publishing houses. First novels are as despised as story collections. But it's even worse than that.

Worse than the first-novelist — who can be excused, because of all the bad advice handed out by failed writers in universities — is the third- or fourth-novelist whose other books have gotten terrific critical reception but no real sales. He's in big trouble. The books that are getting attention are, by and large, foolish books. The writers who are getting a lot of attention are, by and large, fulfilling a commercial expectation, confirming kind of an expectancy.

The last book of any excitement that I read coming out of the States was Norman Mailer's *The Executioner's Song*. Sure, it was too much, but.... I was disappointed by Richler's *Joshua Then and Now*. Stick-figures, conforming to a mechanical vision. On top of that, it was messy, contrived in structure rather than organically complicated. I've liked Hodgins' stories, but his novels? As soon as someone started walking on water, I felt that South American literature ought to get its tubes tied and that we ought to cut down on the number of illegitimate offspring we're taking in. I thought Atwood's *Life Before Man* was very well written but the "world" of the book left me, well, cool, as did the characters. "Unengaged" is the word that comes to mind — the book aroused my expectations more than it satisfied them. But that's the case with even very good books; there probably are not more than a dozen books in anyone's life that exceed your expectations and achieve their author's ambition.

Leaving aside the work of the older Titans — Joyce, Mann, Proust, James, Dickens, etc. — I would say that I derive satisfaction only from Mavis Gallant, among Canadians. Among Australians, from Keneally and from Robert Drewe. In England, Paul Scott and occasionally Anthony Powell. Of Naipaul's work, *A House for Mr. Biswas* is a masterpiece; his other works lag behind, whatever their merits. A writer in the States who I feel has been consistently underrecognized would be Thomas Berger. I think *Sneaky People* is one of the best books I've read in the last decade. Heller's *Something Happened* is a book of drab wonders, with real depth, scary psychologically and socially and stylistically. *The Collected*

Stories of Hortense Calisher stands with Mann's novellas just over my writing desk.

There are a few books around that I would like to see in fifteen years, after all the hoopla gets shaken down, to see what really remains. I have found a lot of consistent interest in reading Ann Beattie's stories, but I don't know if that's not a fascination more with the times and places and encounters we've almost "shared." She too scares me the way Heller does, especially when I see her control of so much waste and aimlessness. She's like an illustration of what Pynchon was getting at in "Entropy" and *The Crying of Lot 49*; you can almost hear a scream in those quiet little stories. Just like you can feel the blood in some of Rothko's geometric canvases.

GH: The landscape that your characters move through is sometimes a grey world, though. It's the way we live now. They always move in an ominous landscape. It's mass-market culture, it's cheap hotels, transitional neighbourhoods. What does that say about the way we live now?

CB: Well, if I use the market world, I don't believe in it whole-heartedly. I've always tried to show that running behind a shopping centre is a creek or a stand of timber and if one simply steps outside the motels or walks behind the franchise stand or simply looks long enough across the parking lot, he will find birds in the trees, fish in the stream, and mud puppies in the swamps; in other words, eternal forces are still at work churning under the surface. You carry out the garbage from McDonald's but it's still the same flies that lay eggs in it. I simply mean that my eye is on dualities more than on satire or put-downs. I've always tried to account for *why* a road dips suddenly or *why* a basement gets wet in the spring. I've tried to account for these things, to be alert to them, because I was a geology major in college and I have a greater sense of subsoil and substructures and determinants from weather and from rainfall and from things like that, things I had to learn, than I do from purely literary sources.

I remember the drawing my younger son, Bernie, used to do before school tried to straighten him out. His stick-figure people would stand on very perilous ground in the middle of the paper, under the usual sun and tree, beside the usual house with the usual smoke in the chimney. But underfoot, he would lavish enormous, intricate attention. Those lines were "worm-roads" he said. His real attention was focussed on the unseen. He was flinging order on the wildest chaos.

I get impatient with satire and with pure realism because I'm a moralist in my own way. I think I've always tried to mitigate the greyness of the landscape by saying that no matter how you transform it with bulldozers and concrete you're still having to deal with permanent forces that are unmoveable and that will come and get you. Those forces are still there to change you, but you're never purely created by them. We are formed by our capacity to imagine, to make worm-roads under our feet that are as important as the clouds and the airplanes overhead.

GH: To move on to your stories, you always have an "I" narrator who is a very intense perceiving consciousness and the events are rendered exactly as the narrator perceives them or even misperceives them, which sometimes makes the narrator appear terrified because the focus is so tight. Is this a correct reading, that an emotional response always precedes the intellectual understanding?

CB: I can't write anything until I feel I have come into

contact with its depth. That sounds pretentious, but I hope all writers are like that. Unless I feel that I have seen behind the stage, so to speak, or grasped the texture of a given situation, which is to say unless I know far more than I can possibly use, I won't be content simply to say, "Here's a street, a house, a car, an attractive young couple." I can't use a theory. I have to have some *other* sense about that street: What is the last thing I can say about this place? Until I have come to that point, I'm not interested in rendering any of it. But once I have come into that awareness, then I can't stop myself from writing it. It simply grips me and that's it, I'm in its full power.

The first-person narrator is a way of controlling a work's power by limiting the world outside the self. I'm not using first-person right now in a novel I'm writing and I didn't use it in my last three stories. First-person at one time seemed a very rich, deep, and natural thing as opposed to third-person. Now I find first-person rather tinny and I can't stand to write in it anymore. I want to link up an individual life with many things outside that life. Third-person is a mode of community; first-person, the voice of isolation.

GH: What kinds of things do you want to connect with that you couldn't before?

CB: I want to connect with randomness. I want unpredictableness, shock, surprise, disorderliness, chaos. I want those things, and happenstance, and the collisions of the most unlikely forces. I want *impact*. So I want to get an illusion of depth. And that sense of spaciousness in a work derives, I think, only from the demonstration of things failing to quite connect.

GH: Do you find you can also use humour and compassion and other subsequent insights with the third-person narration?

CB: Yes. Third-person opens up many, many aspects because the tone of voice can be varied. In first-person the tone is so controlled that you can't really exploit all the opportunities for humour. If you do, then you end up with a funny story. Or an ironical comic monologue. That's all well and good. But if you're less than perfect at it, your comic scenes come off like gravedigger bits, transparent attempts at levity. I didn't want that, either. I wanted more *un*evenness of tone.

GH: Now could you tell me something about the victory of voice? That's what makes your work so compelling for me. There is a voice of an intelligent consciousness dealing with the tones, with the colours. I would also say that the mastery of voice is probably the most important thing a fiction writer can do.

CB: Voice is finally *all* that he has because the other forms of writing have everything else under control. Obviously fact is more "important" — and often more *interesting* — than fiction. Most people would rather read factual, not fictional, accounts of most things, simply because facts work in more bizarre ways and they're more unpredictable and they're richer. The thing that makes fiction *fiction* is the kind of luminous, or at least *suggestive*, space between quite ordinary facts. Other kinds of writing have to lay on facts densely, sentence by sentence, and they have no trajectory, no sprung energy, nothing to sustain them when the informative level is lowered.

GH: Your stories are very visual. The surfaces are almost sculpted with the texture of words. Could you comment on this?

CB: I try to see things in dimension and with texture. I don't feel as though I'm in possession of the detail until I can see the other side of it. "Sculpted" is a nice word, if it's meant to imply the use of space, the "other side" of the familiar surface, and if it also implies the hardness of the surface. Details are there because they have penetrated my own consciousness. And when a detail penetrates, as it so frequently does, then I try to figure out *why* because my life is generally a fog.

When I'm going very well, a number of things stand out. And when I'm in possession of a story, everything stands out and I'm seeing linkages that almost make a story inevitable. Then I go back to my normal fog and to keeping these notebooks in which I copy down random bits that I see, read, imagine, or overhear. Trying to be responsible for those things that leap out at me means that I have to write a story to go with them. I have to find the *why* behind each of them. I have to find a set of characters who can in some way provide a context for those details. It's often that way, finding characters who can justify the details rather than the other way around. I usually start with the light or the physical details that evoke a particular mood. And then the characters suggest themselves more slowly.

GH: Is the image sometimes triggered by an experience, an emotional ulcer?

CB: Rarely, rarely. I get moved by a visual situation. Most of the deep emotional situations that hit me or that hit people I know are too hot for me to handle. I'm in possession of a great number of stories of vast interest. But they're thoroughly useless to me; I would make pulp of them. If they would give me a *detail* instead, then I could invent the situation. I think Joyce Carol Oates probably can turn such stories into fiction. At least I believe that she means that when she says, "Someone told me the story and I wrote a five-hundred-page novel about it." I can't do that. I guess I'm in possession of as much emotional data about other lives as anyone is, yet I don't really use it at all. It's one of those great wasteful areas in my life. I overwork a rather small area of my experience and I ignore vast areas of it that would probably be more interesting and more to the liking of the editors that we were talking about earlier. There's nothing I can do about that. That's how I work.

GH: Yet even working within this small area are you conscious of style? Shall we invent a new term, "Blaisean stylistics"?

CB: Oh, I'm always very much aware of style. The style is the situation. If I want to be true to how something strikes me, I have to be as stylish or as style-conscious as the very thing that I found so gripping. I'm talking about very small things: a hedgerow, say. To do real justice to a hedgerow would require the work of a great lyric poet or Monet or, in prose, Proust — the only author I know who gives every element of nature and of character its proper space. To do real justice to anything is a matter of generosity and character and style. You can't use the language of the butcher shop or the newspaper or the textbook to do that hedgerow justice. That's the great challenge: to find language that fits the things that do not yield to language. We have no agreed-upon formula for that. We do have visual formulas in the arts, in painting and film and music, but not in prose.

The moment we agree upon conventions they become clichés. As soon as we agree that "spun-gold" hair means something, it has already become part of the language of coquetry and of the marketplace, and thus off-limits for art, except for pop art and parody. So the self-conscious or simply respectable writer is continually reinventing the world through language.

I might add as an aside here that most of what critics

and editors call "new" or "exciting" concentrates on *formal* inventiveness, without realizing that one sentence of great writing, in a traditional formal shell, can be as "avant-garde" as the latest breakthrough in form. To put it another way, dazzling innovations in form are simple face-liftings if they do nothing fresh with language as well.

GH: Your opening lines nearly always suggest the opposite of what's going to happen in the story. So if it starts off with a sunny day, you just know that there's going to be stormy weather coming up. You suggested this in your essay "To Begin, To Begin."

CB: A writer is always trying to suggest the *other* side of things. He's trying to create a subject and an object, not only the centrepiece but the frame, and sometimes he feeds the frame first and withholds the picture. Other times he gives the picture and withholds the fact that he's going to hang it in the garage next to an old nudie calendar. Sometimes it may be a very beautiful thing to be deliberately destroyed. There has to be surprise, continually. You can't follow a single course. You can't shoot an arrow straight and expect to get anywhere in fiction. It's always a matter of working by indirection and by surprise and by suggestion, which means that everything you state directly has a shadow meaning, implied. There's an essay I wrote called "The Cast and the Mold," in Metcalf's *Stories Plus*, in which I tried to develop the notion at greater length: the story is a delicate, fluted casting; what the writer is out to capture is the rough, shaggy, and broken-open mold that surrounded it, at least in his imagination. This doesn't necessarily mean that you are committed to a path of irony at all times, but it means that you are always trying to be aware of the sinister and of duplicities and of dualities.

GH: Does that mean then that the writing of the story is a line-by-line discovery?

CB: Oh, it had better be! If the reading of a story is a line-by-line discovery, the writing of it has to be much more. It's not just line-by-line discovery, it's line-by-line creation and it's line-by-line re-presentation. It's not like choreography, with its illusion of spontaneity and its hours of rehearsal. Line by line the writer is discovering the nature of his material and each line is like the finest nozzle point holding back a great force. The best kind of writing — I'm thinking of Gallant, or Calisher, or a few others — is that which comes out like a laser: very fine, very controlled, perfectly placed, able to do retinal surgery, but behind it is the power to knock aircraft out of the skies. You are aware of the power and of the need to be very precise and very controlled.

GH: Because of the choices you have in creating each line, do you do a lot of editing in your head or on the page?

CB: I edit before, during, and after. I am continually editing. I am continually writing and I am continually rewriting.

GH: I am making a distinction between rewriting and revising. Rebuilding the car as opposed to revising which is giving it a new paint job.

CB: I tend to work from the small to the large. I can worry a long time over a word and then the sentence and then the paragraph, but the real progress comes when I realize that all of that was useless. I didn't need the paragraph. I didn't even need the three or four paragraphs around it. I can go from point A to point G in a single leap and a suture, but I don't see it quickly. I have to go from the very, very fine up. That's how I work. I don't have the construction engineer's sense of "Knock this out, knock that out, and it will work." I'm a brick-layer in that sense — I have to go from brick to brick.

GH: As a result of that, your stories seem to point into their centre rather than follow that line towards a rev-elation, climax, or epiphany. Is that a strategy or is that just what happens?

CB: Who knows? It's deeply related to one's own psy-chology obviously; introspective people write inward-turning stories. The stories, in my own mind, tend to-wards the discovery of that which you wanted to keep hidden and to a kind of confirmation of what you hoped was not true. If there is any kind of optimism, it's in the fact that, well, "I" have weathered it and "I" can survive it and before the story "I" would have thought "I" would have died if this had happened. But it does happen and, look, you've survived it! To me that's the central message, if any, in most of the things I've written. Most of my own life experiences have been like that, too. I don't think I would have taken out an option on any year in the past five or six if someone had shown me an outline of what the fates had in store. But I've sur-vived, the family has survived, fire and repeated up-rooting, disease, disillusionment, all sorts of agony and we've swallowed it back and we're not destroyed. I'm older, that's all.

GH: Is that why your stories have a "slice-of-life" ap-proach, in quotation marks?

CB: Well, yes, only if "slice" means "segment." I hope to imply that the world was not created when the story started and does not end when the story's over, but rather there is a continuum and the story is a plucked thread, one of possible thousands, from a sweater that remains indifferent to the process. We tease the story into a very visible loop and we stare at this loop and it bothers us and it disrupts the harmony of the weave but it also goes back into the weave and disappears. End of story. For a while, it snagged at our eye. We even felt sorry for the owner of the sweater. But we also noticed that, snagged thread and all, it remains a handsome sweater. The sweater isn't destroyed. The overall design isn't destroyed. There are thousands of other threads running every which way that will eventually get snagged and that will become exposed and embarrassing. That's my sense of the story. We are not talking about a whole sweater. We're talking about one out of several thousand intricately patterned, interwoven, anonymous threads and if we had the time and the patience in our lives we could look at every single strand, at every single moment of human life, and make of it a densely observed story. But no one has that. The sweater, however, is the shaggy old mold I was talking about earlier.

GH: So that means that rather than a bigger realization or a greater epiphany, again to use that well-worn term, you have little epiphanies, little realizations that light up each moment of a life, each part of a story.

CB: I think that's what I'm trying to do. That's all I can do. I would like to make the big noise, but it's just not in me to do it. I don't have that talent and I don't especially regret not having that talent. It's not in my background either. It's not in my personality. It's none of my concern.

GH: Is every story an allegory about "reality," in quotation marks, or a metaphor for some aspect of reality?

CB: It's not an allegory in the sense that, say, Hugh Hood's stories are. I don't have the moral patience or the scruples for allegory, but I would imagine they are all metaphors. I think of a story as essentially a single metaphor and the exfoliation of a single metaphor through dense layers of submetaphors. My test, when I'm rewriting stories, is that every sentence in some way be a part of that metaphor. I try to understand what the largest metaphor that contains the story is. And that's my principle for cutting out things — certain details may be well and good in themselves, and tangential to the story, but not really part of its central metaphor.

GH: Could you give me an example from one of your stories?

CB: Well, say, "At the Lake," about the leeches. There it all is from the very first page. I say, "I was suckered into it." I use the name "Lac Sangsue" and I specifically say that the name of the lake does *not* refer to the bugs or the leeches, but rather to the shape of the lake. I specifically say of Lac Sangsue (meaning "bloodsucker") that it's named for its leech-like shape, not its fauna. You see, the metaphor is of *naming* things, not *doing* things. My character places his faith, like many academics, in the names of things, in aesthetics. He wants to drain off the "health" of nature. He dreams of transforming himself simply by lying in the sun on his dock in "immemorial torpor." All of it is a denial of reality, all of it is a desire to place a faith in names rather than in reality, so that eventually reality comes, eventually what happens to him is that he is forced to pay the price for his preference to live in a world of aesthetics rather than reality and he ends up with bloodsuckers around his body. My feeling has always been that nature is ruthless and that nature is corrosive.

If I have any kind of "vision," it's a naturalistic vision. Everything will be worn down; every life will be worn down in seventy years, the way continents are reduced to bedrock. Everything that has been suppressed will eventually be exposed. Every doubt will be tested. Every weakness will eventually be exploited. A life consists of about two billion separate seconds; every second is like six months in the life of the planet but with the concentrated time-lapse of Creation to Apocalypse. Every second in a life relates to the beginning and to the end of that life; every sentence in a story relates even more intimately.

Each story is a metaphor. I can't say it's a metaphor with a paraphraseable meaning. It's just a metaphor, an elaborate comparison, a way of suggesting something larger and more permanent. Then I have to create characters to satisfy the metaphor.

GH: Let's talk about some of those characters. A lot of your protagonists are watchers as much as they are participants. They're often detached observers. They're sort of artists if not real artists. They're interested in healthy, mind-improving hobbies: astronomy and chess and all those things ...

CB: I don't think of those as mind-improving. I think of those as anxiety-ridden. Chess! I used to play competitive chess and I never knew a more ego-destructive and tossing-and-turning-all-night-long type occupation than chess-playing. You would replay endlessly your mistakes. I think of chess as the epitome of sickly pursuits, something worthy of Thomas Mann or Nabokov — it's really out of that tradition. And astronomy, too, is the most humbling of sciences. The concepts of astronomy are so humbling to human ambition, to the human frame, to the human context, that I look on it as an apprenticeship either to humility or to cynicism. It's very hard to worry about your mortgage payments when you're also having to worry about calculations in space. So I would dispute the idea of either of those things being mind-improving or healthy. They're meta-phors.

GH: Your characters are in some way trying to triumph over the world's sordidness. What do your characters do to achieve that triumph? What's their strategy?

CB: Cunning, exile, and silence. Their only triumph is that they have imagination and an ability to accept. A low-grade survival principle. They're not terribly ambitious for themselves in a physical, sexual way. In very few of my stories, I think, the characters could actually think of themselves as competing in the normal world. They're on a continent of strangers. The young lover, Keeler, in Europe, wants to compete in all the classic ways, as artist, as lover, as man of the world and all the rest of it, but he's young, untested.

The other characters have more or less seen the eternal footman hold their coats and snicker. The world has provided enough irony about their ambitions — or they have provided their own irony about their ambitions — and they realize the big gesture is not for them. So their survival could be called a very Canadian thing, I suppose, in that the "lesson" of life seems to be don't try too hard, don't want too much, be satisfied with less and you'll get by, too much ambition is a bad thing, and conspicuous success is inevitably going to bring the gods down on you.

I've never been comfortable with the kind of character who really is, let's say, Faustian. That's part of my essential psychological Canadianness, I think. I've always said I'm sociologically an American and psychologically a Canadian. I'll never possess the sociological information about Canada that I do about the States. I'm a trivia whiz if you put me in an American context. I was that moist-skinned, under-the-rock type child who simply knew everything, memorized everything, and listened to everything and never fed it back. I have all that and will always have that at my fingertips — but I think my use of it is decidedly Canadian. I read Alice Munro's childhood stories, or Margaret Laurence's, and that's me just as much as it's her. The issues of *National Geographic*, the maps, the encyclopedias, the mother with genteel tastes, the father who is continually letting them down, the small towns, the hankering after a kind of respectability and gentility that is never really there, the sense that you are somehow superior to your surroundings.

But it's exactly the same world that Naipaul writes about in Trinidad. It's a Commonwealth experience. The very nature of the Commonwealth is, I think, precisely that; you feel you were created for better things but somehow the centre has receded far from you and it's not there to certify you anymore so you're left with this vulnerability. And this arrogance. You've been exposed. You've come out of your shell expecting something and all you're getting is the boot.

GH: How autobiographical is your work?

CB: I feel quite often my life has been an imitation of my fiction as opposed to the other way around. I have such an imagination for disaster that I have merely accepted, until very recently, the shell of "my" life for my fiction — Canada, America, French, English, North, South, and a kind of reflective, observant, fat, and phlegmatic child — simply because I've always found it easy to feed the things that interested me into those frames. The "stuffings," the plots, have been totally invented.

If you have a basically passive and observant and fearful child, then you can create vivid, lurid nightmares for him to fall into. If you create the tension of a responsible and respectable mother and an irresponsible and unrespectable father, you can create confrontations between them. That is again fruitful. If you're talking about such vast geographical compass points as Manitoba, Quebec, and Florida, you can talk quite legitimately about North America. So I've been quite happy accepting the givens of my life autobiographically, but I have not been dependent upon the contents of my own life. I'm a placid bourgeois. My ambitions are purely mundane.

I don't lead an adventuresome life and I don't hanker for it. Adventures have come — the India aspect especially — and I exploit them for all they're worth. For someone my age, forty, I am probably less rooted than most. That is, if someone would offer me a job tomorrow doing something else in a completely different place, I would probably say "Yes." My house here is up for sale. I'm off on leave next year, without pay. But the only consistently adventurous part of my life is its restlessness and the fact that I'm likely to be just about anywhere this time next month or next year.

If all the things that I've written about had actually happened to me, then I would obviously be a very different person than I am. They are merely all within me. I would say I'm beginning to be in touch with the possibilities that can derive from my life.

GH: Another question springs off from this too, and it's a big one, the William H. Gass one: What is your concept of character?

CB: The centre of my stories is not in my characters. The centre is elsewhere and so I do not set out to create character. I do not set out to write a psychological case study. I am really trying to talk about the world, as I understand it, the nature of the world, the nature of event, happenstance, accident, beauty, permanence, change, violence. I'm trying to talk about things like that. In our humanist culture, in our humanist Western traditions, you have to have a human focus for those things or else you are writing allegory or fable. And psychology has told us so much about probability that the character is bound to be fairly recognizable. I'm committed to representational fiction; otherwise you're doing stained glass windows.

GH: Or sociology.

CB: Yes, or sociology. The agreed-upon way of registering shock waves is through a perceiving consciousness and so I do that. That's Jamesian, I guess, tinged with a bit of William H. Gass. It feels natural but that's not to say that I see the character first and then devise a story for that character. Writing would be a lot easier if I did, but my own essential narcissism or egotism gets in the way. Things that really interest me are more aesthetic than psychological. So I'm willing to accept a fairly stable psychological receiver. I don't explore a great range of characterization and I'm willing to accept that so long as I do have intensity and texture. To me that's where the interest lies, not in the characters. Or put it this way: my experiences have led me into interesting places and my subconscious churns up confrontations that I find terrifying. So I follow those strengths into fiction. But what I can tell about character is probably deficient; I simply don't notice that much. And the things that I do notice about disparate lives and about social patterns fail to move me. I'm very underpopulated.

GH: So that leads to the gaps between the author and the "I" narrators of your stories, characters like Dyer and Greenwood and Thibidault, and that also explains the links between the three or the four, including yourself.

CB: I've only written of three characters, really, and

that's my mother, my father, and myself. I am utterly dependent upon the family situation and the family conflicts as the source of my fiction. Now the "myself" character is sometimes female, sometimes male. And sometimes the "myself" character is acutely analytical and cynically intelligent, and sometimes it's reflective and passively intelligent, and sometimes it's only cynical and worldly and abusive, but all those are within myself and I can as easily be one of them as another. The father character stands as all males, older, with authority, with physical power, with experience, with sexual charm, with confidence, with a fearlessness before the law, with a kind of lawlessness, people who *define* or who are continually pushing out against definitions. And my mother figures are always the ones who are pulling in within definitions, so acutely aware of restrictions and anticipating rebuffs, anticipating them so sensitively that they internalize them before they ever do anything. So this is my landscape, my moral landscape, and it has always been enough for me. Eventually it will not be enough for me either — and that's when you notice "crises" and "stages" in a writer's career.

GH: Do you want to be a self-projecting or a self-effacing writer?

CB: It doesn't bother me, self-effacing or self-projecting. It amounts to the same thing. That is, an artist might do two hundred self-portraits or he might do the Rouen Cathedral for twenty-four hours. Which one is more self-effacing? Is a self-portrait any more self-projecting than doing a landscape? I don't think so. The artist is as much present in his landscape as he is in a self-portrait. In fact, curiously, he may even be more self-effacing in his self-portraits because he may be seeing the parts of himself in a disembodied way.

GH: Does that mean that the old notions of plot and character are worn out, that writers have to find a new way of dealing with these?

CB: For me and for me alone, plot is not planned but is the revelation of inevitability, the slow disclosure of something beautifully obvious, though hidden. That's plot and that's the kind of plot I acknowledge. I feel sometimes that you hurtle through the vastness of time — those two billion seconds that we all have allotted to us — towards something you feared and hoped to avoid but was always there. You embrace it, finally, and that's a plot, but until that moment you've had, seemingly, an infinite number of choices and ways to avoid it. With my strong sense of inevitability I obviously have a strong sense of plot, of a certain kind of plot.

GH: Here's a bunch of easy questions. What are your writing habits? Do you have an average number of pages per day or a certain time of day? Do you set aside a certain place? You've mentioned you keep notebooks. Do you type or write in longhand?

CB: Those questions are all too painful. I don't have a schedule simply because I don't have the time to write. Given the ideal circumstance, I would be writing every day. I would begin writing as I do when I've had my month a year to write. I used to go to Yaddo, to the artists' colony in Saratoga Springs, and there I would finish breakfast at 8:30 and I would write steadily till 5:00. When I lived in India and we had servants looking after the house and the kids were in school, I wrote steadily from 8:30 to 5:00. In each of those cases it was ideal. I wrote a lot, I wrote every day, never took a break. I would write about an hour and I would read about an hour and I would play solitaire for about half an hour. That would be my way and I knew exactly where I wanted to get, not in terms of pages but in terms of scenes. I knew I wanted to move this far and if it took eight pages, it took eight pages, if it took two pages, it took two pages, but I wrote very carefully.

But in the last year and a half I haven't written more than three stories, three chapters, some reviews and some articles, because of my teaching job and responsibilities with the kids and the house. So I can't really speak with any legitimacy about work habits. I know that when I first was writing, I was an all-night writer. I loved to start around midnight and write till about 5:00 and then sleep till about 10:00 and then get up and write some more. That was when I was in Iowa. Ideally, I want a circumstance that allows me to write every day, read every day, write letters every day, walk every day, that's really all, and if there is socializing to be done, fine. I like to see movies. I like to see my friends. I think I would like to be in a fairly confined setting, I mean in a fairly small town. I don't think I need the cities, particularly. But if I'm in a city and I like it, I exploit the possibilities.

GH: Do you find the literature of India has an appeal for you?

CB: I'm so restricted to reading what is written in English that I am really not able to say I know the literature of India.

But the *experience* of India is like that. It gives a new range of potential, a new range of possibility, that to these tired eyes is very refreshing. You just can't match on the page the qualities and complications and dramatic pitch of daily life in India. You suddenly find your palette loaded down with new colours. The spectrum that you've conventionally been operating in has been widened and you see what a tiny slice you've been in.

GH: How do you deal with that in your work?

CB: I haven't written much fiction about India at all. I have a story, "Man and His World," and I have a novel in germ with two or three beginnings about Africa and India — and Canadian characters in those places. It's really a matter of feeling confident enough to control those settings and to allow for greater degrees of accident and collision than I've ever done before. I would deal with it by plotting on a larger scale. Character remains character throughout the world. But it is a matter of plotting. Of feeling in command of so many points on the compass that you can navigate much further out.

GH: Would you deal with the African or Indian experience in the same way as someone like Margaret Laurence, Audrey Thomas, Dave Godfrey, David Knight, even Hugh Hood?

CB: I would choose to do it in Canadian terms rather than American because Americans, simply by nature of their national and psychological involvement in other parts of the world, have muddied the waters. It's largely impossible to be an American and still be a neutral creature in those places. The Canadian is a kind of clear veneer that you can put over the canvas. It allows the highlights. It's a good thing to be in those settings because it really doesn't interfere all that much with the native essence of the place.

I think of the Canadian as being your standard, decent, upright soul who doesn't go to the place with great ambition to transform the landscape or to save the people for anything. He goes trying to be fairly open to experience and he goes as a fairly vulnerable person. He can be destroyed more easily. He also has no historical linkage in the place. And to me, lacking a history in a place is almost a formula for vulnerability and destruction.

GH: Is that what you were doing in *Days and Nights in Calcutta* when you created the persona that narrated your half of the book?

CB: Yes, very definitely. I exaggerated the qualities of lostness and wonder and ignorance on the part of the character who carried my name. All the things that I described were true, but I suppressed a lot of things too — things that I did know — to create a character who was capable of wider degrees of wonder. It was necessary if I wanted to move him from a point of absolute ignorance to a point of some comfort and sensitivity. I had to create a character who was perhaps a little more naïve than I was.

GH: To change directions here: Do you think *Lunar Attractions* is an extension of your stories?

CB: It's definitely that. I came to the end point of many of my stories in that novel. I can't see ever picking up on Southern material again. I can't see picking up again on that particular quality of myself: the fearful phlegmatic child, the spoiled but neglected child. I'm writing a story in which the same American/Canadian/Montreal/French/English axis occurs, but here I found the mother character has all the affairs, is an extraordinarily attractive woman with aggressive sexuality. The father is a poor schnook who has been on the lam for years and the son is not myself at all. At least not as I recognize myself. But it's a new variation on my side of reality.

GH: Does the novel have a form for you?

CB: No, not at all. The form has to be like abstract expressionism in painting. Representations for the passions. Metaphoric equivalents. Dramatic equivalents for your deepest feelings. They just come, in the same way abstract expressionism comes for painters. They may come in a rigorously controlled Rothko way, as two big squares, or they may come as they did for Jackson Pollock, but to impose an academic form on it — "This is how it *must* be" — violates the essential reason for the novel. The story is a formal piece. The novel is an experience the story couldn't contain.

GH: Do you feel part of Canadian literature?

CB: Yes. Psychologically this is my home. Culturally I am a hybrid and maybe not bred true to either parent — Canadian or American. But if Canadian literature can't find a place for me, then Canadian literature is sadly self-restrictive.

To Create Histories Around Little Things: An Interview with Clark Blaise [1980]

Barry Cameron

BC: I'm going to wander all over the canvas with my questions, to paraphrase a remark by one of your characters, but I want to begin with a few general questions. Are you writing one novel? Is all your work one book?

CB: Everything that has been published to date could probably fit into one large book with certain breaks and discontinuities, I suppose. You could say that everything I've done has been related to the Oedipal triangle in one way or another and to the cultural dilemma and to the cosmogonic dilemma — how we understand where we have been placed and what we are to become and how we get our ideas and arrive at our conclusions and how we get our *métier*. All of these things have been overriding questions for me, so much so that I haven't concerned myself too much with social issues, with adult marital situations, or with any of the normal things that concern, say, middle-aged people as they confront their everyday reality. I've really been involved with childhood and adolescence and with the origin of things rather than with the middle of things.

BC: Yes, a good ninety-eight per cent of your work is, in fact, in an autobiographical mode — personal fiction that uses the first person — and you seem to have consistently used yourself for the material of your fiction.

But you think you're moving away from all of that now?
CB: I haven't written in the first person in the last year and a half, which tells me something anyway.
BC: Yes, I notice that your most recently published story, "Man and His World" — which is in the same issue of *Fiction International* as the "Writers' Forum," to which you contributed, that discusses John Gardner's book *On Moral Fiction* — is in the third person.
CB: Yes, and there's a story coming out in *Toronto Life* — I gave it the title "Partial Renovations," but they're calling it "Prying" — that's from a female point of view in the third person, and the novel I'm working on is in the third person. The exception to this is a long, overtly autobiographical piece I've been working on this year. It's even nonfictional.
BC: In what ways do you see your stories as a response to the history of the short story, and in what ways do you see your novel, *Lunar Attractions*, as a response to the history of the novel? I mean, how conscious were you that you were bouncing off a tradition, say, or trying to do something that hadn't been done before?
CB: Hadn't been done by me before anyway. Well, so much of it is simply the background necessity that a writer carries with him. There is, with any writer, an awful lot of sophistication and craft and a deep, intimate knowledge of the form and an awareness of the millions of words that have been written in that form before he even sets pen to paper. But *where* and *how* you tap into this enormous grid is what makes your work unique. The choice of a point of entry is probably unconscious. I couldn't sit down to write something about which I didn't carry a deep illusion that it had never been done before and that the language had never been used in that way before and that the form had never

been discovered before — even though the conscious part of me knows that that's horseshit.

BC: Are you saying, then, that you're really not consciously aware of the history of the form itself when you write, say, a short story?

CB: Well, there are some stories in *A North American Education* and *Tribal Justice* that if you were to ask specifically about them, I could tell you. In writing certain stories included in *Tribal Justice*, for instance, I was quite aware of working within specific genres.

The first one, "Broward Dowdy," is one of my earliest pieces of writing. I wrote the core of that story as a sophomore in college when I was nineteen. But I put the frame around it when I was at the Iowa Writers' Workshop. In saying that my father was away at war and all that, the frame is inviting the reader to see the central incident as really a "separate peace" kind of story in which a child is trying to understand dislocations in the world and in his own personal life by riveting on a very difficult social adjustment that he has to make. That frame was part of a more conscious, later generic development.

A story like "Relief" is written very much in the mode of Faulkner. If you take the first paragraph of "Relief," for example, and compare it to the first paragraph of William Faulkner's "That Evening Sun," you'll see that it's almost a word-by-word transliteration:

Those with radios were safe from hurricanes, in their snug bungalows on landscaped streets. They nailed their shutters down, parked their cars under protection, and threw a card party till the storm blew over. In the morning, bleary-eyed but fresh with adventure, they'd drive down the cluttered streets, detouring around power lines, trees, temporary floods, then go home to sleep. Schools closed, and the kids gathered behind the fallen trees, firing kumquats at the clean-up crews of Negroes. The next day, blue skies and an autumn coolness returned; the town appeared cleaner, almost freshly painted. Errant hurricanes did that when they chanced across the state — made the townsfolk feel akin for a day to the blizzard-struck residents of upper New York who had also licked the adversity with candles, fortitude, and a supply of good hard liquor.

But with us things were different.

Monday is no different from any other weekday in Jefferson now. The streets are paved now, and the telephone and electric companies are cutting down more and more of the shade trees — the water oaks, the maples and locusts and elms — to make room for iron poles bearing clusters of bloated and ghostly and bloodless grapes, and we have a city laundry which makes the rounds on Monday morning, gathering the bundles of clothes into bright-colored, specially-made motor cars: the soiled wearing of a whole week now flees apparitionlike behind alert and irritable electric horns, with a long diminishing noise of rubber and asphalt like tearing silk, and even the Negro women who still take in white people's washing after the old custom, fetch and deliver it in automobiles.

But fifteen years ago....

Now, "The Fabulous Eddie Brewster" was written very much as a *New Yorker* "my crazy uncle" type of story; you know, "When I was a young boy, we had a visitor from overseas...." It's that kind of story, written in the first person — that is, urbane and recollective and, at the same time, focussing on someone whose personality and ways are bizarre and whose actions "illuminate our times" in some way. That's the *New Yorker* formula. So these three stories were written very distinctly as genre pieces.

Although less crafty than these three, a story that's a little bit closer to my deeper concerns — but written with much less of a sense of indebtedness to the form — is "The Seizure," which, like the Thibidault stories, although much more disguised, is a story I extracted and reworked from the Thibidault novel that I spoke to John Metcalf about in our interview. The story ends on a passionate note, a plea for knowledge, and if there's anyone to whom I owe a debt there, it's Isaac Babel, especially his story "Crossing into Poland" which ends, "I should wish to know where in the whole world you could find another father like my father?" I wanted to have a sensitive and sort of wimpish character who is involved with crude and violent people in a crude and violent world, and who has to take responsibility for that world because — even though he doesn't want any part of the seizure of the furniture — he's the owner's son. What, finally, is the right response? This is the question I wanted to throw back to the reader. It strikes me as the artist's dilemma: to be aloof from the nastier social, political, and economic realities, to be *weaker* than so many people he writes about, yet to possess total power and responsibility over them.

BC: The burden of moral responsibility really becomes the reader's at the end of the story.

CB: Yes, that's why I deliberately threw the problem back to the reader. Now, in "Grids and Doglegs" I wanted to talk about the bewilderments of adolescence. Again, the wimpish artist-figure sees himself as a worm, but he behaves more like a snake-in-the-grass.

BC: That story is very close to, or part of, the world of *Lunar Attractions*, isn't it?

CB: Well, yes, you could say that the grids and doglegs of that story are, in several senses, my world. I mean, it's the desire of the orderly intellect to lay out patterns, but the recalcitrant body and the physical world keep insisting on doglegs. There I was dealing with a world in which I wanted it all to come out: astronomy, baseball, fifties Americana, hopeless infatuation, arrogance, embarrassment. I suppose I was trying to deal with a kind of male analogy to a lot of Alice Munro's work in which you talk in the first person about your adolescence and you're deliberately trying to recapture that moment, say, of intense embarrassment. You know, you're saying, "Yes, I was pretty awful, and, yes, this is a terrible scene of gawkiness, but I want to give it all to you, and here it is."

BC: Is there anything personally cathartic involved in such writing for you? Do you need to write such fiction? Do you need to come to terms with such things? There is, I think, a strong sense in your work of a voice that needs to speak, that needs to utter in order to understand.

CB: Well, there are levels of compulsion in writing, of course, but I hope I don't write out of a compulsive therapeutic need. I don't think that would be consistent, anyway, with the enormous amount of hard, frequently unrewarding rewriting that goes into my work. Yet there may be at the core that compulsion. I'm dealing right now, for example, with a character in a novel who is a writer. He doesn't have much to do with me, but he realizes that his writing is an act of revenge, and I do think there's a lot of that in me. So it's not compulsion so much as it is really revenge — that is, I'm going to get

my side of it out, and I'm going to speak for those in-
articulate souls that died because they couldn't speak.

I'm very much aware of the fact that I am an accidental writer, that I'm an accidental Canadian, an accidental American, and an accidental survivor in any
number of ways. I realize that many of the writers I know
have come out of a more promising background for
writing than I have. For them, it was a more natural
act; with me, it was a very unnatural act. And I also think
I should have died physically many times, like one of
those characters out of Marie-Claire Blais — some hopeless, spiritual, sickly, orphan intellect who can piece
together extraordinarily insightful associations, but
who is doomed to die a lingering death or is doomed to
never speak of his insights or to suffer for having had
them. There's a lot of that in my writing, you know, the
kid who suffers for his intelligence, his insights, or
whose insights are more correct than the indicated
ones. That's the French side of me speaking. Think of
Jack Kerouac, of *Doctor Sax* and *Visions of Gerard.*
BC: Your central character is also often an artist figure
of some sort. Is that because you're writing out of your
own sensibility? Or is the artist a symbol of humanity?
CB: No, not artist as symbol of humanity, but artist as
unifier and synthesizer, quester and questioner. The
writer is aware of chaos and randomness and senseless-
ness, and he tries to re-create a world in which *his* sense
of balance and motivation and inevitability has a better
chance to operate. After that comes the business of
craft and style.
BC: The distinction between the primal material of art,
vision, and artistry?
CB: Yes. I suppose I have been rather passive before my
own autobiography — that is, accepting it as being as

good as anyone else's for what I do as a writer, not realizing that it's quirky and eccentric and relates really only to me. I mean, there's nothing universal in my autobiography unless I choose to make it that way. Otherwise, it's a thoroughly singular and useless one. I don't know why I'm so involved with my own background. I've known many writers with vastly more interesting stories to "tell" who have avoided their private stories altogether.

BC: But there is a tendency in your work to make the experience of your central character paradigmatic in some way. In fact, I seem to recall your saying that those people who might want to read, say, David Greenwood's story in a paradigmatic way might sense an allegorical dimension in your work. I'm not saying that it's conscious allegorical design, but merely that that's the way people could respond to it.

CB: They can respond to it either as a specialized study of utter alienation or as a study of a kind of possible Everyman or possible paradigmatic figure, as you say. I have seen reviews that have offered both points of view. I'm aware of seeing these possibilities in my own life. I can speak with assurance as a Southerner, an American suburbanite, an American ethnic, a Canadian, and I can speak with assurance in some ways as someone with a memorable experience of India and certainly as a wanderer through Europe. In other words, I can sit in fairly sophisticated North Atlantic company and feel at ease, and I can also feel at ease with a carpenter in New Hampshire. Probably, however, the only place I'll feel truly at home is in sitting down in a baseball stadium and letting it wash over me for the thousandth time.

BC: But you write in and speak for my time, despite the experiences you have had that I haven't.

CB: But this is what I've had to evolve, had to work on. In this sense, I've not been passive before my own auto-biography: I've had to do an awful lot of enlargements and variations upon it to make it even passingly accessible to other people.

BC: What about distinctions between the novel and the short story as fictional forms, other than the obvious things such as length?

CB: I think that if we're lucky we're seeing a kind of collapse of definitions, of distinctions. Earlier in the century, of course, there were distinctions, not just in terms of length, but in terms of any number of intentions — social aspects, for instance, social functions of fictional forms. But, as the short story market disappears and the urge to write short stories is even more intense, we're witnessing a collapse of any workable distinction between the two except length. I notice, for example, that this year's edition of *The Best American Short Stories* contains two stories by Mavis Gallant. Now, I've never seen that done before. A hundred or so pages of Mavis Gallant: put the two stories together and you've got at least a half of a novel there, and what, pray tell, is the difference between a Mavis Gallant story when she's working at her richest and fullest and most polyphonic and someone else's novel? It's just that the novel becomes smaller and thinner than her story.

There's no way in which I can be convinced that the standard definitions are useful anymore. A John Cheever short story, for instance, contains as many points of reference, as many individual events, as any novel. The short story, I suppose, has to work a little bit more by association, suggestion, and indirection than the novel does. A novel has to use its greater length intelligently — otherwise it's merely an inflated story. *The*

Autumn of the Patriarch, say, simply needs its dense texture. *Something Happened* needs the variations on its repetitions.

BC: Does the novel, then, have the licence to be more discursive than the short story?

CB: It has the licence to be, but I think people who are capable of ringing all the variations in forty pages, either writers or readers, are not going to tolerate having to go through three hundred pages. I think a novel, to be epigrammatic about it, has to be at least as rich as the short story. And, frankly, most novels aren't. Most novels are watery, diluted, and bloated, and they do not have anything like the richness of a short story. I think there are only a few rich ones around. One way out, of course, is what the South Americans do: use magic and suspensions of conventional realities. Another way out is what the Japanese do: what is three hundred pages in Japanese comes to us in a hundred and ten pages in English, and we see it as marvellous, dense work.

BC: Your own novel is incredibly dense! I've been teaching it as a matter of fact, and I've been three weeks on it and I'm not past page eighty.

CB: That's wonderful. But, on the other hand, I got a review of *Lunar Attractions* this week from Doubleday Canada that appeared as a comment in the year's round-up of fiction in the *University of Toronto Quarterly*, a remark that in effect said that the book is merely another story of adolescence written in direct simple prose and that it's not terribly interesting, but does have some funny things to say about the adolescent predicament.

BC: That's hard to believe. Perhaps we could come back to the topic of Canadian criticism and Canadian culture in general a bit later. In your interview with John

Metcalf, you refer approvingly, it seems, to John Hawkes's "assumption that the true enemies of the novel were theme, plot, and character." Would you still agree with such a postmodernist aesthetic?

CB: Well, there is something in Hawkes's remark and in much of what John Barth says — Barth who is far more articulate on these matters and who is, in a sense, the pinnacle of a kind of anti-humanist tradition, the post-modernist tradition I suppose. Both of them would believe that the only possibility for freshness in literature is to view literature as literature: you know, the novel as a statement on literature, not a statement on life. I'm somewhere in the middle; I like vision, voice, and texture; maybe to play off one kind of conventional vision against the jazzier kind.

BC: Metafiction.

CB: Right, metafiction. And of course such people as Barth are all anti-Gardnerians — and John Gardner is not his own best advocate by any means. I guess I've read as much of it as I can understand and as much of it as I care to, and I must say that I simply do not *have* a position on it. Hawkes is of course right that an awful lot of meretricious junk is written to give us a pulpy, palpable feel of life and that all of it is terribly conventional and simply perpetuates lies and frauds and limitations on the reader — it speaks down to him and to his experience. Yes, that's there in the humanistic tradition, in the tradition of realistic fiction. On the other hand, my mentor, my closest and dearest friend in writing, is Bernard Malamud (to whom *Lunar Attractions*, incidentally, is dedicated), and Malamud comes out of a very different tradition that, when well-handled, is one that speaks for me. I am still not *that* interested in these terribly intelligent sophisticates: I find something cold and alienating in them; I find something just as meretricious in their world.

BC: Intellectual exercises?

CB: I don't know. Surely there is room in fiction for intelligent, concerned people working at the best of their abilities, however it may be. I *like* the notion of having, say, a William H. Gass around. It's lovely to be able to pick up his stuff and know that you're being whipped into shape by the ringmaster; same thing with Nabokov. Yes, I can read Nabokov's lectures, his sneerings and posturings on modernist and contemporary writers, and say, "Yes, wasn't Mann pompous, a fool, and isn't this unbearable and unreadable?" And yet when I want a sense of what fiction can be at its best, I frankly go to Mann, not to Nabokov. Nothing wins me over more than the novellas of Mann.

BC: What you're speaking of here is related to a remark you made in *New Canadian Writing, 1968*: "Joyce and Hemingway distract us from the discursive tradition, from literature compounded of cold observation *and* subjective passion." The discursive tradition is the one in which you would find Mann, right?

CB: Yes. I like the sense of discursiveness always nozzled through a critical intelligence and craft. But the sense of discursiveness and randomness and the ability to exploit and to make something of everyday life are what I like most. Now, obviously, Joyce and Hemingway do that too — I read them myself all the time, and I'm always telling my students to read them — but I still prefer things that have a kind of sponginess to them, a sort of softness and unresolved quality. The high ground is nice, austerity is attractive, but I guess I'm a swamp-dweller.

BC: Well, I am genuinely attracted to both traditions. I

enjoy reading books that are humanistic, to use your term, and books that are metafictional. And I like books that fuse both traditions in interesting ways.

CB: This is related to a problem I've just had to confront. For the first time in years I have to teach, in the second term here at Skidmore, two heavy hard-nosed literature courses. Not writing courses, not form and theory courses, but strict undergraduate lecture courses in modern fiction. One in recent fiction and one in Commonwealth fiction: Canadian, Australian, South African, Indian, African, and Caribbean. Just this week I've had to make up a list of about twenty books. What twenty books do I want to live with next term? And it's hard. Who in recent world fiction — I mean, I don't have to confine myself to British and American fiction — can I justify thrusting forward? From Canada? From Australia?

BC: It's a hell of a question.

CB: It's a hell of a question, all right, and so I've had to decide, do I want this year's sleek low model, or do I want the twenty-years-ago boxy chrome-fendered model? Now I think someone like Peter Handke — his novella *The Left-Handed Woman* is to me a miraculous combination of all that is heartless and cold and sleek in the French tradition with a workmanlike, daily, compassionate, minute observation in the tradition of realism to give us a sense of what fiction can do. That is a beautiful thing. I'm putting two of Peter Handke's books on, *A Moment of True Feeling* and *The Left-Handed Woman*. I also want them to see Tom Berger's work and, say, a Naipaul novel. I want them to see so much.

BC: Well, how do you choose just twenty books?

CB: I have to start with what I've "liked." And I want to make a selection that combines the metafictional with the humanistic.

BC: Do you see yourself working out of a particular literary tradition — Canadian, American, British, European, or otherwise?

CB: The literary tradition to which I feel the closest in its many forms is the French tradition. I feel religiously, alas, very close to Pascal; I'm a Jansenist. I also feel very close to Céline, to Stendhal, to Proust, and to Kerouac, so that every time I turn around that is the tradition that speaks to me.

BC: Do you mean in terms of both philosophical perspectives on the world and artistry or craft?

CB: All of that. I would, for example, like to be a dirty saint. I would like to be a Céline, I suppose — that is, to take what is in a very minor key a Proustian sensibility and smudge it in a Célinesque way. I have a lot of Céline in me; I have a lot of dirt in me. I am not attracted, however, to any of the perfumed decadents like Genet.

BC: What about non-literary artistic influences?

CB: Because I started as a painter, an artist, I have been affected by painting, especially Dutch painting.

BC: Do you think films have had any particular influence on your work?

CB: No, I don't think so. I'm a schlock consumer of film. I don't have much of an intelligent understanding or any kind of formal understanding of film. I'm also turned off immediately by film criticism. The only film maker who speaks to me with any kind of passion is Satyajit Ray — but not really because of film as such. I mean, it's the entirety of his vision. If I understood every film the way I understand every minute or foot of a Ray film, then I would take up film criticism. But no other film maker, it seems to me, has that human vision. Now someone like Ray may be the best antidote for too much Nabokov, Gass, or Barth, for Ray's work is entirely humanistic. It is totally concerned with real people dealing with real problems in a real world. It is an understanding of gesture, sympathies, compassions, and hungers — all those old unchanging human things.

Speak to Ray about *Star Wars* or any of the technological advances that film is supposed to have made, slick things, and he wouldn't understand. That isn't quite fair; he understands perfectly. But his attraction to it would *still* be story and character: What does this tell us about humanity, as opposed to presenting mere spectacle or entertainment? If you asked him "Did you do this shot because of the need to inject more alienation?", he would probably answer "No, I did it because the camera broke down" or "I did it because it was necessary to her feelings at the time." It's entirely a world of the feelings of characters for Ray.

BC: I asked you that question about film because I have been wondering about the epigraph to *Lunar Attractions* from Frederick Feirstein's "The Film Maker to His Father":

> ... No matter what others take
> For intellect, art; I know
> That for each illusion I make
> There is one scenario:
> It's our unresolved debate
> About where love must leave off
> And how much freedom to take:
> That's what my craft contains.

CB: Well, Fred is a very close friend of mine. And I was also involved there in trying to speak to my father, who was dying during the writing of the book.

BC: You mentioned Pascal a moment ago, reminding me

of another remark you made in *New Canadian Writing,
1968*: "Pascal ... would insist that infinity suspends reason and that to cope with the 'infinity of things' lying
beyond reason requires grace. And if faith or grace is
not forthcoming, silence and fear alone are possible."
Are there any of your characters who have this faith or
grace? Why are so many of your stories "about men
with only passing claims to promise and potency"?

CB: That remark of Pascal's and perhaps fifty others
when they hit me as an undergraduate did so with the
force of immense fertility. They were seeds that were
really small trees the moment they were planted. They
were immediately right for me: I'd never heard those
fears articulated before and the dilemmas stated so
acutely.

BC: They're personally powerful insights for me as well.

CB: I had been struggling on my own towards a very
imperfect, very crude understanding of the dilemmas
of which he speaks, and he simply pushed me light-
years along. As I recall, however, the religion course I
was taking presented these ideas as curiosities, her-
esies, and simply well-formed French epigrams. And
they are of course religious dead ends; they don't really
tell you how to live.

BC: Religion implies a comic vision, I think, but in many
ways you could say that Pascal's vision is tragic — or at
least that his comic vision is in tension with his tragic
vision. In the "Writers' Forum" about John Gardner's book
On Moral Fiction, you speak of morality as "a mythic
structure[,] ... a narrative force, an older and ... trustier
tool than psychology for the plotting of inevitability,"
and then you go on to say, "morality is a great and enduring myth, it is the lone universal myth ... out of
which spring all notions of religion, ethics, conscience,

duty, and neurosis." The thrust of your entire comment is that the moral vision opposes the natural order.

CB: This is the old grids and doglegs problem. Doesn't morality oppose nature? It's our only way of fighting back. Otherwise, our very "natural" deaths would make a mockery of all human activity.

BC: Yes. Are you, however, always on the side of the natural?

CB: I try not to be. Part of what I had said in that response to Gardner's book, which did not get printed in the "Writers' Forum," is that I try to be an "altruistic pagan." Altruism: a sense of sacrificing oneself, one's desires, one's tastes and appetites, one's lusts, for other people's benefit, for the social good, or even for the intellectual cleanliness of it all. This is what morality is all about.

All our myths and all our neuroses are really about this. That is the tragic dilemma. Am I always on the side of the natural? I don't know. The book on which I'm working now is called *The Book of Lusts*. It's about lust and about sexual lust and about hunger and about art. It's about a person who has been pretty nasty, who has foregone much of his altruism.

I am personally repulsed by the natural order. It's just that I think that my experiences have weighted me strongly toward an understanding of the natural world. My childhood in Florida, the bizarre marriage my parents made — these were mired in the physical world. I'm talking about being aware of the worlds that went into my making.

BC: The tension between morality and the natural order you speak of can be defined in so many ways: chaos and rationality, freedom and order, the natural world and civilization in several senses of the word. What is fiction, what is its value I mean, why should we read it? Is fiction more or less important than other literary forms? What is the most important literary form in 1980? Poetry? Drama? Fiction? Film? Television?

CB: Pascal said there is nothing to substitute for a man alone in his room with his writing desk. There is no reality more important than what a man can confront at his own bare table, and I don't think we need eight-million-dollar budgets and shooting schedules and all the rest to tell us things. I mean, film and television are garbage. Poetry has a value, of course, but I'm not a poet.

BC: But you used to be, didn't you?

CB: Oh, yes, I started out writing as a poet, but who doesn't?

BC: Right. I wrote poetry myself as an undergraduate. It's an apprenticeship for being a critic, too.

CB: It's an apprenticeship for any number of things: many are called, but few answer. There are times, however, when I've gone back to it, times of fairly recidivist tendencies in my life when I've known that I really didn't have the opportunity to sit down and fully write — as in fiction — and I've envied the poet's ability to be so promiscuous with his material and to turn so many things into a workable moment. But, you see, the habit has died in me to be able to treat things free of contexts. I want to create contexts and resolutions. I want to create histories around little things. So I may see them as a poetic possibility, but they immediately become transformed into something else.

BC: Do you see the fiction writer as having a social function?

CB: I have two absolutely opposing views. It's all meaningless; if it has any virtue at all, it's that it keeps me off the streets; it's a hobby that I could just as easily fulfill by taking up stamps or some such thing again. That's one sense that I have of it. What the hell good does it do? All these books? A kind of tax collector's view of it: You know, why should we care, why should we publish it, why should we pay you to do it, why should we exempt you from the human carnival simply because you say you're a writer? It's increasingly hard, in other words, to cloak yourself in Joyce's, Proust's, or Mann's mantle and say that you're above it all. On the other hand, I realize it's a disaster to go down and become a Günter Grass writing political speeches. I mean, for whom are you going to write speeches anyway? Barry Commoner? The NDP? There's something ridiculous about the dead end we've gotten ourselves into in North America. I'm living well — not through my writing but through my teaching.

All that being said, all the sneering aside, I still feel there's an audience out there, people who want to see more clearly than they can in any other way — than in film, television, newspapers, or magazines — their lives, a life, or life in general. And they can only do so through the medium of the written word, through reading real books. All the rest is, finally, unsatisfying; it may be more intense, but it's unsatisfying. I don't want to write for purely my fellow practitioners. I have a desire to reach a general audience of my fellow "élite" — not my writing élite and not my academic élite, but an élite, say, of sensibility, which numbers many millions. I don't see millions in sales, mind you, but I would like to think that I'm stamping a currency that could be passed in, say, law offices, accounting houses, banks, and universities. BC: But how do these people get to know about your work, except through academic channels? OK, so I've got both your books of short stories on my short story course and I've got your novel on my novel course. Is that the only way? And how appropriate, really, is my adoption of your books? I mean *Lunar Attractions* was published in 1979 and I've got it on a 1980 course.

CB: Actually, we're probably better off now than we were in the past. Still, I have to have an idiot faith that, in some way, all the stuff that we do, all the hopes and prayers that we have, will eventually be answered. We send these books out on a long trajectory — and what we get through the filtering process of academia is very small potatoes — but eventually they come down. Eventually they will come down and people will be able to see them. We shoot them in the air, never knowing where they fall. I think it was a French writer who said that writing is a lottery, that you draw the ticket not for next year, but for a hundred years from now. If this year you have a thousand readers and if in ten years you have a hundred readers, then you will endure. Flannery O'Connor said something similar, too.

BC: Is recognition, then, important to you?

CB: Oh, sure. The kind of recognition that I would really like — this sounds very arrogant to say — is to have created a world by which people can apply an adjective: you know, we have a Kafkaesque world, a Faulknerian world, a Dostoyevskian world, a Cheeveresque world. It seems to me that this is the highest praise you can give an author — that he has created a mood, something, that you recognize exists in its essence uniquely in that author's world, almost a kind of gestalt, which I think is what moves me in my reading. This is the humanist impulse. You don't really talk of "a Hawkesean world," but rather of "a Hawkesean sentence."

BC: I think I can see the beginnings, or the shape, of a Blaisean universe in your work.

CB: Perhaps, but there are many more points of reference that have to be laid down — for instance, what I was suggesting in "Man and His World," that if you live long enough, you lay down enough experience to permit coincidences to become possible and, in fact, become expected, and suddenly life seems to be nothing more than a series of significant coincidences.

BC: Jungian synchronicity.

CB: Yes, in a way. I've never done anything systematically with Jung, but I once took the first couple of paragraphs of *Lunar Attractions* and explained them to a class in terms of both Freudian and Jungian motifs. There are in that book the classical Freudian postulation of replacing the father and all the rest of it and, at the same time, a Jungian sense of subsuming the dualities, the crises, the conflicts into one. And each of the "pictures of my mind" concerns simultaneously playing all the roles. You know, sometimes you are the camel, sometimes you are the lion, sometimes you are the Arab, sometimes you are the crayon, sometimes you are the drawing.

BC: Affinities converging, eh? I'm very much aware of your concern with texture — "detail arranged and selected and enhanced," as you described it to John Metcalf — and, of course, texture "probably rules out most satire," as you said in the same interview. Now, in *Lunar Attractions*, there is a lot of material that could have been developed in a satiric way — all the authoritarian figures in the novel, for example, the principal, the teachers, and the detectives. Is there a tension between the aesthetics of texture and a satiric impulse in the novel?

CB: Oh, I'm sure there must be. But I didn't want to write just another high-school thing in which the teachers are the heavies. They are heavies, but heavies in a heavier way; they're not caricatures. Now I enjoy reading satire, but I don't really like it. I think there's a chill in it. Take Evelyn Waugh, for instance: I don't like his prose at all, though everyone says it's the greatest prose in the twentieth century. I don't see it; I've read all the books, and I don't see anything there. I have no interest in his characters. I mean, I know what his targets are, but I don't respect his means or his position.

BC: Are the people who admire Waugh the people who don't like Faulkner, say?

CB: Exactly. And they don't like Kerouac either. This is the great divide, you know. I'm not sure that Waugh-lovers are not envious of his certainties, and a little uncomfortable with their own disorder.

BC: It's not a question of a comic or a tragic vision, is it? I mean, many satirists really have a tragic vision.

CB: Now, I like Anthony Powell's *A Dance to the Music of Time*, but that wasn't to me essentially a satire. It was a rendering and ordering of an entire society by means of shrinkage that necessarily, inevitably, involves the ironical. Now, there are ironical shrinkages and ironical expansions, and my vision is ironical for the purposes of complicating, not simplifying, for expanding, not shrinking.

BC: Everything in the novel is there in the last page and a half, isn't it?

CB: I hope so. But "everything" ideally should be present in *all* parts, and I know that's not the case. It's in the beginning and the end, but there are thin portions that don't deliver. It's like drawing blood for purposes of testing. *Everything* should be present, no matter where you draw the sample. Most of the book went through an enormous number of drafts, and then I only had the last twenty or thirty pages to finish, but in my last year in Montreal I wasn't able to get more than one or two hours a week to work. So I said to myself, "I've simply got to get this thing finished." Consequently, I went down to Doubleday's office in New York and had my editor book me into one of their seminar rooms, and they gave me a typewriter and paper, and I told myself, "I am going to finish this book here in three days." I normally write in longhand first, but those last pages were done straight out on the typewriter.

Actually, I cut out a lot of stuff I originally had, particularly material with the teacher, Virginia Pritchett-McQuade. I had a much longer scene in mind for the very end, too. And I had an epilogue. But then I thought, "That's it." There have been some objections to the ending, but none of it matters if the book is strong. That's one of the advantages of the novel over the short story, I suppose: if the experience is strong, if the voice is strong throughout the book, you can have all sorts of objections to parts of the book and it really doesn't matter. The whole thing can sustain little excursions.

BC: Speaking of voice, I think that there is far less dialogue in *Lunar Attractions* than in most of your stories, not that there's much in them either.

CB: I have a great many problems, in fact, with relinquishing control, and in many ways I would like to have more dialogue in my work. But I find most dialogue so vapid, so vaporous, and so uninteresting. This is in many ways the Mann impulse: if I'm in the hands of a guy who has got the goods, I would rather he does it than have him split himself up into five or six parts.

BC: Any theories about the language of fiction?

CB: Well, I just gave a lecture here at Skidmore this week about fictional language as opposed to any other kind of language and about the necessary cracking of grammar, how grammar must be cracked in order to layer in temporal and spatial and psychological and social aspects — not to mention everything else. English grammar as it's handed down to us through the grammarians and teachers does not really permit such things. It's the evolution of prose styles, the evolution of fiction, that enables us to do something like this: "It's the man, his hand bleeding, who salutes the flag." It's the ability to suggest, to see, "his hand bleeding," a remark which has nothing logically or grammatically to do with the rest of the sentence, that gives this sentence its fictional weight. "The man with the bleeding hand saluted the flag" is a different order, conventional grammar.

BC: Although one might call your first example, in grammatical terms, the absolute construction.

CB: Yes, but you're really beginning to play on more than one keyboard; you're beginning to realize that you can play on five keyboards if you want to. You begin to learn "The man, his hand bleeding, saluted the flag, the pole still greased from the day's activities," and then you realize, in fact, that language is capable of infinite refinement, infinite directions, and that the only way to get the polyphonic quality of life itself into the sentence is to break the grammar, break the back of the sentence, crack it open and stuff it with these other things. Once you develop this ability, however, there is a tendency to overdo it at first, and then you have to learn the value of the simple sentence "The man saluted the flag," which becomes a kick in the gut, a powerful understated sentence. But until you can crack the grammar, you're dealing with only conventional thoughts and conventional language. You're not going to achieve anything until you do, but once you have, then you can go back and use a perfectly plain sentence that will be as effective as a gun going off.

BC: Any theories of chapters?

CB: I certainly have a strong sense of parts, but, really, I would like to break an action where I want to break it — as in, say, free verse. Page breaks, chapter breaks — these are the *invisible* structural supports in a narrative. They impose a pace on the action the way sleep, say, structures our lives.

BC: You do use white space quite a bit in the novel, and I don't feel that the book would have been as effective had sections, parts, or chapters been numbered throughout. I see, however, that you're using numbering in your most recently published story, "Man and His World."

CB: I looked on that story as a deliberate developmental sequence. Steps have enormous consequences; deliberate steps have direct and predictable consequences, and totally accidental steps have even more far-reaching and long-range consequences. The man dies for any number of reasons: for the sins of the British colonials upon the Maharajah's grandfather, for his own amorality or immorality, for having discovered that life is coincidence and useless, for a small act of passion in a Westmount park. I am trying to talk about the enormous number of random events, and correspondences between random events, that can destroy human life at age forty — which I do feel myself, the only autobiographical aspect of the story.

BC: It's a strange story, and it seems so radically different from your other work. This is the direction in which you're moving?

CB: Yes. The story is part of a planned book of stories, the book after the new novel, and it's characteristic of a lot of the stories. The book will be about Canadians in the world. I have my own version of Naipaul's *In a Free State* in which we have a couple of Canadian diplomats out in a kind of Madagascar or New Guinea world. An utterly foreign, mythologically potent, physically unbelievable world in which human fauna lead a life of supreme degradation. Mythological like the myth structures in "Man and His World" about the camels, motherhood, and the brother murdered in the womb. In fact, I've been making up a lot of cosmogonies. It contains the long autobiography, focussing on my Winnipeg years, and then the Montreal, Toronto, and Indian experiences, and the decision that Toronto was unworkable for us. I won't be trying to evoke the physical world first-hand in it as I was in, say, my Southern stories. If I need an ordinary tree, it will be there; if I need an impossible tree, it will be there because I'll just invent it. Before, in describing Florida, I was trying to give an accounting of a world that I knew was there but that no one else knew was there, a world being destroyed by Disney and condominiums.

BC: Speaking of foreign climes, what place does *Days and Nights in Calcutta* have in your canon? How important is that book to you?

CB: The importance of *Days and Nights* was first of all technical — I had to integrate a narrative and a set of feelings and responses and build up a series of characters, plus I had to read and manipulate a lot of factual materials. In other words, it was a novel for me, very much a nonfiction novel, with a clear sense of myself-as-character, making me a little more naïve than I was, a little more priggish than I am, in order to, I hope, create a believable transformation of character by the end. I didn't want to be a Vedantist from the beginning — I wanted to respect my considerable reservations about India and to show that I went to India not from prior vulnerabilities but under the compulsion to understand my wife and myself. Writing that book showed me that I could do a book-length study and that I could discipline my prose to be nonfictional and that I could string together a few thousand sentences with the injunction that they be continuously "wondrous," as Dunstan Ramsay might say, meaning that they show people back home, who share none of my problems or my autobiography, the simplicity of some very complicated situations.

Secondly, the book informed me of my own feelings: through writing it and the discipline of preparing myself to write it — while still living it, in India — I learned that I have a "shadow" that India touched. I endured more in India than I could have elsewhere. And I also resisted and fought back and demonstrated more vociferously than I have since. It taught me something of life-as-theatre. It also brought something out of me, an affectionate side that one must repress for the most part in North America. It did all those things for me that India is supposed to do — dented me, even smashed through me. I haven't known such freedom, emotional freedom, since.

It is by far the most important book to me — it freed me, for I started with two advantages that I can never have in my fiction: one, I'm an absolute amateur here, and know *nothing* about this place and will *never* know anything but the most superficial clap-trap about it; two, everything about the place is fresh, fascinating, and of absolute interest, and all I have to do is find a voice, distance, a vantage point, and let my eyes do the writing. You can see that these two conditions are precisely reversed in my fiction, where I labour under the

burden of being an expert in *myself* and the further burden of having *nothing* fascinating to be dealing with.
BC: Oh, I wouldn't say that, considering *Lunar Attractions*
in particular. But I want to return to the question of
Canadian culture. I read your Mermaid's Inn column
in *The Globe and Mail*, in which you say,

> The deeper forces hurt anyone who writes seriously
> in this country, be he or she honoured or forgotten.
> The enemy out there is (to be kind) the amateur spir-
> it, which translates to a love of mediocrity. And I
> mean as well its necessary corollary: a fear of ambi-
> tion, an embarrassment with excellence. Layton
> would have called it constipated and masturbatory;
> I'd call it a decayed gentility, others might excuse it
> as a neo-colonialism. The point is, no one escapes it.

You go on to say, "Professionalism and a long apprenticeship are an embarrassment." Do you want to add to
these remarks in any way?
CB: Well, the corollary is more important than the observation. I mean, everyone can love a genial, clumsy
fool; a kind of oafishness combined with an awareness
of one's oafishness is a genial thing. What we often lose
sight of is that those people who are amateurs and who
are aware of their amateurism and who are continually apologizing for it are also vicious. That's something
that good writers and good artists have always known:
that underneath the egregiously apologetic fool is quite
often a person who is very proud and very comfortable
— too comfortable — with his particular kind of foolishness and who will do an awful lot to maintain that as
the standard.

BC: I know exactly what you mean: I've seen it everywhere in the academic world, too.

CB: And when you first experience that kind of homespun quality, you think, "How very nice, how very pleasant, how very humane this all is," and you discover that it's a genial and tolerable atmosphere in which to live. But the point is that the frustrations we feel with our impotence, the frustrations we feel with a lack of real place and real power in the world and real recognition for our talents lead to many forms of perversion. For those who truly succeed — the Northrop Fryes, for instance — there is a marvellous openness and warmth and total lack of jealousy, but for anyone beneath that level there's nothing but implicit contempt or the most grudging acknowledgement.

The real Canadian spirit is that you have to have been born here, raised here, and had five different generations of blue-eyed ancestors to understand what Hugh MacLennan is saying. And if you say that Hugh MacLennan is a tedious writer, then you just don't understand. "Of course he's tedious, but he's our kind of tedium and we can only explain that in our terms." *Tout comprendre, c'est tout pardonner.* Well, I understand that; I know exactly what's being said. But Bharati and I sadly discovered that Toronto was impossible for us to live in, given the racial facts of our marriage and the climate of the city. That, too, is related to the defensive-mindedness of Canada, which I understand but can't forgive.

Room for Anything:
An Interview with Clark Blaise
[1993]

Sherri Telenko

ST: In the past you have claimed to use autobiographical elements only as a springboard into your fiction. Now, with *I Had a Father*, you have written an autobiography. What is the difference between autobiographical fiction and autobiography?

CB: First of all, true autobiography means everything in there happened and is documented and verifiable. But also, the impulse behind autobiography — as I said in the introduction to the book — is to establish consciousness as the control over experience. In autobiographical fiction you are using autobiography to explore experience and then trying to use that autobiographical entry to create or to imagine experience. In this book the experience has already happened — either to me or to my father.

I'm trying to re-establish distance and control to extract a meaning, a set of patterns, and perhaps even a message from it all. In fiction you are pushing experience to a point of confrontation, but you're not necessarily resolving or surmounting it. It is enough to expose the situation and let the reader make the resolutions. However, in autobiography there is an impulse built into the form to surmount the distance you have established.

The point is that no one is interested in me or my father. We are anonymous people. The reader can only be interested in so far as our experiences *touch* their experiences. My consciousness has to reach out to their consciousness because the experiences in the book are going to be unique. They're only going to be my experiences — that's what autobiography is. I am not trying to find experiences which will tie other people to my book. I'm trying to explore a tone of voice, a consciousness, that will bring people into my book.

ST: Do you enjoy reading autobiographies?

CB: I do. When they're good. I have no interest in what I call "self-narrative" as opposed to autobiography. That is the General, the politician, or the movie star who is setting down the events of his or her life because she or he is so famous, powerful, rich, or has achieved something in the outer world. I'm interested in the anonymous stories of anonymous people who are compelled to write because of some crisis in their life that forces them to go back and reassess everything in their life before they can go forward again. The autobiographies that I admire are those that come upon you in mid-life by surprise.

I started *I Had a Father* with the smell of cigarettes in an apartment that I was living in — suddenly I was back and my father was speaking to me even though he had been dead for years. I began by conjuring him up from memory and smoke, and then going out and documenting him from the historical records in Quebec, and then seeing how foreign he is to me and yet how much I am his son. It was a way of helping me out of the crisis I was in during the eighties: poverty, joblessness, being in a sense forgotten — having gone from a very comfortable life in Toronto and Montreal to being a nobody and feeling that I had made a ghastly mistake.

I felt I had no real future. I was facing my own crisis and that's what started the book.

ST: Is the book, then, a type of self-realization?

CB: All autobiography is coming to terms with the cards you are dealt. You are born into a time and place and people that you might not have chosen on your own. I would not have chosen to be the things that I am. But after rebelling against it, exploiting it, or whatever it is you do for thirty or forty years, you are going to have to come to terms with it and accept it. You can't enlarge upon what you are given. You can investigate the angles, and all of the implications, but you can't really expand on it too much. What you have to do is to examine very closely all the cards that are in your hand rather than saying, "I'm not going to play with this deck."

ST: You have given *I Had a Father* the subtitle *A Post-Modern Autobiography*. What do you mean when you use the term "post-modern"?

CB: The post-modern aspect comes in all the time in the book. First, post-modernism accepts all levels of information as equally valid, so that if you have historical records, memories, pop culture, all of these things have value. It's not as though I'm going to sit down like some nineteenth-century novelist and try to write in an elevated language or from an elevated position about time, eternity, religion, fate, society, and culture. I'm using a discontinuous method of narrative — here you can open the book anywhere and read it. There is no building narrative. Things are layered. I'm using juxtaposition rather than organic growth. There is no consistent plot or characterization.

ST: You also take a very post-modern approach to history and historical recording.

CB: Yes. It is as important for me to talk about the epic

qualities of nineteenth-century French-Canadian life or the frontier of Manitoba as it is to talk about events in my own life. To me, these things are now equally important. I have surrendered the desire of modernism, or conventional literature, to evaluate what's important and what's not. The pink rabbit in the Duracell commercial is a very important autobiographical statement to me. The record of the *New York Times* editorials against French Canadians is very important to me. Baseball is very important to me. The literature I have read — both the serious literature and the pop culture — and the moves I have made throughout my life are equally important to me.

The other thing about post-modernism is that it is very conscious of the act of its own creation. Rather than trying to play the game that you are writing this from a room somewhere that is not intruding upon your text, I acknowledge that this week I am writing on a laptop computer in an airport in New Zealand, or Finland, or Canada, or New York, or Iowa. I'm seeing the book as sort of a soft-sided bag into which everything can be put. I can find room for anything that is happening to me while I am writing this book. Those are all post-modernist assumptions that would be thrown out of a conventional or traditional literary work.

ST: You have written books in the past which have involved an interesting combination of essay and fiction — *Resident Alien*, for example. I get the same sort of feeling here, in *I Had a Father*, particularly at the end of Part One when you discuss borders. Is this mixture of narrative and didactics conscious?

CB: It's just part of saying that the voice of this book is polyphonic, that I'm using many voices to illustrate the same thing. I want to illustrate certain academic truths,

certain literary truths, certain notions of what autobiography is. I want to talk about my father's life. I want
to have a historical record of French Canadians and of
Franco-Americans. And I want to be responsible to my
own life, too. So if there are many voices — some of them
academic, some of them less so — it's conscious. I am a
border mentality. I don't want to give allegiance to
either side. I want to live in a place where store owners
wait on you in one language and then turn and count
up in a different language at the cash register. I'm comfortable with those kinds of people, who are totally
English-speaking to a customer and totally French-
speaking among themselves.

ST: So how do you feel about finding your books in the
Canadian literature section?

CB: I'm perfectly happy with that. The only alternative
is the American literature section. I think I say in the
book that until there is such a thing as North American
literature, I probably belong more on the Canadian side
than the American side. Psychologically I am more Canadian. Sociologically, more American. I know more
about American pop sociology than I know about the
Canadian equivalent. I know American history better
than Canadian history. And although I know both geographies pretty well, I probably know American geography better than Canadian geography. On the other
hand, I have lived a longer period of time in Montreal
than anywhere else. And imaginatively I keep returning
to Montreal as a subject matter. However, the next
thing that I'm writing is set in New England, with
French-speaking characters, in a 1920s or 1930s world.
But I'm still dealing with the effects of French Canada
in my life.

ST: You speak often about the number of times you have

moved throughout your life, about places and boundaries and areas as being significant overall, but is there
one place in particular that was more of an influence?
CB: Montreal is the most influential place I think I've
ever lived in. I would say, though, that I would be a very
different person if I hadn't had those Florida years in
my childhood. And I would be a very different person
if I hadn't had the Pittsburgh of my adolescence. And
very different if I hadn't spent a considerable amount
of my adult life in India. All of those things are so mixed
up in me that it would be impossible for me to say that
one is more dominant than another, more important
than another. I simply wouldn't be the same person if
they hadn't happened to me. Those are the significant
ones: Montreal, Pittsburgh, Florida, India, and a lot of
European — French, German, British, Scandinavian —
travel and living in between.
ST: Are you more comfortable with newness, with experi-
encing a new culture like India? I can imagine that someone who has experienced as much diversity as you have
would be more inspired than alienated by difference.
CB: I'm never alienated by difference — though sometimes I'm alienated by familiarity. If I'm in a totally new
place, it's a challenge and a stimulation to me. I immediately want to start familiarizing myself with it. I
start riding the public buses and trams and subways to
feel that I'm a part of that place. I spent a lot of time on
the Seoul and Tokyo subways just last January, because
that's how I wanted to get around, to feel that I belonged
there. It's an outrageous statement, but there are hardly any Western European cities that I haven't spent a
good deal of time in, that I'm not comfortable in, that
I don't know fairly well.

ST: Does Iowa's International Writing Program, of which you are the Director, take you to these places?

CB: The reason why I got the job at Iowa is because I had those languages and experiences and I had that comfortableness with the foreign world. Since I've had that job, yes, I've willingly gone to any number of other places. In Iowa, the International Writing Program has grown very much as part of that, because it puts me in line for an awful lot of invitations to international gatherings and conferences. I have an academic duty to go to a lot of them and also to open up agreements with international arts agencies and with the national arts councils of various countries so that they will bring writers to Iowa and pay for them.

ST: One final question about *I Had a Father*. Even though you have talked about the many elements that went into the book, I do get a feeling that your father is central to the work or at least the inspiration for it. Do you think you could have written it if he were still alive?

CB: Probably — though I likely wouldn't have felt the need to. But there's nothing in it that I would have changed had he still been alive. That would be asking an awful lot. He would be eighty-eight if he were still alive. But no, there's nothing I would have changed. I would have hoped that some of the resolutions that I felt were still possible would happen in life. Instead, they have happened in death. I've had to reinvent him, in a sense, as being far more like myself. In fact, maybe I've even made myself him in order to achieve these resolutions. But that's what resolutions are all about. I see myself becoming a lot more forgiving of him and even admiring of him and maybe even like him in ways that I wasn't when he was alive.

ST: So what's in store? Will there be more about him? About French Canada?

CB: Not overtly about him. But sure, there will be more about French Canada. It's the immigrants and the first-generation and second-generation children of Quebec who are lost between languages and between worlds and without identities that I want to write about. And maybe bring it up-to-date with someone my age, although in a sense I'm first-generation. However, I know a lot of people in New England — even some relatives of mine — who have French names, identify themselves as French, but have never been to Quebec, don't speak a word of French, and feel that they're not part of anything larger than their own parish in the town in which they were born. The Manchester, New Hampshire, Lowell, Massachusetts, Lewiston, Maine areas, about a dozen cities in New England that are still predominantly French-Canadian. That's what I want to write about, sort of the world that Kerouac wrote about.

Too Canadian for the Americans and Too American for the Canadians: An Interview with Clark Blaise [2002]

Alexander MacLeod

AM: We'll start off easy. How does it feel to be back in Montreal? By the time this week is over you'll have given a reading at Concordia, delivered a lecture at Mc-Gill, met with students at Dawson College, and participated in a book-signing at The Double Hook. It seems like the city's literary community is certainly embracing you, but in what measure is Montreal still part of your imaginary landscape? Does this city still feel like "home" to you?

CB: It feels like a potential home. Over the last three or four days I've revisited every neighbourhood that I've ever lived in here. Although the city has transformed itself remarkably and there has been, of course, twenty years of social and political history between the time I was here and now — twenty-five years actually — I feel it is still the only possible home for me. It's the place where I was engaged most completely as a writer, as a teacher, as a husband, as a father. It's where my children first went to school and where I learned the names of all their classmates. It's the only place I've ever taught where I learned the names of all my colleagues and my wife's colleagues. And it's the only place in my life where I've written about what I was living as opposed to what

I was remembering or fantasizing about. So it's the place where I was engaged fully on every level and where I felt I was a young princeling. I felt as though I had a claim on the city as well as the city having a claim on me.

AM: I would like to extend that same query to Canada as a whole. Can this country still be a home for you? Recently, it seems there has been a new surge of interest in your work here. Your book about Sir Sandford Fleming, *Time Lord*, has been nominated for numerous prizes and was recently back on *The Globe and Mail*'s nonfiction bestsellers list. And this new series of your *Selected Stories* by The Porcupine's Quill is introducing you to a new audience or perhaps to your old audience in a new way. Do you feel that your relationship with Canada has evolved or changed in the last decade? Would you say you feel more or less comfortable today being classified as a "Canadian writer" than you did ten years ago or twenty years ago?

CB: Well, I never have fought being classified as a Canadian writer. I probably could have chosen to, but I never have. I've always been satisfied with that designation because I think it does describe my psychological state if not necessarily my content at any given stage in my career. I've always seen myself as a Canadian writer and bringing a Canadian sensibility to America, or vice versa, sometimes an American sensibility to Canada. So it's the proper designation for me.

Now whether there has been a change, I'm not the best person to ask perhaps. I know that John Metcalf at The Porcupine's Quill has always wanted to get all my stories back in print in one place, so that's no change. He's just simply able to do it now where he wasn't able to do it before. Sandford Fleming was not, of course, a choice foisted on me by a desire for Canadian public approval. It was something that really boiled out of my unconscious as a matter of very odd circumstances. The fact that it was received so well — I don't know how much that has to do with me or how much it has to do with the discovery of an authentic Canadian hero at a time when Canada, maybe, is in itself going back to having a new appreciation for its old Scottish "Proud and Presbyterian" origins. Canadians are no longer ashamed of their origins in the same way.

AM: I'm interested in this idea of bringing a Canadian sensibility or a Canadian sensitivity to America, or, vice versa, bringing an American sensitivity or sensibility to Canada. You've been performing this function throughout your career, purposely straddling the border, and it has been underappreciated in both countries. In your essay "The Border as Fiction" — and this is just a parenthetical comment within the essay — you write, "At one time, I made something of that formulation: the Southerner and the Canadian, back-to-back brothers with the belt of individualist, ahistorical Yankeeland in between."

CB: The point I was making there was when Faulkner put Shreve McCannon (a Canadian) and Quentin Compson together as roommates, it's Shreve's continual questioning that gets Quentin to open up. "I don't hate it," he says. "I don't hate the South."

AM: But I guess I'm wondering if you *still* make something of that formulation? Is there something more there? As a person who has lived deeply and experientially in the South, in Quebec, in Manitoba, in the Midwest, in California, do you still feel that such a kinship exists? Southern writers have always translated very well in Canada.

CB: Well, it's there I think. If you simply take a different map of North America and don't run the dividing lines the way they are, but run them in different ways, you'll see that there are maybe not two countries, but twelve countries, strongly differentiated by region and accent and proclivities one way or another. You would run a very different map than the one that exists currently if you followed people's historical migrations. Certainly New England and the Maritimes have an awful lot in common. Quebec? I don't know where else it could fit except Quebec. But the South shares with Canada, obviously, its confederacy, its confederation: a strong regional sense of separation and specialness and resistance to federal authority. At least it used to historically. Things have changed with time. I don't know how much more deeply it goes than that.

Canada was for a very long time resistant, far more than the North of the United States, to immigration and to changing its "national colour" or its "national colouration," just as the South was. It was not as welcoming a place in the nineteenth century at the same time that the North of the United States was transforming itself so enthusiastically or so completely. The South didn't change. Canada didn't change nearly as much in the same years. You look at what was happening in the North of the United States in 1885 and what was happening in Canada in 1885 and you have very, very different pictures. Canada, on the other hand, has now had this later wave of transformation, which is significantly, percentagewise, probably more deeply transformative than anything America has ever gone through. So it's not as though Canada is unwelcoming anymore to the idea of immigration and transformation, but it was at one time, and I think that's the Canada I remember, the Winnipeg I remember, the South I remember. Now, of course, it has all changed.

I don't know how much more deeply one should go into the ethnic roots, the Scots-Irishness, the Protestantism, the racial exclusions, all those things, but they're all part of it. The edgy way in which the South existed racially probably has some parallel in Canada. The relatively larger role that Native Americans played in the South and Canada compared to the North of the United States: these are all aspects of it, too.

AM: I want to talk a little bit about recent events in your career. I think that what Metcalf and the people at The Porcupine's Quill are doing with your short fiction is pretty much unprecedented in Canadian literature. They're taking your whole life's work in the short story — a period spanning more than forty years — and effectively re-indexing it according to the various cultural geographies that you have represented in your career. The whole series is projected to encompass four volumes. The first instalment presented your Southern stories; the second, your Pittsburgh stories. I was wondering if you could talk about what's next? Where will the next volumes be situated and how do you feel about the entire project?

CB: The next one will be the Montreal or the Quebec stories. And the fourth one will be the international volume: India, Europe, Asia. I feel very good about it. I was thinking about all of this today when I was speaking at Dawson College and I think these are my time zones: the time zones of North America, the time zones of my life. That's what started me writing about Sir Sandford Fleming. I had written a line, "Our lives are time zones." Then I looked up "time zone" and saw that it came from a Canadian engineer in the 1880s and I realized that just as in time zones, there is only one time. Time is not divided. There is only one time and yet we have to divide it arbitrarily in some way. And it's the same way with life.

I've had only one life, but myself as a Southerner, myself as a Pittsburgher, myself as a Canadian, myself as an international traveller seem to be like Pacific, Mountain, Central, and Eastern — they almost don't relate. You are significantly separated from yourself in each of those guises. I was only a child in Florida; I can't claim even being an adolescent there. I was only an adolescent in Pittsburgh; I can't claim being an adult there. I was only a young pushy aggressive husband-father-teacher in Montreal; I can't claim having a childhood here. I was never on St. Urbain Street. And as an international older gentleman, I can't claim that I was an immigrant from central Europe. So in each of these places, I've reinvented myself. I've lived in a different time zone, a different psycho-zone if you wish.

AM: Back to this series of your stories. I think I was a little suspicious when I first encountered *Southern Stories*, the first volume. I was afraid — the way you're afraid when one of your favourite musical groups comes out with their fifth "Greatest Hits" collection and you know there are only one or two new songs on the record and you can't help but feel like they're trying to get you for a couple more bucks.

CB: Like being the Don Ho of Canadian literature.

AM: Yes, that was my fear. But when I started to get into the new book, I don't know why, but I began to think about, or maybe just to play word games with, this idea of a "re-collection" and a "recollection." I began to think about the way a reader's memory of a story or understanding of a story can be changed or challenged when it is "re-presented" to us in a different way. When you re-visited older stories from decades and decades ago and juxtaposed them with newer pieces that were more "fresh," did you enjoy that experience? How did you get across that bridge between a Pittsburgh story written in the sixties and a Pittsburgh story written last year?

CB: It's never a pleasure for me to revisit old work. I can't really do it comfortably. In fact, quite often, I can't even read it aloud. I start stumbling. I feel like a bad actor with a script rather than reading my own material. I vastly prefer to read stuff that's unpublished and brand-new.

Answering your question is very difficult for me. I'm aware of what you're saying. I'm aware of the truth, in fact, in what you're observing. But how much I contributed to that, I'm not sure. It's going to be something for the reader to consider. I think perhaps a story like "South," which was in *Resident Alien*, probably loses something by being now just a Southern story. For something that is gained, something else is lost. "A North American Education" gains perhaps from where it was originally placed in *A North American Education*. But now, again, it's just another Southern story. You win a little, you lose a little.

I do feel that geography is fate or that geography is destiny in some way. I felt that the larger overall classification or locating of my psychological centre in each of these places was probably a more important thing in the long run than any individual losses or gains as a result of moving particular stories out of their original contexts. Because those original contexts were arbitrary as well.

AM: Right. By putting the stories into these volumes, by dividing the geography up in this way, it does give each of these places a new weight, a substantiality that they didn't have before. This leads into the question that I'm most curious about. I would say that you are more interested in place than any other writer in English Canada today: interested both in place as a physical site and in how we "orient" ourselves in places physically, intellectually, and emotionally. Despite this overwhelming interest, however, your work has never really been identified with the term "literary regionalism." You've repeatedly identified Faulkner as one of your greatest influences and you've written intensely about the South, the Midwest, Quebec, and other locales, but unlike other people in Canada like David Adams Richards, Robert Kroetsch, Jack Hodgins, or even Alice Munro, you aren't normally considered a regionalist. What does the term "regionalism" mean to you? Is it a word that carries negative connotations of limitation or is it something you've always aspired to? Would you like to be a regionalist writer? Do you think you "deserve" to be one?

CB: Well, these books will make me four different kinds of regionalist. I'm hoping The University of Pittsburgh Press will bring out *Pittsburgh Stories* in America because these books — *Southern Stories* and *Pittsburgh Stories* — are Canadian. They don't exist in the United States.

AM: That's revealing, don't you think? It says something about this relationship between the two countries and your place in them both.

CB: Of course. As you say, there is something unique about my status. There's also something painfully unique about it: I've always been too Canadian for the Americans and too American for the Canadians. I don't have a home. So you could say that my stories have been crying out for a regional identity that I'm not allowed to have, that I was never allowed to have. I was ripped untimely from all these places. It's my particular signature to be the kid who desperately wanted to belong and who desperately learned everything he could about every region, every place he was in. He was very, very observant about all the places he was taken to, but he didn't have the dynastic roots there, didn't have anyone to tell him that he belonged there. The only place where I had that sense was, in fact, Quebec. My father was from here, my parents met and married here, and I was conceived here. So all of those things put together give me a sense that I belong to Canada and Canada belongs to me naturally in ways that I've had to forge in the United States.

AM: But my point is that this is a legitimate form of regionalism. In an interview with Tim Struthers, you say, in reference to your Southern stories, "... I wasn't even writing in those stories as a Northerner transplanted to the South. And I wasn't writing as a Canadian transplanted to America to the South or as a French and English Canadian transplanted to America to the South. I was writing as a Southerner from the South." One of the things that made those early collections so distinctive was the fact that the voice from the South and the voice from Pittsburgh and the voice from Montreal are all local voices. That's what the reader is being asked to engage with. How can this regional consciousness be from more than one place? It challenges the standard notion of the purest environmental determinism. The collections seem to say, I can write a regionalist story about anywhere because a regionalist story is always about trying to know something. You don't need the dynastic roots, you just need to get in there deeply enough, experientially.

CB: It also speaks negatively, I suppose, of a fragmented consciousness. In other words, it can operate independently or untethered from regional connectedness. The place that I'm most connected to, I mean the place that I know in my heart and in my soul and in my bones, is Winnipeg, and I've never written about Winnipeg. This is the place where, when I was out there this spring doing publicity for *Time Lord*, no one knew that I had ever lived in Winnipeg. My mother and four generations of my family are buried there. My cousins are all there filling the bookstores when I read. When I was going around with the media escort, I was saying, "I used to go to school here," or "Didn't this used to be here?"—I mean, I knew Winnipeg better than he did. And yet, I've never been moved to write about it. So there's something here in Montreal that's special.

It's not just a matter of knowing something well. It's a matter of knowing something well plus maybe *not* knowing something well. It's a matter of being moved by the mystery of a place as opposed to just simply its transparency. I think this is probably what all regionalist writers who then transcend their region—say an Alice Munro—do: they find something continuously mysterious or unknown about what they know so well. The bad sense of regionalism is when somebody is telling you something they know very well and they want you to know it very well too. And so you feel as though you're being jerked around on a tour led by a tour guide. Or that something is being held up to you for admiration or for disgust, whatever the case may be, because there are negative regionalists who only want to show you the worst.

It's always a question in writing, in good writing I mean, of what you don't know about what you know.

Grace Paley said it, I think Eudora Welty said it too: it's what you don't know about what you know, not what you know. Take Flannery O'Connor. Take any number of people who never transcended their geographic space and yet they write universally of it.

AM: Up to now, the major critical commentators on your work have portrayed you primarily as an autobiographical writer. With your blessing, critics have posited a fairly close correlation between Clark Blaise, the man, and many of your male narrators. But lately, with *Time Lord* and this new series, it seems that your work is shifting a bit, slightly changing its focus. In 2000, you released this piece of nonfiction that essentially details the "invention" of time as we know it in an industrialized North American culture and now, with the series, you seem to be, more explicitly than ever, encouraging your readers to think about your work in spatial terms, in terms of changing places and the various ways we locate subjectivity. Have your interests changed? After mapping out the topographical details of your own life in such painstaking detail, are you now starting to consider the broader question of how anybody, anywhere, becomes "placed" in time and space?

CB: Yes! [Laughter.] First of all, it's impudent of any critic, even though I'm probably friendly with whoever said it, to assume that what I wrote about is what I lived. In my own mind, even when it was at its most apparently autobiographical, I was inventing all the way along. You can't invent dialogue that may or may not have happened forty years ago and say "I'm just recording what was said." Obviously, it wasn't said. You're situationally autobiographical and you're situationally imaginative or inventive. The situation either calls upon you to invent out of whole cloth something that absolutely never happened and never could happen or it imposes on you that sudden memory that ... oh my god! ... that did happen. And I would imagine that very inventive writers, like say Tom Boyle or someone like that, are probably as dependent upon their autobiographical observations as someone who seems overtly autobiographical such as myself.

AM: Is the key word there "seems?"

CB: Yes. My strategy as an author, as a fiction author, has always been to make you believe that it was autobiography, that I was using an autobiographical voice.

AM: That's a technique then.

CB: Yes. It's a technique. Right. I gain credibility by saying, "I'm going to confess to you something that is deep and dark and that has been on my mind for a long time and I won't understand it until I write it, and then once I write it, I will get it off my chest." But it's not my chest and it didn't happen. I invented it. Even though it follows the shape of my own life up to a point. Now, maybe I've exhausted all of the easy nuggets that were lying on the ground, so I have to dig a little bit harder. Now, when I write fiction, I'm not at all dependent on anything that ever happened to me. I'm perfectly free to invent everything. I was talking to Mavis Gallant about this a long time ago in Paris and she said, "You know, as we get older, our sensuality simply diminishes. What we can taste, smell, feel, remember, hear, see: all of these things, they just get blunted after so many years of trusting them. And we finally have to substitute for the sensual apparatus something like wisdom or some cogitation or something like that." Without wanting to become a Henry James about it, it simply is true that things no longer surprise me or shock me with the same kind of fresh-born eyes that they once did.

AM: Going back to terminology, similar to what we did with "regionalism" and "autobiography," I was wondering if you could talk about "postmodernism" for a while. You have always been a self-reflexive, self-conscious writer. Some commentators, such as Fenton Johnson in his introduction to *Southern Stories*, have said that you were postmodern before there ever was an official postmodernism or that you are a pre-modern postmodern figure. You have also used the term to describe your own work, you have glanced at it in other interviews, but I was wondering how you would define "postmodernism" as it is reflected in your fiction now? Maybe this is a tough one.

CB: It's not so tough really. To me, it's the creative usages of disjunction and separation and leaps that you can assume the reader will follow along. It's also grouping your experiences in different ways. I'm thinking of a story like "Meditations on Starch." Potatoes, Corn, and Rice: the staves of life. You're talking about the whole of the twentieth century, every horror of the twentieth century, but you're talking about it under a rubric that joins people by their preferred carbohydrate. Well, that's postmodernist in a certain way. Also using, as I do in the last two Pittsburgh stories, a lot of deliberately separated subtitles, subheadings, subchapters. But I did that years ago as well in "Extractions and Contractions." I've done it a number of ways. So, yes, I've always been aware that it's not enough to simply present material. And I don't necessarily want to present the material with a mediating adult consciousness, or a mediating writerly consciousness, that says, "Oh how foolish I was then to think that." But I want to get that same effect across.

AM: So, do you think of postmodernism primarily as another technique?

CB: I think of it as a technique. Right.

AM: Rather than as a world view?

CB: Well, I don't know how to separate technique from a world view. I think the two are significantly entwined. It's all a matter of how do you get this large and compelling material out in the shortest possible way, in the most economical way. I think these postmodernist techniques, however old or clichéd they are by now, offer one way of doing that.

AM: I guess I'll end with a tried and true interview-concluding question: What's next? This has been a very active period for you, but what else have you got on the burner now? What projects do you currently have in the works?

CB: I have, of course, the next two volumes of these stories for The Porcupine's Quill. They require me to write a couple of new stories for each of them so that the idea of all the books including new and selected stories will have something to hang on. I'm writing two new Montreal stories and two new international stories. But beyond that — and I don't look on those as insurmountable challenges although I do have to find a way of returning to Montreal, returning credibly to a world that I've left, and I don't know exactly how to do that, it's a technical question again — I have two other things.

One is very actively underway. That is a nonfiction book, also set in 1884, about America's first Black serial killer who was operating in Long Island in the 1880s. I don't want to just write a story about him because pathologies are, finally, not terribly interesting. But I want to interrogate — there's a good academic word — I want to "interrogate" *Huckleberry Finn*, the book which came out at exactly the same time, and the Supreme Court's nullification of the civil rights laws, the civil rights protections of the Reconstruction Era, which set Black/White relations on their tragic course back toward segregation and sent the Black population northward and caused enormous hardship for everybody.

I want to make it an intertextual study, if you wish, where we have the melodrama and high drama of the actual murders and the chase and this man and what I can discover from the record — which has taken me a year, so far, to accumulate the hundreds of pages of research that I have — and then I want to look at the social history of the times, at the literature of the times. I think I have new things to say about *Huckleberry Finn* that have never been said before: about it as a response to the nullification of these civil rights, and about Twain's attempt to head off what he saw as the new stereotyping of the Black as a brute and a fiend. At the same time, he wanted to update the old cliché of the Black as Uncle Tom, forever forgiving and unaccomplished.

The other thing is a novel on nineteenth-century Quebec. I've been working on it now for ten years or so and it's hundreds of pages long. French-Canadian village life taken across the border into upper New England and into Franco-America. It ends in the 1970s, starts about the 1870s. So it encompasses "the *Sentinelle* Affair" in Providence, the whole union organizing problem. It's a real classic old multi-layered Victorian novel. I may never finish it. Things keep growing, new members of the family keep arising. Maybe I'll do it as a three-volume set.

So those are the two things, I guess the three things, that I'm working on now.

AM: Great. And thank you very much for sparing some time from this busy schedule you have here.

CB: Thank you.

Expressions of Your Breath:
An Interview with Clark Blaise
[1988]

J.R. (Tim) Struthers

TS: A decade or so ago, Clark, in 1977 to be exact, you and John Metcalf put together for Oberon Press an anthology called *Here & Now* containing some of your favourite "Canadian" stories from the 1960s and 1970s. The authors represented in the book, just about chronologically by age from the oldest to the youngest, were Norman Levine, Mavis Gallant, Margaret Laurence, Hugh Hood, Jane Rule, Alice Munro, Austin Clarke, Leon Rooke, Audrey Thomas, Dave Godfrey, John Metcalf, Russell Banks, yourself, and Ray Smith. Then in 1978, 1979, and 1980 — the year when you and your wife, Bharati, left Canada for the States — John and you collaborated on picking the contents of Oberon Press's then brand-new annual series *Best Canadian Stories*. I'm wondering if, at this point, let's say in your imagination, you had a chance to assemble a collection of your favourite stories from around the world, stories that had reached you and had stayed with you, what some of them might be?

CB: Well, I think there would still be a large number of Canadian stories in a world anthology that I would put together. I read so many stories. I must read thirty or forty a week, even now, because of my duties running writing workshops. And then I also teach short stories sometimes. So I have a lot of short stories in my mind. Oh, goodness ...

One area that I had ignored totally in the short story was the Japanese, which I now appreciate with far more sincerity than I ever did before. The Japanese short stories — that I've read at least — are absolutely stunning. They really do represent an alien mode of presentation. The effects are the same, but there is a clarity there. And there is something like the Japanese woodcut, if you wish. There is something of a floating world of emotion that just takes my breath away.

I would attempt, if I possibly could, to get to that kind of presentation of material that is just so sudden. Allegorically, it's a lot like the Hiroshima or Nagasaki bombing — that one minute you are this and the next you are incinerated. There is that sense that without motivation, without premeditation, without warning, your life at any given moment can be totally wiped out. And that sense of the tentativeness of human existence is something we still don't understand in the West, something we still can't appreciate. So that would be one whole realm of world literatures that I think I would want to make my own if at all possible.

I get some of the same feeling in Arab culture — in Arab short story writing, North African and Middle Eastern. There, again, I didn't know that area ten years ago. And I think I have a firmer appreciation now than I did then of contemporary European ironists. I mean the Calvinos and the Levis and people like that in Italy. Appelfeld of Israel. A number of authors that, again, I hadn't read sufficiently in. I do read in the Latin Americans. And I do read in the Caribbean area, too.

So if I were to put together an anthology, there would be Canadians. There would be some Americans, certainly.

The short story is a thriving art form in the States at the present time, although I think there's more heat than light there. Then I would insist on all these other areas being heard from.

Of course I've always felt that the most moving author in the world to me, personally, for some reason — and I think I could begin to understand it, but I don't think I could do justice to it in an interview — is Peter Handke. I continually read with pleasure, and re-read with pleasure, all of his books. They're not exactly short stories, but they're not exactly novels either. They're sort of in the novella range of fifty to sixty to seventy pages. And that's a very flattering and conducive length, I think, to the kinds of statements I would like to make, although it's very difficult to publish at that length in the U.S.

TS: A particular Canadian writer or European writer or world writer whom you have spoken of very highly in the interview by Geoff Hancock first published in a special issue of *Canadian Fiction Magazine* on her is Mavis Gallant.

CB: Yes.

TS: What are the features of her work that you find most powerful?

CB: With Mavis, I'm just struck by her sentences. It's nothing more complicated than that. I think she has the most beautiful sentences, the most chiselled prose, the most disciplined prose of anyone writing in the English language at the present time. I'm not always moved by her characters. But I'm always *convinced* by anything she writes. There's that authority that just knocks your socks off. It's not the characters that I'm attracted to. And it's not even her plots, necessarily, that I'm attracted to. It's the authority. It's the sitting you down and telling you to shut up while she's writing [laughter] and you do and you're rewarded by it.

It's not the humane presence. We're not talking about a Chekhovian kind of warmth. It's a cold world — ironical. But I still think that if you enter her wavelength in any given story, it's likely to be the fastest and cleanest ride you can get in the English language.

TS: Writers, I've found, have a special sense of the most fascinating and the most significant portions or elements of other writers' bodies of work, their *oeuvres*. And this often differs from whatever is most widely commended by journalists and reviewers or most widely examined by teachers and scholars. If you were to encourage someone to read a few stories by Gallant, and to concentrate on certain aspects of them, what would you suggest?

CB: Oh, I don't know if I have eccentric choices in her work. And I haven't read all of her work by any means. I just can't keep up, with all the other things I have to read. I've always been very drawn to the post-War German situation, so the stories in *The Pegnitz Junction* are very personally meaningful to me.

TS: *The Pegnitz Junction*, Gallant's third book of stories, was published in 1973, the same year as you released your first collection, *A North American Education*. Her two earlier books of stories, *The Other Paris* and *My Heart Is Broken*, had appeared in 1956 and 1964. I find it interesting that the opening piece, the title piece, of *The Pegnitz Junction* is a novella, the form that you said has a special attraction for you. And the story "An Autobiography," in that same volume, is an extremely intricate and highly charged example of first-person point of view, a technique that has great importance for you. Indeed, "An Autobiography" is the work by Gallant that you and John Metcalf selected for your anthology *Here & Now*.

I'm wondering about further parts of Gallant's work — of her world — that would also generate a strong personal connection for you. You and Bharati lived in Montreal from 1966 to 1978 before moving to Toronto for two years and subsequently departing for the States. For you, what would be particularly compelling about Gallant's portraits of the culture and the landscape of Montreal?

CB: I also, being an old Montrealer, had a kind of appreciation for her Linnet Muir stories that spoke right out of my mother's world. That cold grey Sherbrooke Street — those cold limestone fronts on Sherbrooke Street were still there when I moved to Montreal, although they're vanishing now. That sense of Sherbrooke Street as a kind of sullen mile of propertied homes that would not have admitted Westmount people to their company. That sense of the stratified, slightly colonial, thoroughly snobbish world of Montreal of the twenties and thirties that Mavis inherited is something that my mother came into in the thirties and suffered from.

TS: Gallant's six Linnet Muir stories were first published serially in magazine form in the mid- to late 1970s — mainly appearing in *The New Yorker*, but with a final, more comic story, "With a Capital T," included in *Canadian Fiction Magazine*'s special issue on Gallant published in 1978. The Linnet Muir stories were then collected in 1981 as the final third of her book *Home Truths*. Could you describe your response as a writer to Gallant's fictional re-creation, in these stories, of the Montreal that she knew during her childhood, youth, and early adulthood in the twenties and thirties and forties, before she left for Europe in 1950?

CB: In reading those stories of Mavis Gallant's, it's as though you have been given a map of a place you love very, very much. However, it's the authoritative map that precedes all the things you don't like about that city now. And this map that she made has all the names of all the streets and all the particulars of the buildings and houses and rooms and just the kind of people who worked in those buildings and served tea in those rooms. It seems to me that's exactly what fiction writers have always tried to do — first of all create the map, and then put the buildings and all on — and that's one of the things she has done so well in those stories.

TS: I'm interested in learning from writers what their conceptions or intuitions about the form of the short story might be, what it involves from the inside, in terms of the many years of writing experience that people like you — the generation or perhaps two generations of Canadian short story writers represented by the anthology *Here & Now* — have now had from your very early stories onwards. I'm wondering if you could bring to mind your sense of the possibilities of the form over the nearly fifteen years that you spent writing the large body of stories from which you made the selections published in 1973 and 1974 in your first two solo volumes, *A North American Education* and *Tribal Justice*.

CB: I felt I was simply an inheritor of the form when I started writing. I suppose you would call it, loosely, the *New Yorker* form: personal voice, personal reminiscence, trying to be distanced, looking back over some experience that was probably still molten at its core, trying to poke it into life from a distance now. And there was kind of an elegiac sense of all the things that are past and cannot come back.

I felt that way until — I remember the moment very

intensely—Milton Kessler, an American poet, came to Montreal in the late sixties for a reading. He was not very well-known, but he came to Montreal for a reading. And I think Milton at that time was maybe having a second childhood. He had taken on a kind of late-blooming Beat Generation quality. This was someone who had been, before that, a rather typical academic poet, I think, and he was suddenly taking on what would seem to be an "unseemly" kind of Beat Generation attitude. A lot of people were turned off by that. But somehow or other I was very charmed by it. I think it also had a lot to do with the poetics of breath that Robert Duncan and all were talking about. In other words, Milton had taken on a lot of West Coast poetry aspects.

I was so struck by it that I wrote a story—it's in *A North American Education*—called "The Salesman's Son Grows Older" that tried at the end to resolve the action just by slowing the character down to listening to his infant son's breath as he recalls hearing, earlier that day, the sound of the windshield wipers going on a parked taxi and the sound of a girl's boots while she's running along Sherbrooke Street over the sandy gravel of winter. Somehow or other, slowing the character down to being able to live within the span or the arc of just the human breath—to being able to see the whole world collapsing into a breathing rhythm—gave a character who was somewhat overburdened at that time a sense of continuity and of how to go on.

TS: And this story, "The Salesman's Son Grows Older," is the one by you included in the anthology *Here & Now* that you co-edited with John Metcalf.

CB: So that was an important moment for me and it was part of the story that I think is still valid. And it led, it seems to me, to a series of desired conclusions to stories. I do want to bring the story down to the human voice or to the human presence. Even the story I read last night, "Meditations on Starch" — in which the entire tunnel through the twentieth century has sort of passed through this man's life — ends in Vienna with, really, just some kid thumping a tambourine at the edge of a fountain a short walk from the former office of Dr. Sigmund Freud. That's all that it amounts to. That's all that he's able to pass on. So a very important way of resolving a story's action, for me, is to bring it down to the human voice, if at all possible.

TS: Many of the stories collected in *A North American Education* and *Tribal Justice* were originally part of an unpublished novel that you called...?

CB: *North America*. A lot of the stories were part of that. Not all of them. But a lot of the stories were, yes.

TS: Can you be a bit more precise about the chronology of the composition of that novel and the other works?

CB: The first time that I went through that novel was back in 1962-64 in Iowa. Then I did a lot of stories that were not related to it. But that's what I was writing for a while in Iowa. And then we moved to Montreal in 1966. And that first year, when I was not teaching except evenings at McGill, I wrote another version — "North America 2," you might call it. That's the one, I think, that there are parts of in my archives at the University of Calgary, because "North America 1" I destroyed one night in Iowa City. I've written about that in *Resident Alien*.

TS: There you explain that the actual title you gave to the novel's first version, the one written in Iowa in 1962–64, was *The French and Jewish War*.

CB: *North America*, the version of that novel that became the ur-manuscript to *A North American Education* and to parts of *Tribal Justice*, was written in Montreal in 1966-67. *Tribal Justice* pre-dated, really, *A North American Education*, though it came out second. Most of the stories in *Tribal Justice* were considerably earlier than the stories in *A North American Education*, because the stories in *A North American Education* did, in fact, grow out of that novel. But there were just a few pieces in *Tribal Justice* that were also part of the same novel. "The Seizure" was part of it.

TS: Which stories in your first two collections, *A North American Education* and *Tribal Justice*, would you identify as being most typically and most strongly what I like to term "signature pieces"?

CB: Of course if any author is trying to be honest with the form, every piece will have the author's signature. *None Genuine Without This Signature* — right?

TS: To give a nod to the title of the story collection that Hugh Hood, one of your former fellow Montreal Story Tellers, released in 1980 with ECW Press, which emerged out of the journal *Essays on Canadian Writing* at York University in Toronto. You had just finished the two years that you spent teaching at York. I remember that you had participated in a panel discussion on writing and publishing during The Hugh Hood Symposium that ECW Press hosted at York in October 1979 — the symposium at which ECW's and my own first book, about Hugh Hood, *Before the Flood*, was launched. *None Genuine Without This Signature* indeed!

CB: And if a story doesn't have your signature at some level of it or in some little corner of it, then you're not ever going to collect it or honour it or claim it. There are some stories I've written that I haven't claimed or reprinted. They are just more or less out there as fugitive pieces, some of them published, some of them in

Calgary [laughter], whatever the case may be. But I would regard "The Thibidault Stories" of *A North American Education* very much as "signature pieces."

TS: *A North American Education* consists of three sections of stories about a multiply named, in some particulars differentiated, but in essence the same protagonist/narrator. The book begins in the time present of his early adulthood with the section called "The Montreal Stories": "A Class of New Canadians," "Eyes," and "Words for the Winter" — stories told respectively, and progressively, in third- then second- then first-person point of view. It continues in his early adulthood in Montreal, and, eventually, a little ways back in time, and in space a long ways eastward, with the section called "The Keeler Stories": "Extractions and Contractions," "Going to India," and the fifty-page "Continent of Strangers: A Love Story of the Recent Past," which I see as another example of the form named in the subtitle of the last piece in the book, "Snow People: A Novella," even though the form goes unnamed here in order to have a subtitle that would function in various ways. And finally the book proceeds much further back in time, and in space southward, to his childhood in the American South, in the section called "The Thibidault Stories": "The Bridge," "The Salesman's Son Grows Older," "A North American Education," and the forty-five-page "Snow People: A Novella."

Significantly, I would add, the last piece describes him heading north — ultimately, readers expect, to what they know from the start of the book to be the protagonist/narrator's home as an adult in Montreal. That is, the last piece has him and the book coming full circle — very appropriately, I would say, for what I like to call a story cycle.

CB: I think all the parts of that book are probably "signature pieces" in that there is a recognizable character, the sort of standard character that I evolve for myself, and the various settings, the Deep South, Montreal, are me.

TS: Your twelve-year continuous residency in Montreal from 1966 to 1978, excepting periods spent in Calcutta in 1973-74 and in New Delhi in 1977–78, was the longest and I suspect the most satisfying that you have had anywhere, at any time in your life, as a child or as an adult. At age twenty-eight you officially launched your writing career with the volume *New Canadian Writing, 1968*, comprised of several works apiece by David Lewis Stein, yourself, and Dave Godfrey, a classmate of yours in the Writers' Workshop, the MFA program at the University of Iowa. The selections by you included in that début volume, in addition to a brief "Author's Introduction," were: "The Fabulous Eddie Brewster," first published as "The Mayor" in *The Tamarack Review*; "How I Became a Jew," which you have described as a tribute to Bernard Malamud, teacher of the writing class that you took at Harvard in the summer of 1961 and a very important personal mentor for you; "The Examination," which you did not elect to collect again in either of your first two solo volumes; and a favourite of mine, "Notes Beyond a History."

In Montreal you were an active member — with Hugh Hood, John Metcalf, Ray Smith, and Raymond Fraser — of The Montreal Story Teller Fiction Performance Group for much of its full run from late 1970 to 1975, as re-created in the memoir essays that each of you wrote for the collection *The Montreal Story Tellers* issued under my editorship by Véhicule Press in 1985 and launched with a reunion reading by the entire group at Concordia University in Montreal on the 14th of February the next year. I remember that date because earlier the same afternoon I got Irving Layton, when he came into The Double Hook while I was shopping for books there, to sign, as a Valentine's Day present from me to my wife, Marianne Micros, a copy of *The Love Poems of Irving Layton*.

While living in Montreal you published, back to back in 1973 and 1974, your first two story collections, *A North American Education* and *Tribal Justice*, followed in 1977 by a first nonfiction volume co-authored by you and Bharati, *Days and Nights in Calcutta*. And you established the graduate-level program in Creative Writing at Concordia University in Montreal. But at a deeper level, familially let us say, in terms of your father and mother, what did taking up residency in Montreal involve for you personally and as a writer?

CB: Montreal is the natural home of my parents. It's their city. When I say in *Resident Alien* that I need the shelter of my parents' marriage to imagine my own life, I mean I need them, in a sense, over the story. Even if they're not there, they're in the story — in order to draw out an awful lot of images.

TS: The next two books that you released were novels, your first and second published novels: *Lunar Attractions* in 1979 and *Lusts* in 1983. These were followed in 1986 by *Resident Alien* — a work intriguingly, and perhaps uniquely, comprised of both memoir material and fiction — and then in 1987 by a second nonfiction volume co-authored by you and Bharati, *The Sorrow and the Terror: The Haunting Legacy of the Air India Tragedy*. I would like to get comments from you about each of these two published novels, but before that I want to pick up on the description you gave of the first of these, *Lunar Attractions*, in the brief interview by Geoff

Hancock published in *Books in Canada*, as "the final work of my personal quest for identity." In retrospect, nearly a decade later, do you still consider that statement to be true?

CB: Maybe I was premature.

TS: [Laughter.]

CB: But, actually, I think that statement, in some way, is true. *Lunar Attractions* was an attempt to establish, or to assert, an identity. Now I think it's a more complicated question. In *Resident Alien* it's more the rejection of an identity — it's the man *sans identité* that I'm writing about. And it seems to me that the next novel I write is going to try to be quite horrific on that.

Lunar Attractions was a very painstaking attempt to piece together an identity out of fragments that were given to him, to piece together in an impasto way layers and globs of identity, taking on whatever he desperately can. Now it's more a sombre realization that a very few of us are denied an identity, and denied a community or a country or a history, that is truly our own. Now I'm a little bit more interested in the demolition of identity than I am in the establishment of identity or the painful accretion of shards of identity.

So next I'm going to take someone who seems to have a very clear sense of identity and systematically strip him of all layers of assumed identity or of assumed purpose in life. It's going to be a reversal, if you wish, of *Lunar Attractions*. A little bit like what happens to the character of Porter/Carrier in *Resident Alien*. But there I excluded so much of my real life in order to write that character. I was simply isolating him with his disease and his twisted life in order to concentrate, really, on the polarities of his parents and what that made of him.

I would like to talk about someone who is equally

twisted, if you wish, though not just because of his parents but because of a whole host of larger things. I want to amplify in some way, to make it a novel rather than stories or a novella.

TS: Could you give an account of what you wanted to bring to writing your second published novel, *Lusts*?

CB: In *Lusts* I wanted to create something outside my experience. The character and his background are very much different from anything in my own experience. It's a totally imagined work. I had a sense of a character, I think I had always carried a vision of him in my mind, born in the centre of America — really working-class armpit America, Pittsburgh in the era of the 1940s and 1950s — who lusts for inclusion, lusts for a finer thing, lusts for just the will to lift himself into a finer, nobler world. But because of class, and because of the urgencies and hungers in his own background, he destroys just about everything he touches.

I wanted to talk about the limits, perhaps, of that kind of hunger. I mean it can carry you a long way, but it does create moral monsters. And while I don't think of him as a moral monster, I do think of him as eventually responsible for the death of his wife. He does need redemption. Lust is a sin and I felt very strongly that he was a sinner, even though it was never clear to him why he was a sinner. In a sense he's a lot like my father. That is, he's more a portrait of my father than he's a portrait of myself. In a very Americanized way. But it's the same thing, I think, that drove my father to be that kind of a violent person.

I wanted to have the counterpart to that character — the wife — be someone born on the rather effete rim of America who wants very much to enter the centre. The wife is someone who is born with all the privileges of America. She has been spared all the grime of America, but she then wishes to have it. So for her and for him there is kind of a tragic transection.

I've realized more and more that it's a portrait, really, of my parents more than a portrait of myself. Some people thought of it, of course, as the story of Sylvia Plath and Ted Hughes, which I had no interest in writing — or as the story of Bharati and me, but it's not that either. To me, it's far more a story of people fated to collide because each represents an idealization of what the other wants.

TS: I found *Lusts* to be a very powerful book and I found it worked for me on different levels — "mythological" or "mythopoeic," I think, would be the keyword I would use to open up that book.

CB: I wasn't aware of that. That is, I was certainly working with the myth — to me, very vulgar myths, pop myths if you wish — of America. That was as far as I could carry it. I do have some overtly mythological stories in the collection I've just finished.

TS: And are you writing another novel?

CB: Yes. I am. That novel would be finished. In fact, two drafts of it have been finished. For want of a better term, it's an espionage novel. I mean it's an adventure novel.

TS: What are you calling it? And would you say something about it?

CB: Well, at present it's called *Embassy*. It's about a corrupt embassy on a Caribbean island. It's very much based around our living as Canadian diplomats in New Delhi in 1976-77. So I saw the embassy world up close. I saw how easy it would be to corrupt one. Had I finished that novel this summer — that is, had I finished the third draft of it, because I've changed the point of view into a single unified first-person point of view, whereas, before, it had several points of view — I think it would be going right now. But I couldn't finish it. I had two teaching jobs and it was too much.

The novel that I would like to start, had I world enough and time, would be the one where I'm talking about the lack of identity. It's called *Brothers and Sisters*. It's all very much planned out. I know exactly who its characters are. It's a big family. It's the first time I've ever taken on anything with brothers and sisters. Again it's an invention of something that I never was, never could be.

TS: You have already commented about your conception of, and your experience of, the short story as a form early in your career. I'm wondering now if you could describe any impression you might have of an evolution in your sense of, and your practice of, the short story as a form while you have continued to work ardently in a widening range of forms including the short story, the novella, the novel, as well as the memoir essay, nonfiction, criticism? Or to focus this, perhaps I should ask you to discuss the components of *Resident Alien*, a book constructed of a powerful middle sequence of fiction — "The Porter/Carrier Stories," climaxing with the novella "Translation" — framed by memoir material that provides a penetrating critical gloss on the fiction in between at the same time as standing forcefully by itself.

CB: Let me answer the implied question before the overt question. I think that as one proceeds with one's career — and I'm now towards the latter part of the middle of mine, I suppose — you feel greater confidence and greater urgency in getting the stories to be almost expressions of your breath, expressions of your most casual thought. So you don't have to construct an elaborate form to pour the molten story into, but rather you want the form to be an expression of the impulse behind the story.

Like a poet who starts out as a rigid formalist and ends up as a jagged-edged impulsive poet or lyric poet, then it's the same sort of thing, I think, with a story writer. You become more and more confident that you can simply turn event or impulse into a story. And you don't worry about the form because you have so internalized formal messages that you don't have to think about the form anymore. You know that the story will have its form simply because you have written it, that there will be a form in there.

You don't want to commit casualness to the page, but you want to have the sense of casualness or the sense of a story sneaking up on you. I think that's one of the things I get about the Japanese story — it just seems so authoritative in its brush strokes that all sorts of light things can happen to it.

Resident Alien is a strange book for me. Some of it had to do with just fulfilling exercises. I was teaching out at the David Thompson University Centre in Nelson, British Columbia — the late, lamented DTUC of Fred Wah's imaginings. And it was the most marvellous teaching experience I've ever had. I was living in a motel and it was unpleasant in many ways. This was in the fall of 1983, just before the provincial government closed the Centre down. But what Fred had there was a fully integrated writing program, in which everyone was writing stories, everyone was writing poetry, everyone was running a press, everyone was putting out a magazine, everyone was expected to do reviews and feature articles in the local newspapers. When people came out of that program, they knew how to do things. [Laughter.] Not just how to write things but how to do things.

And the teachers had to present papers or little think-pieces to the students every week. *We* had to write something to share with *them*. So it was out of that, in fact, that I wrote many parts of the first section of *Resident Alien*. Simply to share the mentoring thing about Malamud, for example, and other parts that I wrote there and that got me thinking about the fictional parts.

TS: The middle section of *Resident Alien,* "The Porter/ Carrier Stories," consists of a sequence of three short stories, "South" and "Identity" and "North," followed by the astounding fifty-page novella, "Translation," in eighteen numbered parts — a miniature *Ulysses*, if you will, involving more than one sort of homecoming for the protagonist and, arguably, for you.

CB: The story called "South" had been written earlier. Bob Weaver used it on CBC Radio and then it was put into his *Small Wonders* anthology, along with stories by Margaret Atwood and other writers. "Identity" was written just about that time and it was used in one of the *Best Canadian Stories* volumes — I forget which year. And "North" was written at that time out at DTUC. *Saturday Night* published that story.

TS: "Identity" appeared originally in the 1981 instalment of Oberon Press's ongoing series *Best Canadian Stories*, the first of the two consecutive volumes of it that John Metcalf co-edited with Leon Rooke following the three John did with you. I remember this because Louis K. MacKendrick of the University of Windsor has written an essay on the 1981 volume for a collection that I'm editing on the Canadian short story, *New Directions from Old*. And "North" was republished in the first of the two volumes of the unfortunately short-lived series *The New Press Anthology* that John and Leon co-edited for General Publishing after leaving *Best Canadian Stories*.

CB: Writing "North" was a matter of coming back to Canada, after being out for a couple of years, and having that sense of the urgency or the particularness of Montreal flooding through me — perhaps also I was giving kind of a tip of the hat to Mavis Gallant — when I was sitting out there on the shores of Kootenay Lake in B.C. [Laughter.] I was writing that story then and feeling very close to a world that I never knew. I mean I never went to school in Montreal. And, especially, I never went to school in Montreal in French. All that was totally imagined. So I was quite pleased with being able to imagine it.

I think I was responding sentimentally — in the good sense of "sentimental," in the Flaubertian sense of "sentimental" — to the realization that Montreal was now lost to me, was now taken from me. I also was responding sentimentally — positively — to the notion of Canada. And I was responding to the tragedy in my life of being torn up from Canada. People should not be uprooted from their home because of prejudice, because of racism, in the twentieth century. But that's what happened to us. Life in Toronto was simply unbearable in the late 1970s. So, in a sense, I was projecting into a different character what I was going through.

TS: Could you talk a little more about that dilemma as it registered for you?

CB: It was a matter of having to choose between where I would make my home, the States, and what empowered me as a writer, which was Canada, the idea of Canada. That part of *Resident Alien* about needing the shelter of my parents' marriage was written as part of the DTUC assignment talking about what empowers you to write. Well, I don't have that in the States. I was responding to the realization that Canada was no longer an option and that I was now in this rather confusing situation. Not confusing, the U.S. isn't confusing to me. I understand it in many ways better than I understand Canada because, sociologically, I'm a very American guy. I understand it all as well as any American does. But it doesn't speak to me in that sense that Alice Munro was talking about in your interview yesterday — that there's a special kind of memory a writer has.

TS: When you returned to Canada during the fall of 1983, however, to teach at the David Thompson University Centre in Nelson, British Columbia, memory and feeling and imagination combined and you found yourself writing new memoir material and a new Montreal story, "North."

CB: I think I have a memory of Canada, even a memory of places I've never been. That is, I can imagine a Canadian reality such as French Montreal, or my mother's prairie Canada, or whatever it may be. I can imagine a Canada as though I'm remembering it, even though I haven't passed through it ever, whereas the things that I remember perfectly about many aspects of the U.S. lack dimension for me. I'm not particularly interested in writing about them. It would simply be an exercise in nostalgia or recall.

So that density of recall that's in Alice's stories and that density of recall that's in Mavis's stories is something in a small way I can do also. But I don't have as much of it is the problem. I simply do not have that long vertical mine shaft of experience in Wingham or Montreal or whatever it may be. It's in glimpses. So I have to write of fragments of those intensely felt moments. That's what my fiction is: it's fragments of intensely lived-in or imagined realities that are always tentative, are always provisional, can always disappear.

TS: I'm wondering about the actual process of constructing *Resident Alien* as "a complete, whole book" — to borrow the phrase employed by Kent Thompson to describe Hugh Hood's 1967 story cycle, *Around the Mountain: Scenes from Montreal Life*, and Margaret Laurence's 1970 story cycle, *A Bird in the House*. At the beginning you have a one-and-a-half-page introduction followed by the thirty-page "Autobiographical Fragment: The Voice of Unhousement." At the end you have the twenty-page "Autobiographical Fragment: Memories of Unhousement," an abridged version of the piece first published in *Salmagundi* and then anthologized by Bill Henderson in *The Pushcart Prize VIII: Best of the Small Presses.* Could you comment on how you came to use this memoir material as a frame for — and we might say a metafictive gloss on — "The Porter/Carrier Stories" in between?

CB: I even had a long middle essay in it called "Tenants of Unhousement," which was published in *The Iowa Review.* It's a good piece. It talks a lot about my mother's European background. But we didn't use it, finally.

TS: I would like to read that uncollected memoir essay, "Tenants of Unhousement." And afterwards, I may have something further to ask you. Would it be OK to follow up with you on that and to insert your answer?

CB: OK.

TS: Here goes, then — I do have something else to ask you. Right at the end of the long opening section of memoir material in *Resident Alien* called "The Voice of Unhousement," there is a scene containing two characters, father and son, in which you have the father address the son with these words: "'I'm so lost, son, it's awful!'" However, in the uncollected memoir essay "Tenants of Unhousement," a closely comparable scene involves not just these two but three characters — father, mother, and son — and, although almost the same line occurs, it is the mother, not the son, whom you have the father address: "'I'm so lost, Anne, it's awful!'"

In my view, there are good reasons within the respective contexts for presenting these scenes in the different ways you have chosen. What I wish to know — not that fact has a higher value than fiction, of course, but that knowing fact can give us a better appreciation of fiction — is: What happened in fact? What was said? Were just your father and you there? Were all three of you present? Or are both scenes, perhaps, largely invented?

CB: I know he said it to me when we were alone and I'm pretty sure he said it to her when I was with them. I can't really swear to the particulars, but the address to me very much happened, and it struck me as a sincere line, for him. The same thing to my mother is not without a certain manipulativeness.

TS: As strong a piece as you considered the memoir essay "Tenants of Unhousement" to be, separately, you didn't in the end include it in *Resident Alien*, conceived as a working whole. Was that a result of necessarily redirecting your attention at the later stage from one sort of activity to another, indeed almost from one set of principles to another — from imagining and writing and rewriting assorted pieces individually to imagining and organizing and shaping them as a book? You turned to arranging these pieces, making alterations of one kind or another to them, if required choosing a smaller selection of them, in the interest of creating a lucidly structured, well-proportioned, high-impact book.

CB: Cynthia Good at Penguin Canada thought it would be better just to keep the book with a front and a back but not a middle essay. I also had two other stories in it that she felt were best left out. They were good stories.

TS: The two stories left out of *Resident Alien* were...?

CB: One of them is the title story of the next book, *Man and His World*. That story was published in *Fiction International*. It's about a Winnipeg guy who ends up getting killed by a Rajah in his palace.

TS: And the other?

CB: The other story is the one that's set in Toronto. It was done in *Toronto Life*. They called it "Prying." It won a nation-wide magazine award. My title for it is "Partial Renovations."

So those two stories are in the next volume — if it's ever published. I don't know, because it's eight or so stories and it's very Canadian. It's an intensely Canadian volume all written in the States. It's too Canadian for an American publisher, but I think I've more or less lost my Canadian publisher. So it may be an orphan, an orphaned book. We'll see.

TS: *Resident Alien* and *The Sorrow and the Terror* were published not by Doubleday Canada, as had been the case for your five books up to and including the novel *Lusts*, but by Penguin Books Canada.

CB: Well, I had to change because I was rejected by Doubleday Canada. After *Lusts* did so poorly, they had no interest. I submitted *Resident Alien* to Doubleday Canada and they didn't even open it. The book should have been out a couple of years earlier than it was. It knocked around for a year and a half before I ran into Cynthia Good of Penguin Canada at a party in Toronto. She was, by that time, bringing out Bharati's *Darkness* volume. And I said, "I have a book." And she said, "Well, send it to me." And I said, "I don't know where it is. I think it's in the Doubleday Canada office now." And, sure enough, it was. Unopened. [Laughter.] So they just couriered it across Toronto and she read it and accepted it.

TS: And now you have completed a volume's worth of new stories.

CB: The interesting thing is that my agent right now is attempting to market two books — that is, three chapters of *Embassy* and the book of stories — and they are such different works. One is an adventure novel with an intellectual quality, sort of a Graham Greene-esque kind of adventure novel. And the other is this tortured book of stories, such as the story "Meditations on Starch" that I read last night. A number of other stories like that are in it. Alzheimer's disease is one kind of underlying theme in it. And, certainly, dislocations and violences of the century. There's an awful lot of Asia, as well. I mean these are characters who have voyaged out from Canada into the world. So that it's *Man and His World*.

The same publisher could not bring out both works is what I'm saying. One is commercial and would require commercial handling by a fairly commercial press. The other really looks like an academic press book. [Laughter.] So the people who are attracted to the stories don't want to handle the novel and vice versa.

TS: You would expect to use *Man and His World* as the title for this new collection of stories.

CB: I think the title of it will be *Man and His World*. The ideal title for it would be one of Tagore's: in Bengali, *Ghare Baire*, or, to use the English title of that novel, *The Home and the World*. *Ghare Baire* means the little world and the big world, the world outside the door of the home. The big writers often steal our titles. I remember Roth saying the ideal title for his second novel, *Letting Go*, would be *Disorder and Early Sorrow*.

TS: However, the title *Man and His World* does return to and repeat the wording of the theme for the World's

Fair held in Montreal during Canada's centennial year, from mid-spring to mid-fall of 1967, a period corresponding to the end of the first year and the start of the second year of your twelve-year residency in Montreal. This may be a good place for us to finish — I like the idea of things such as a story cycle or a conversation or a person's imagination circling back and then proceeding, of endings that represent beginnings.

In that spirit I would like to bring to your attention what I see as an exciting development, one I hope you would view as a good opportunity for yourself. John Metcalf, John Newlove, and I have begun working on two series of books to be published by The Porcupine's Quill: the one reissuing important Canadian prose and poetry, the other presenting new books of criticism. I know how highly John Metcalf regards your stories. If he could speak with you about this, I know that both of us would be pleased to have you consider some kind of arrangement.

As well, I would like to thank you for flying up from Iowa City to participate with John Metcalf and the other distinguished writers — Keath Fraser, Douglas Glover, Hugh Hood, Alice Munro, Leon Rooke, Ray Smith, Kent Thompson — and critics in this four-day conference entitled "Coming of Age: John Metcalf and the Canadian Short Story" that I've organized and hosted here in Guelph ending today, on John's fiftieth birthday, Saturday the 12th of November 1988. A conference meant to celebrate John Metcalf's extraordinary achievements as a writer, a critic, and an editor as well as to honour the important contributions that all of you continue to make to the Canadian short story in particular and to Canadian writing in general.

We truly are intent on helping as much as we can to

cultivate the audience that you want, and greatly deserve, for your work — John Metcalf and I and Catherine
Sheldrick Ross from Western, who has joined us in order to ask you about some background details for use
in the introduction she is writing to a planned book
listing your archives at the University of Calgary. And
we definitely wish you the very best in personal terms.

CB: OK. Well, thank you.

TS: We're with you!

CB: OK. Thank you, Tim.

TS: Thank you.

Looking East:
An Interview with Clark Blaise
[1992]

J.R. (Tim) Struthers

TS: Welcome again to Guelph, good sir. And allow me to say it's great to see that your latest volume of short stories, *Man and His World*, has now been published by The Porcupine's Quill.

CB: Just to reverse the questioning for a moment, let me ask you about this new book, because no one has read it yet so I haven't had any kind of response from anybody. What are your feelings about it? I notice on the jacket blurb they say "a departure" and I can see how in many ways there are departures, stories in this book that are unlike anything that people who know my work will have read. How do you think it is likely to be received? What stories are likely to be enjoyed? What stories are likely to be problematic for people?

TS: Let me talk about it in this way. When I was walking over for this interview and rehearsing in my head how I might begin, I imagined myself saying to you: "I would like us to go back and then come forward. I would like us to look West, South, North, then East."

These compass points are obviously very important to the rendering of your life beginning with the publication of your first solo collection, *A North American Education*, in 1973. For the record, I would like to say here that as I studied that book with great care a decade or so ago when writing a long chapter on it for my Ph.D. dissertation at Western on the Canadian story cycle, I felt it was the most densely textured collection of short fiction I had ever read, bar none. It demanded more of me than any collection I had read before. And I also felt a strong sense of gratitude in finding a work I could stay with for as long a time as I could with it. Yet if someone were thinking in terms of a Clark Blaise myth — and thinking in terms of how that myth is set out in *A North American Education*, though you do include "Going to India" there in the middle section called "The Keeler Stories" — I suspect that this new book, *Man and His World*, in its direction, in its imagery, would seem quite different.

I see *Man and His World* as a book that looks East. I think the East is the unknown, the unnameable, the magical, the mystical ...

CB: The erotic.

TS: The erotic. And I think that like the character Paul Picard, the Asian expert in the absolutely haunting story "Did, Had, Was," this book travels East and comes back with reports.

CB: In this new collection, I try to talk about the dark erotic force. The book goes from naming it as Leo, the father, in the first story, to being Leo Libido, the Love God himself, at the end. To me what you see is the revelation of my own erotic relationship with the surface of the earth. So the stories are set everywhere that I have ever had the least ability to define or authorize because it's as much erotic as geographical and in many ways they are becoming one and the same to me.

TS: So in terms of how I would see this new book, and comparisons I would make, I think I would describe it as a more mythical book — in a broader sense of that word than I mean when I speak of a personal myth. I found that some of the images in the last two stories reminded me of D.H. Lawrence. The mythical snake-god in "Sweetness and Light" reminded me of the snake in D.H. Lawrence's poem "Snake." The mythical horse-god in "The Love God" reminded me of the horses at the end of his novel *The Rainbow*. And the first two stories, "A Tour around My Father" and "Meditations on Starch," are, like your earlier collections, obviously mythical in the sense of tracing and enacting a personal myth. One deals with the inheritance from your father; the other, with the inheritance from your mother. But in the last two stories this book is transformed into something else. It becomes part of the territory of universal myth.

I would see this book as mythical in the sense of taking on the world, embracing the world, imagining its origins and destinies. There's a lovely passage from the title story, "Man and His World," about a kind of creation myth, about twins, about twin brothers:

> It is said that one brother was evil, but which one? They had struggled in the womb but the secret was kept. The tribes of animals divided. Those giving allegiance to the survivor became his servants. Others retired to the oceans and to the air and to the underworld, growing fins or scales or feathers, or shrinking themselves to become insects. They all kept faith with the one who had died.
>
> It is said that the survivor, be he good or evil, is born with sin and with guilt and is condemned to loneliness. Nowhere on the earth will he find his brother or anything else like him.

I think the last two stories in the book, "Sweetness and Light" and "The Love God," look to the Eastern material, the Indian material that you have acquired through marriage to Bharati Mukherjee — as does "Man and His World." I suppose I see the last two stories as companion stories that complete the volume, just as I see the first two stories as companion stories that open the volume. But in the course of the book something personal has evolved into something universal.

I found that I was very taken with the third story in the book, "Did, Had, Was" — the title of which seems to represent a nod in the direction of Faulkner's story "Was." Your story is about an acclaimed journalist who is seen at the end of the story to be succumbing to Alzheimer's disease. I thought you handled that beautifully.

CB: "Cold cherry soup" is the clue there.

TS: In the case of the story "South," in your collection *Resident Alien*, when the narrator's mother is described as walking across town from the other direction, I knew to ask "Why?" That is, I seemed to be able to detect sooner or to infer sooner — at a more conscious level — what was going on. But with the story "Did, Had, Was," I was kept in suspense longer. Retrospectively, I can see that I was responding to various clues that you provided; however, I was responding at what I would call a less conscious level. There was, for example, the passage in which you say of Paul Picard: "He remembered driving his mother around North Hollywood, Florida.... One day she'd turned to him and said, 'I know you're very familiar and I'm sure we've met.' She'd been sixty-two years old." When I first read that passage, I didn't know the entire shape of the story. And therefore initially that passage didn't hit me with as much force as it did when I remembered it a few paragraphs from the end of the story upon recognizing what was happening to Paul Picard.

I think it's very interesting to examine the process or the progress of one's responses as a reader, to see how details like that surface again later — when one gets to the end of a story and things click, though you know that those things were registering earlier. I felt "Did, Had, Was" worked perfectly — as a result of giving us almost at a subconscious level the details we needed.

CB: It's a very difficult thing to do when you have a character whose mind is failing him but who is at the same time a very brilliant person. "Meditations on Starch" and "Did, Had, Was" and in a sense "Dunkelblau" all deal with my mother going through that and with my becoming aware of the terrible tragedy when a life as rich as hers is gone, when she's just some granny that a Ukrainian nurse hauls around a retirement home in Winnipeg and she's just a burden on her like all the other old people. And you want to say: "But this is a woman who did, who had, who was," whose resources and whose responses are in fact exquisitely well-trained and there's no evidence of that anymore. And you realize that each mental death of a person like that is in fact the death of the world as we know it, the death of Western civilization as we know it.

So I created for her the persona in "Meditations on Starch" — which is also a meditation on the failure to heed Freud's insights into pathology and into dreams and into dysfunction. While they may in fact be revised into non-existence by further research, they nevertheless are a clue. The fact that we are now willing to disregard how his family could be gassed and he could be exiled, the fact that we are now willing to laugh at some of his proposals, is done at our own peril. And the fact that a woman who has been through all that experience is now just a kind of babbling idiot is a tragedy of the same scale.

And then I created a mental image of what my own fear would be, for I have the same inheritance after all. Namely, the fear that all of the knowledge that I've accumulated, all of the experience that I've had, would be lost. At least I'm trying to get it out on to the page should I … should it be lost. At least there will be some evidence of it. With Picard — that character is strongly there.

TS: Just at a time when he is coming into his inheritance in this world, if not yet an inheritance of some future kind, he starts to lose the intellectual powers that allowed him to establish his reputation.

CB: I had done a satire years ago — it was published in 1965 in *The Colorado Quarterly* and was never collected — called "A Scholar's Work Speaks for Itself." In it a university gets a grant to bring a major major major scholar to its miserable campus and they buy the biggest name that they can get and he comes and they rebuild his whole house for him to hold his enormous library and finally when he is asked to speak he goes ————, shows that his vocal chords are gone and that he can't say a word. The satire was an early working of the same idea, not that the mind was gone but that the notion of him giving a public lecture or of him even being able to confront a classroom was impossible.

TS: I felt on a first reading that *Man and His World* was a very carefully sequenced book — starting out with a story about your father and a story about your mother, setting up, to begin, the poles of your own experience. How did you describe your relationship to your parents in the long opening segment of autobiography in *Resident Alien*? "I need the shelter of their marriage; their complications and polarities. They are the heavens of my imagination, the indispensable maps leading north and south into Quebec and the Prairies and the Swamps, and even to Europe. To their Moral Atlas, I have added only India."

CB: Yes. And that's what this book is.

TS: Yes. Adding India. Looking East. And to finish that quotation: "They are endlessly available and compliant; they survive transmutation and still bounce back, pure and unknowable. They are the light source, the solar energy to my lunar self; they keep me not quite modern and combatively at odds with the meta-literatures and strenuous fabulations of an exhausted imagination. I want literature even now to teach me about life, not about itself." So I felt that *Man and His World* was a very carefully sequenced book — beginning with the way you deployed the first two stories, "A Tour around My Father" and "Meditations on Starch," as a pair, then the way you had the second of those followed by two other stories, "Did, Had, Was" and "Dunkelblau," that also owe a good deal to your mother's experience.

"Dunkelblau" portrays Willi Nadeau's life as a young boy — starting at his nadir, lying in bed under the care of his mother until he's nearly five years old. What impressed me most about that story was the feeling of excitement, the joyful quality, that you were able to generate in the course of the story — finishing with the scene on New Year's Eve 1945 when Willi, now a year older and now fully mobile, wakes up and rushes over to join his parents at the party next door. I also appreciated the legendary and artistic qualities of gypsy life which you evoked in that story.

But I think the word that I am most inclined to use to describe "Dunkelblau" and the collection as a whole is "mythical." I probably sensed the mythical power of the book first when I got to the joyful picture at the end of "Dunkelblau" of Willi bursting into the party next door, naked inside his mother's fur coat, embodying the New Year. That's myth of a certain kind. And the story deals with it in terms of ritual, in terms of the calendar, in terms of ancient folkloric elements with which we can still, if sometimes only barely, connect — yet deals with it forthrightly, confidently, without apology.

CB: And after the atomic bomb. It's the post-lapsarian world, too.

TS: In terms of sequencing, "Dunkelblau" is obviously a story about very early childhood. And it's the first of two consecutive Pittsburgh stories here. It's followed immediately by "Snake in Flight over Pittsburgh," which takes the book through adolescence. Then the four remaining stories — "Man and His World," "Partial Renovations," "Sweetness and Light," and "The Love God" — carry the book into adulthood, seemingly towards a final apocalypse.

I was wondering if "Sweetness and Light" didn't perhaps connect with — if the personal resurrection that the main character goes through in that story, and if the intersection of East and West in that story, didn't perhaps connect with — your second novel, *Lusts*?

CB: No. It didn't in my mind. "Sweetness and Light" was written fairly late. It was written in the late eighties.

I have always felt that what I have not sufficiently done in my work — and I intend to address this in the years remaining — is to talk about the erotic, is to talk about resurrection as an erotic thing. In the first story here, "A Tour around My Father," the idea of love breaking

down barriers is something I have not talked about before. I have talked about the pathologies of sexuality
and the kinds of voyeurism and the kinds of incest and
all the Oedipal things that afflict the sensibility of a boy
growing up in the kind of family I grew up in. But I have
not talked about marital love. I have not talked about
adulterous love. I have not talked about the other kinds
of sexual activities. And I didn't want, I don't want, to
return to the cloistered humid sexuality of the adolescent, or of the child, but rather I want to break out, to
break out even into the destructive and heartless and
cruel sides of sexuality. So that's what "Sweetness and
Light" is about.

I've only read that story once. I read it as the keynote
address at one of the Learneds in Winnipeg and Helen
Vendler kind of walked out and said it was anti-femin-
ist, it was a sexist piece. And, of course, yes, the main
character contemplates his wife's death with pleasure
and takes on a teenage Indian girl with pure colonialist
and white-man intentions. It's rather brutally sexual.
What she does for him is what a courtesan did for an
old Rajah, bring life back to him. And, yes, he becomes
a devotee of the monkeys and of the incredible snake-
cult, really a low kind of sexuality. But to me that was
only the sign of how deep his life had been allowed to
sink into paralysis: an alcoholic wife, an academic career that meant nothing, writing a book about *Contingency and Character in the Contemporary American
Novel* [laughter], a life that was totally pointless. And
now he has a focus. It's a crazy focus to have, to try to
resurrect a manorial estate in Uttar Pradesh. But he's
happy, it seems to me.

TS: Faulkner's Sutpen did it. [Laughter.]

CB: Yes. [Laughter.]

TS: But not in the same place.

CB: Yes, he's a Sutpen. In his way he's a Sutpen. And he's treating life as Sutpen would. But he's not saying to the girl, "I'll give you a place in my stable." He is in fact doing everything he possibly can for her and for her family.

TS: "Man and His World," which is not only the title story of this book but also the earliest story written for this book, was the first story to intimate or to chart something of the Eastern direction — the erotic direction — that you want your work to take now. That story was published in *Fiction International* in 1980.

And "Partial Renovations" was published under the title "Prying" in *Toronto Life* in 1982. "Partial Renovations" may strike some people as a more abstract, more difficult title, but it's a much subtler and more resonant title than "Prying."

CB: Yes. I didn't even know until the story was published that they were choosing the title "Prying." Titles are apparently in the hands of editors not writers. Commercial magazines employ editors for captions and headers who have control over such things. They said they changed the title to "Prying" because they didn't want their upscale audience to think the story was another renovations story.

TS: Perhaps we could get on record the times of composition and the places of composition of all the stories in this book.

CB: If I remember them.

"A Tour around My Father" was probably written in Atlanta when I was the writer-in-residence down at Emory University in the mid- to late eighties, sometime between 1985 and 1988.

"Meditations on Starch" was probably written in

Saratoga Springs in 1983-84 because it was published in *Salmagundi*. Or it might have been written right after in Iowa City. It was probably written in Iowa City but published in *Salmagundi*.

TS: You read it here in Guelph in November 1988 at the four-day conference on the Canadian short story that I organized in honour of John Metcalf, and it had just been published at that time.

CB: In *Salmagundi*. Yes. So maybe it was written a little bit later. Right. There had been two years or so between the time that I had written it and the time that I submitted it to *Salmagundi*. I had submitted it to a number of magazines, and it had been rejected by all of them, so I felt that there must have been something terribly wrong with it. I didn't look at it for about two years. Then, after having put it away, I read it again and I said: "There's nothing wrong with this — it's just that it's obviously not a commercial story." So I sent it to Bob Boyers, my friend who runs *Salmagundi*, and he published it, and since then it has been published all around the world in many languages.

"Did, Had, Was" was a story that I'd had many desires to write. That is, it had many notebook entries over the years.

TS: When did the title come?

CB: In the writing of it, in the writing.

TS: You say that you had been thinking about this story for many years.

CB: Oh, yes. Some of the scenes were triggered by a visit to Paris in 1985. I was staying with an old friend of mine, Sara Mitter. So a lot of my feelings for Sara, who has been a friend ever since Malamud's class at Harvard in the summer of 1961, went into that. Sara and I go back such a long way. She has just done a book,

Dharma's Daughters, about labour unions for Indian women. It's published by Rutgers University Press. It's sociology, although she's a poet.

So staying with Sara in Paris and going around with her and her son and daughter ... She's married to an Indian, strangely enough, a Bengali, a physicist. But I didn't want to get into that tight little coincidence, so I made him *malgache* because my wife and I had been to Madagascar in the late seventies and I had a strong feeling about Madagascar. I also wanted definitely to get the sense of Bruges, the perfection of Bruges thirty years ago opposed to what it has become now with all of its German tourists. And on top of that, the sense of a failing mind. That was sort of the organizing principle: What kind of character was going to convey all of these experiences? And it was not until I had buried my mother ... That was in 1987. So this story had to have come out of the buried mother.

TS: You give the date of your father's death in *Resident Alien*: December 30th, 1978. What was the date of your mother's death?

CB: 1987. February 5th, I think it was.

TS: On the topic of dates ... You were born in April. What day?

CB: The 10th.

TS: April 10th, 1940. The exact same birthdate as that of my good friend and fellow Canadianist here at the University of Guelph, Doug Daymond. Another Clark Blaise *aficionado*, I should add.

And the next story, "Dunkelblau"?

CB: It's an Iowa City story. 1988 or 1989. All of these were revised, however, in the summers when I was teaching at Emory in Atlanta. So they were all in a sense finished at Emory, wherever else I wrote them.

"Snake in Flight over Pittsburgh" was, again, part of that same stretch. 1987, 1988, 1989 — something like that. There were one or two other stories that I didn't put in this collection that were also set in Pittsburgh. I had a sudden re-burst of interest somehow in Pittsburgh. I don't know why, I don't know what triggered it, but I did one or two other stories.

TS: Specifically...?

CB: "The Unwanted Attention of Strangers" is what I was thinking of. It's a very Thomas Mann-like story about Pittsburgh.

"Man and His World," as you know, is the earliest of the stories in this book.

And "Partial Renovations," as you know, is an early story.

"Sweetness and Light" was, I guess, about 1987 or so. It must have been done in Iowa City because I came up to the Learneds from Iowa City with that story.

And "The Love God" was the most recent, 1989 or 1990. But it, too, had been with me for a long time. The image of a woman in bed and a man passing by her window who was obviously fifteen feet tall and who was just holding out his arms and having her come to him had been with me for a long time as something I wanted to understand.

TS: Splendid.

These Little Moments:
An Interview with Clark Blaise
[1996]

J.R. (Tim) Struthers

TS: It's always a pleasure to meet up with you, Clark. But it's a special pleasure for me to catch up with you on your home ground, as it were [laughter], since 1989, back in Iowa City.

CB: Right. It's as close as I probably have right now to a home, or maybe as close as I've ever had to a home.

TS: I hesitated about using the phrase "home ground," however fond I am of that sort of notion. I suspect that with you it's more appropriate to speak of the world as your home ground.

CB: I've never written about Iowa, fictionally — and in fact I've written very little nonfiction about Iowa. In some fundamental way I haven't claimed it, I suppose, and maybe that's what keeps it kind of an intellectual idea of home. All the other places that I went to as homes, I had either a genetic or linguistic or some national reason for being there. Then they all in one way or another drifted away, or I let them drift away, or they disappointed, or whatever it may be.

TS: As I've been reading the typescript of your new novel, *If I Were Me* — a delightful title, a puckish title [laughter] — I found myself forming an argument in my mind that *it* might in some sense be considered "an

Iowa novel" or at least "a University of Iowa novel" or "an International Writing Program novel."

CB: Certainly a lot of the information in it, a lot of the data, a lot of the sense impressions and all come from my job here as Director of the International Writing Program. And doubtless some of the inspiration for some of the characters would never have occurred had I not been in this privileged position of seeing the world and travelling around it as much as I do. I go to about fifteen to twenty countries a year and I am on e-mail and fax and everything else with an enormous number of people in those countries. So certainly this book is a homage in some way to the IWP.

TS: I noticed with interest an explanation, at one point in the novel, of the meaning of the surname of the main character, Gerald Lander: the explanation of his last name, meaning "farmer" and someone who delighted in a particular sense of place.

CB: A native of a place is a "lander," yes. I gave him something I don't have myself.

TS: And what about the first name, Gerald, that you selected for him? What echoes or suggestions did that have for you?

CB: Nothing special. Gerard is a family name on my father's side, becomes "Jerry" or "Gerry" as Lander's does. More generally, I remember Saul Bellow's observation, maybe in *Herzog*, that Jewish immigrants of the first generation were very accommodating to "American" names. Unlike, say, Indian immigrants who would never name their America-born sons "John" or daughters "Elizabeth" unless, of course, they were Christians. Bellow was also aware that a certain amount of distinction was desired, thus "Von Humboldt Fleisher" in *Humboldt's Gift*.

Overall, the choice of names for immigrant or half-immigrant or minority children is of great interest to me. Bharati was insistent on American names for our sons, whereas in Iowa the half-Indian kids — the father was invariably Indian, the mother mid-western American — all had fully Indian names. Our younger son, Bernie, wasn't even recognized as "Indian" because of his first and last names not computing, but he was as Indian as the Vikrams and Sanjays and in fact had gone to school in India and knew far more of India than they did.

African-American given names are marvels of invention, perhaps because the family name, in many cases, doesn't confer the same kind of information that ethnic names do. I had an Irish student at Iowa, Tomàs Murphy, who was struck in his first weeks by the comedian Eddie Murphy and a host of other Murphys, all of them African-Americans.

TS: In your writing you seem to be occupying, defining, enlarging a kind of intermediate zone or border zone between autobiography and fiction. In that context, I wanted to ask you specifically about two works: your 1993 book, *I Had a Father: A Post-Modern Autobiography*, and the book that will be appearing next year, 1997, *If I Were Me: A Novel*. I wanted to ask about any sense you might have of different purposes or overlapping purposes or possibly identical purposes in those two works.

CB: Well, *If I Were Me* is a novel. And so I can say of Lander that I am Lander but Lander is not me. I've created a character, given him a lot of my baggage, a lot of my background, a lot of my ideas, a lot of my speculations, some of my experiences. But once I've created him, he's not me. Certainly the character of "me" in *I Had a Father* is me. That is, I created "me," I am Clark, and Clark is me, and there is no attempt there to create something other than myself. And of course everything that I say in that book is verifiably true, whereas I think *If I Were Me* is as thoroughly imagined a work as I could possibly have come up with. There's nothing in it, really, that happened to me — I mean, to me, the writer.

The title *If I Were Me* simply refers to seeing oneself as an object instead of a subject. It's also a take-off on the old phrase "If I were you." You know, as kind of an admonitory phrase — "If I were you, I would ..." — and usually some sort of stern advice follows. I always thought, "Well, if I were me, what would I advise myself to be? If I were really me, if I were really in firm control of myself, if I really knew what I was or who I was, where would I take that knowledge? And what would I do with that knowledge?" That's what this novel, partially, is about.

TS: You have enjoyed a remarkable degree of productivity as a writer since returning to Iowa in 1989, despite — or possibly because of [laughter] — the excitement of your day job. In addition to completing the collection of stories *Man and His World*, published in 1992, and producing *I Had a Father: A Post-Modern Autobiography*, published in 1993, you gave a series of three lectures in Japan in 1994, which you tell me were collected that same year under the title *Here, There and Everywhere*. And now you have produced this new novel, *If I Were Me*. Before discussing it, however, I was wondering if you would say something about the particular subjects of those three lectures, since tracking down that volume is, I suspect, going to be even more challenging than keeping up with Clark Blaise. [Laughter.]

CB: Well, they're three lectures, each about an hour in length I guess. They were written up — so it's about a seventy-five-page monograph, each of them around twenty-five pages I suppose.

The first one was on contemporary American fiction, particularly as the eighties closed and the nineties dawned. The deaths of Raymond Carver, Bernard Malamud, Donald Barthelme, and John Cheever all seemed to me to close a kind of branch of American writing — of American imagination, you might say. And so the questions are: What is taking their place? What kind of writing is likely to emerge from their followers, their creative descendants? Or are we at a point where the masters have all decamped and we have to start afresh? What traces have they left behind that others could pick up on?

The second one was on Canadian and Australian fiction — but not broadly so. It was mainly on Michael Ondaatje and David Malouf. Especially the Ondaatje of *In the Skin of a Lion* and *The English Patient*. And Malouf's *Remembering Babylon*, but looking back over some of his other work as well. Some mention of Keneally and other writers from Australia.

Particularly, I was interested in these authors' rather benign view, how they skirted apocalypse in one way or another, how they did not push. For example, when the character swims all the way up the viaduct in *In the Skin of a Lion* and *doesn't* kill the water commissioner in his office. Or the atomic bomb going off at the end of *The English Patient*, causing not a similar rupture among the group, just a long slow parting. And choosing rather to see it in terms of a child dropping a spoon at the end, with the Indian character remembering that years later.

These are all resolutions of plots that would have been irresistible for an American to push in a very different way, or for many other cultures to push in a very different way. It seemed to me that what we really had here was a desire almost to push the novel into historical realms. Just as history is a long continuity of events, although history doesn't end like a novel does. It seemed to me as though these writers were really historians. They were writing history, maybe, rather than fiction — beautifully done histories, of course, but historical nonetheless. And the historical strikes me as being, by extension, present in a lot of Canadian and Australian work.

The third one was comments having to do with postmodernism and post-deconstruction, post-feminism, post-Marxism, post-everything. That was the *"Everywhere"* part of the title of that monograph. It was largely a reading of Gayatri Spivak's work, along with some French critics, to see how applicable I thought those stances were to contemporary fiction. Trying to understand something that even at that time, two years ago, was perhaps past its prime in the university world and has skidded downhill since. Trying to understand what gave it at that time so much currency and so much academic power if not any other.

TS: What was your sense of Spivak's theories?

CB: Well, I found them narrow. And in many ways I felt they followed programmatically, with the result being the assassination of literature, the assassination of the imagination. I think the desire to deny an author the ability to do the very thing I did in *If I Were Me* — to dare to imagine one's self as being different from the author — would make the writer incapable of rendering anything that he or she is not autobiographically heir to or autobiographically gifted by. So Bharati cannot write of a poorer person than she is because that would be appropriating a voice of poverty when she was born rich. And she cannot write of village people speaking

Punjabi because she was a Bengali person speaking English. It goes on and on and on like this.

TS: Of course, these things will only die in the academy if people are willing to let them die and if people are willing to change their thinking.

CB: Well, academics are no less petty than anyone else, and also there's a great deal, I'm afraid, of turf-building and turf-protecting going on in a lot of the academic areas that have recently opened up. The oldest of those forms, I suppose, would be Women's Studies and Black Studies — African-American Studies, whatever you want to call it. In all of these fields, valuable work has been done. In all of these fields, the rediscovery of forgotten texts, obscure texts, the celebration of authors who have been long ignored, the creation of a canon within each field has been very useful and we have all profited. I mean, the whole study of literature has profited from what has been rediscovered in a lot of these fields. In fact, one could easily say that this is maybe what saved literary study.

But while all that is being done, there is the publicity angle, the part where it's not just enough to say, "We have discovered a brilliant new woman from 1840 who hitherto was totally unknown and who died in obscurity but left behind this wonderful diary that was so full of rich observations and wit and colour and all the rest of it." That's wonderful. But then to take it or hundreds of other examples from any number of other fields and say that the reason *why* it is obscure, the reason *why* we don't know her name, the reason *why* it hasn't been celebrated is because of hegemonic males or because of White-this or because of Anglo-that. So the celebration of a rediscovered text, or of a rediscovered author, leads so often then to the vilification of others and the refighting of battles that were already perhaps fought in an earlier time.

It becomes impossible to talk about one thing without calling attention to another thing. Then of course you have created little internecine battles within English departments, or within whatever other departments you're talking about, and everyone gets their backs up. And it becomes very hard then to study such a work. If one is to say, "Ah, yes, I enjoyed reading this book, but it was seriously flawed in this way or that way," well, as soon as you say that, then you are told that you have revealed your own prejudices and that "You cannot read these things, because you are incapable — coming as you do from the place and time and society and structure and university and language and religion and eye colour that you come from, you cannot be expected even to understand this."

So then the thing we immediately lose is any sense of a universal approach. We are then sunk into simultaneous multicentralities, and simultaneous oppositional camps, so that everyone is validated variously — so that only a gay can be expected to understand this work, only a Black can understand this, only an Asian-American can understand this, only a woman can understand this. And then it becomes even finer than that. Only a woman from a certain ethnicity or class or country can understand this. Only a this can understand that. And, finally, you're really saying, "Only a North Dakota-born quasi-French Canadian can read this book." You know what I mean?

TS: And maybe in that case, perhaps even I can't understand me. [Laughter.]

CB: Yes. Exactly. Wow. That's very much a part of what I'm saying. Yes.

TS: You taught at York University from 1978 to 1980. And in 1982 Michael Ondaatje, who had a long connection with York including those years, published the memoir/autobiography *Running in the Family*. I wanted to ask if that book had come your way at some point and if you could remember when? And, if so, would you see it as a work that in various ways opens up the possibilities of personal writing?

CB: No, I in fact haven't ever read that book. I've heard parts that he has read from it at readings and I'm aware of parts that others have spoken about. But I've never sat down to read the book. I was, however, present at the germ of it, at the moment in which that book was born. That was at the Canadian High Commission New Year's Eve party in New Delhi in 1977, when Michael and Kim Ondaatje were there with Bharati and me and with Eli and Ann Mandel. We were at a table together and we had been drinking Canadian champagne for much of the night and Michael went out to go to the bathroom, slipping out of the tent — quite literally it was a tent on the ground. He came back a long time later. We almost started to worry about him.

He said he had just had a *madeleine* moment, a Proust *madeleine* experience, smelling the *beedi* cigarettes, the typical servant cigarettes that you have all over South Asia. He smoked one with one of the servants who had been squatting behind the tent. And he hadn't done that since he was twelve years old in Ceylon, now of course called Sri Lanka. Then suddenly it all came back to him. Until that time, he had really *not* dealt with his Asian background. In fact, he had been very reluctant to exploit it in any way or to write about it. He had been very carefully a Canadian writer, even an American writer for that matter, but not a Sri Lankan writer. And suddenly that was the moment at which it all started. He has confirmed that. I know this is true because I introduced him a couple of years ago when he was here in Iowa and he verified that this indeed was true.

TS: You mention Eli Mandel, who also taught at York University and also was a very important presence there. Eli is the author of such works as *Out of Place*, *Life Sentence*, *Another Time*, and *The Family Romance*, with a tribute to Freud in the title of the last of those —books which combine poetry and autobiography, autobiography and criticism.

CB: With a great sense of place and geography.

TS: And I note with considerable interest that you have elected to dedicate your new novel, *If I Were Me*, to Eli Mandel. I was wondering, therefore, if you might say something about that connection.

CB: Well, all of the things you mention are reasons. Specifically, I was thinking of his work on the double. We had talked about that at great length at one time. Because seeing one's double, in most cultures, is synonymous with dying, with death. One always suspects that one's double is out there somewhere in the world and if you finally meet it's almost like an obliteration of the two of you. And he had seen his double on a beach in Buenos Aires. He was swimming in the ocean and he looked at the beach and he saw himself walking on the beach. He had been so shaken by the vision that he went to a Rabbi. And the Rabbi said, "No, in *our* tradition, it's not a sign of death—in fact, it's a blessing, it's a good thing." So Eli dealt with that. He felt he had maybe passed through the superstitious part of the vision and broken through into something else. So that was maybe even more of a significant part.

Also, I've always been very much interested in the story of the Hirsch colony in Saskatchewan, as well as that of the nearby town of Estevan where Eli was born, and that of the Baron de Hirsch. Here in the program that I operate, we are beneficiaries of the Hirsch South American foundation. It brings us every year Argentine, Chilean, and Brazilian writers. Not Jewish, by any means, anymore. The money came out of the Hirsch and the Hochschild foundations, great South American families. These are two of the fortunes that were based in Buenos Aires at one time — maybe even based in Paris and operating out of South America, I don't know. But their foundations are in fact the largest cultural foundations in South America. And they operate for the benefit of the whole society and are totally secularized.

TS: In *If I Were Me*, Gerald Lander sees his double twice: in sort of a nightmare vision in the "Prologue: Strangers in the Night," and then close to the end of the book's powerful second-last piece, "Dark Matter." I suppose that would be one way of talking about the shape of the novel.

CB: Yes. Well, he saw his double and the double took him, in a sense, on a ten-year trip, between age fifty and age sixty. A ten-year trip that is meant to be a pretty thoroughgoing investigation — in fictional terms any-way — of what the brain is perhaps capable of being, of how deep or how far it's capable of reaching. And by the end of a certain number of adventures, and a certain number of speculations, Lander has come to the con-clusion, almost, that the universe is somehow inside the brain. A lot of adventures keep telling him that as far as he travels, and as deeply as he travels, in certain ways everything seems to be housed within his own skull. The brain seems capable of reaching into the future

— seems hard-wired, as he says at one time, for clair-voyance.

He starts off solving the riddle, or solving the sup-posed muddle, of Alzheimer's language and goes on from there. He's in the tradition of Freud, someone who takes what is presumed to be irrational muttering — dreams, in the case of Freud, or whatever it may be — and finds reason in it, finds order in it, or, in other words, reduces the level of chaos in the system. In Lander's case it's language, it's not dreams. But as he goes deeper he finds that language perhaps is just, as one of his col-leagues says, a fiber-optic. Language is the thing that carries even more meaning than language itself, so that rather than stopping with language, as a linguist might, he can push language even further — as the Indian says, into certain tribal formulations, or as his Japanese friend says, into ideographic as well as spoken language. There are a number of other ways of pushing language.

TS: Lander seems to have pushed himself through to a different way of knowing as well.

CB: Certainly he did. When the unwelcome visitation of his double came, he was a self-satisfied fifty-year-old suburban researcher, married and with children, mak-ing his way as a respected person. By the end he has destroyed his family, more or less. Or his family has destroyed him. He has a daughter and a son and a wife — but they're all "ex," you could say. He has made love to the dog. He has made love to hundreds of women. He is tired. He has found, finally, the home that he wants to return to: Israel. Or not return to, but turn to. He has found the woman of his long questing: Aviva. He has found all of these things, he has reached some conclusions about the brain and what it's capable of and about what his remaining work is going to be, and he's willing to confront the fact that he's probably going to be called a quack or a mystic or something else like that when his journey is ended for him.

As the author of all this I had the same feeling, maybe, that the world did for Lander, that I didn't want him to die. So I created a "yahrzeit" — a memorial to him — at the end, in which it's possible for the world to keep believing that he still exists, that he's still out there. And like people leaving tickets for Elvis at certain concerts, they still leave tickets for Lander in the hope that he'll come, somehow, out of the desert, bearing the tablets of some new revelation. It's not going to happen, I don't think, but who knows?

TS: What does the word "yahrzeit" mean?

CB: "Yahrzeit" means, in Yiddish, a year's time. After a person has died, you have a memorial a year later. Lighting candles and saying prayers.

TS: In your years in Montreal — 1966 to 1978 — did you happen across the wonderful poetic novel by A.M. Klein, *The Second Scroll*?

CB: I crossed it, yes.

TS: The Zionism and the apocalyptic sense and the question of autobiography in this new novel of yours — all brought to mind Klein's *The Second Scroll*.

CB: I wasn't thinking of it at all when I wrote this. I had read it early in my Montreal years. Jerry Newman had told me, "Oh, when you want to learn everything there is to learn about the Canadian novel, this is one of the great novels." A lot of people pressed that book upon me in Montreal in those years. A lot of people still knew him, remembered him very well. Mesh Butovsky, who teaches at Concordia — I said "Mesh," Mervin Butovsky is his name — Mesh is a big expert on Klein. And Norman Levine spoke highly of it at one time. Of course Eli spoke very highly of it, too. And I read it. I could certainly respect its great moral seriousness. But I must say I was not moved particularly by it. I was not, probably, listening to it at that time. I should go back and read it. I don't remember very much about it at all.

TS: Gerald Lander is a clinical psychologist, a theorist of both memory and what you call "anticipation." Two principles, I would note in passing, that are remarkably important in fiction. What I find myself contemplating, however, is the ultimate focus of your new novel, *If I Were Me*. There is a passage in the second-last story, "Dark Matter," where you refer to material from the brochure for the conference in Israel in which Lander is participating, material that includes the statement "call it language-making, brain-chemistry, or the subconscious, they all point feebly at times, insistently at others, toward a god, or away from it." For whatever reasons, I would put something like that side by side with, to me, a very important image from *I Had a Father*, in which the Clark Blaise of that book remarks on looking in the mirror and seeing the face in that mirror and increasingly realizing that the face he sees there is his father's face. But as well in that scene — and this is completely my own interpretation — it strikes me that perhaps at some level he is also seeing the face of God. So I was intrigued by that description in your new book, "call it language-making, brain-chemistry, or the subconscious, they all point feebly at times, insistently at others, toward a god, or away from it." And I was wondering about your sense of the centrality of that passage and the way in which that passage can reverberate.

CB: You've isolated a thought that Lander considered. It may well be a thought that I have too, at times — what I would call a religious feeling. That would mean a transcendent feeling or some sense that there is an order and a hierarchy and a kind of conjuring act or something up there — "the Cosmic Prompter," I've called it here. There's someone, something, there's some force that is larger than our individual experience. I said this, also, in *I Had a Father* — that autobiography was consciousness achieving sovereignty over experience. I feel that there is a difference between consciousness and experience, unlike what John Locke would say [laughter], although I'm not as serenely confident of it as a Descartes might be. I feel that there is consciousness almost without experience.

Somehow or other there's a link. I don't know what the link is. I don't know when consciousness takes off. I don't know if consciousness is achieved by anybody or if it is achieved by a small minority of people. To me, the act of writing, of putting together words and images, is as close to being in contact with consciousness as I can get. When I see metaphors are coming to me, metaphors that never existed before are suddenly coming to me. Or when I see parallels that I'm aware of, but then you read it and you are finding more parallels in it than I did. I know they're in there. I'll probably be aware of some of them until I die that no one else will have discovered. But you always take great pleasure when others find things in it that you were not aware were there. And as soon as they say it, you realize, yes, it's true. So if God is in the details, or the devil is in the details, or some larger force is in the details, somehow this, I think, is quite true. That's really good enough for me. I don't want to call it a religious sense, although the word used in the line you quote is "god." Just call it a larger consciousness — some sort of sense that there is order, an order to be discovered, a rationality to be glimpsed, perhaps a clarity out of all the confusion.

In this book Lander has many moments of that. For example, in the story "Drawing Rooms" when he realizes that he is really inside the brain. He's inside his own memory in a house that was in fact a mansion. With all the partitions and the drywall, and the dot matrix printers and all going off in every room, it's in fact something like a brain. Anyway, he has a number of these moments in the book. And each one leaves him absolutely blank. He had that feeling when he discovered algebra for the first time: he had that purple light and he realized that it's possible to put an equals sign between any two things and say they are equal, if you have the right numbers. Or when his friend Joel Kaminsky had the same feeling about ratios, that you could logarithmize the world in a certain way. These are all similar moments. And certainly he would have had that experience when he was able to translate his mother's Alzheimer's gibberish. Or when he feels Aviva Golan's breasts hitting him in just the place where he hadn't been touched in forty years. All of these are similar. All of these are times in which you have had a divine moment.

TS: Meeting his old girlfriend forty years later, again in Israel, on his return there.

CB: Those are all moments that I tried to put in there.

I would certainly say that a lot of this is like — I think I used the image — like a child finding bats flying out of a hillside, and realizing that there is a dark cavity underneath, and you go in, and suddenly it's room after room after room that had always been there but never been explored. It all starts where there's just a cold rush of air coming out between two rocks.

TS: But a darkness that becomes luminous.

CB: Yes. Can, anyway.

TS: I would like to ask you about the form and the impact of *If I Were Me*. Some books one could speak of as involving a kind of letting out. And yet what I sensed here, perhaps at the same time, was an equal sense of letting in: a letting out of the self and a coexisting letting in of the world. I was wondering if that would make any sense as a way of talking about the form and the impact of this novel.

CB: Yes, I think that's very close to it. The drive that has always motivated me, that I think motivates most writers, is that, yes, you're out to express. You're expressing something inside yourself and projecting it on as wide and bright a screen as possible.

Yet there *is* something far more mystical going on in this book, where you really are passively listening. You have your ear out to what seems to be the scientific evidence of things — the somewhat mystical, somewhat mathematical, somewhat astrophysical, somewhat psychological mysteries. And I think I wanted to create a character who was at that point in his life not just having a male mid-life crisis — but was at that point in his life when the world entered, unbidden, and gave him a great gift, made him an improbable millionaire, made him an improbable world figure. Not that he wasn't bright, not that he didn't have the right goods and tools for it, but a lot of people have the right goods and tools and never make it. He became like Hawking or Rushdie or Eco, one of these people who also got the good fortune of having a public life now thrust upon him.

The whole idea of creating a character — a standard novelistic character, a standard novelistic hero — just didn't appeal to me in this book. I'm doing something in my novel right now that's very much more traditional, very much more conventional, where I'm happy to do it.

TS: Can you tell me a little bit about the novel in progress? Have you given it a working title?

CB: Yes, but that novel title was taken about a year and a half ago by a very successful book, so I can't use it anymore.

TS: What was that?

CB: [Laughter.] I'm not going to use it. And I'm not going to tell you. I still use the same title, though I don't want to commit myself in any way to it. I'm going to have to come up with something else, but I haven't yet. I'm just hoping that somehow or other something in the text will suggest a new title.

What I've said about this novel in brief comments at other times is that a contemporary crime forces the alleged perpetrator to go back into history to prove his innocence. Something that happens today that he's accused of makes him go back into his own family for three or four generations, and into the family of the so-called victim for three or four generations, to discover what the truth is and how the original crime from the last century has been passed on and how the effects have deformed two families in the process. It's French-Canadian and Franco-American. So it's based in upper New England and Quebec, mainly in village Quebec and a little bit in Montreal but not much.

TS: And did the research for *I Had a Father* open up all of this for you?

CB: Yes, it was that, and the friends who have provided a lot more, and books that I've read. I've been reading almost exclusively books in that field for the last couple of years.

TS: In contrast to the novel on which you're now working, *If I Were Me* aims for and achieves effects that are powerfully unconventional.

CB: In this book I wanted to talk about that countervailing moment in one's life when the world rushes in, the tide comes in. I used that image once at the end of *I Had a Father*. The sense that every now and then you find yourself almost naked in the universe. You're this little creature under a huge sky, or in front of an ocean, and things are crashing in on you and you're very much aware of your smallness and your insignificance.

You're also very much aware of the intricacy and the beauty of the created world, of the surrounding world. And you wonder if there is any coherence or any consonance between the little bit you know inside you, and the little bit you know inside other people, and what seems to be the sometimes organic wholeness that surrounds you. Every now and then you have these little moments — that's why I go back to Pascal. The very origins of my own writing are probably always in Pascal, in the little moments of insight in Pascal's *Pensées*.

TS: Mythic moments.

CB: Yes. Mythic moments. Exactly. I know there are a lot of such moments in this book. No one has read it all except you and the editor and my agent, so I don't have a sense of how people are going to respond to it. I know in the case of the story "Doggystan," which just appeared in print in *Salmagundi*, some people read it and thought, "Shame on you, Clark, for such language!" The idea of man making love to dog is very politically incorrect. And consider also that it's happening in India. There's a whole bunch of things happening — either the style or the place or whatever it may be — that can be seen *in segments* as being politically discomforting. I was not, of course, intending that. I was intending to take a man down to some sort of fundamental level.

But I can see how people are going to say, "You have

a daughter here who is lesbian and Black. You have a man who is hanging out with some real tough right-wing Zionists. You have him killed off by an Arab bomb. You have all sorts of Holocaust imagery. You have all sorts of stuff here that would lend itself, politically, either to some pretty right-wing interpretations or to in some cases politically incorrect but in other cases politically involved positions." And, again, that's not my position. I wanted to create a character who was in the position to have the world suggest itself to him in many ways. He was not a particularly political person until his first lover, at least the first lover that we talk about here, offers him wine from a Nazi cup.

The world is out there, all of these things are out there, and it is creating a consciousness. He does reach some degree of oneness or fatherhood with his very difficult daughter. He does reach the same thing with his totally destroyed son. He does learn to say no to sexual advances when offered to him. He does know to take a stance on the side of his daughter when he meets the man who had in a sense ruined her life or at least changed her life. There are moments in this book where he is, I think, a decent character or, in other words, a recognizable human character with a particular family and a particular set of biases. But I also wanted to create someone who is a free mind — I mean, a very deep-thinking mind — who is constantly using the ironies and the almost humorous situations of his life, the ironies and the tragedies of his life, not just to get back at people, not just for his own advantage, but actually to make some sort of philosophical or scientific point.

TS: There's a very powerful sense of — would you call it "mentality"? — in this book.

CB: Yes, he's a mind. He's a mind. And I didn't want to lose that. He's a *kop*, they would say in Yiddish. He's a *kop*.

TS: I'm interested in how the parts of this novel emerged — and then how they merge into this single unit in ten parts, including the "Prologue: Strangers in the Night" and the "Epilogue: Yahrzeit." Many of the early parts of the book are very short, half a dozen pages or so in typescript. Would you regard those as short stories or as having resemblances to the form of the short story?

CB: Well, I don't see them as short stories, no. I see them as chapters of a work. And I always did. I was much impressed by a writer we had here in the program, a woman from Colombia named Carmen Suárez, who wrote a book called — I'm trying to remember the whole title — *A Red Dress for Dancing Boleros.*

TS: And in the original Spanish?

CB: *Un vestido rojo para bailar boleros.* She had written a short novel, shorter than my new one, made up of very, very brief chapters — a paragraph or two, sometimes two to three pages at most — describing a very, very intense love affair. So the separate takes of the love affair really did seem to be almost breathless. There was in fact an organic similarity to sex: to panting and heavy breathing and orgasm and release and all the rest of it. And she read them here. We translated some of them. Wonderful book. Not at all, in content, what I was expecting. When I heard her, it was very strange. She read one week at the little cabaret we have here in Iowa City, in which our writers and the writers in the Writers' Workshop all get together for about two or three hours of readings in a night with a lot of drinking, a lot of music, in between. Carmen read and then the emcee said, "And next week Clark will read!"

TS: [Laughter.]

CB: And I had nothing. I said, "How dare he!" So I wrote "Kristallnacht" and "A Saint" that week, very much under the sense of Carmen's work, and read them the next week at the cabaret. At the time I was thinking that I could probably do a whole book of brief takes like that. There are a number that I wrote that are not in this book.

There's one that has been haunting me, and that may end up having to be its own novella or something, called "The Most Beautiful Thing in the World." In it Lander meets a photographer whose commission is to take photos of the most beautiful thing. She has a huge bank account to be able to do this, to take pictures of whatever people suggest to her is the most beautiful thing in the world. So they meet up at a conference in Korea — this was set in Seoul — where he meets her and she's asking him, "What is the most beautiful thing in the world?" He's looking at her proofs, the photos she has already taken, and some of them are the clichés, you know, Taj Mahal by moonlight and all, but others are in fact quite interesting: love-making moments, or babies sleeping, whatever, it could be a flower, it could be a hummingbird, whatever is the most beautiful thing. And the question, of course, is: What is beauty? And can a picture be taken of it? Is beauty an abstraction? Is it symmetry? Is it devoid of sentimentality? Is it devoid of human touch? Is it possible to say something is beautiful? Or is everything beautiful? Is one thing more beautiful than another? Is a mangy dog on the street of India less beautiful than a hummingbird bejewelled in front of a wonderful flower with a drop of nectar on its beak? Well, who knows? These were some of the things that I was trying to deal with. And Lander and the photographer naturally become an item briefly.

There was another one that started getting too long, one in which he's in Russia with another woman. He's there, in some ways, trailing his daughter before she got to Poland. He's meeting some of the people whom his daughter knew. He's out in one of the provincial cities during the time of *perestroika*. I was very interested in all these countries in Eastern Europe at that time when people's lives were changing, when their whole cultural history was in the balance. Communism was gone but nothing had replaced it. Revanchist sentiments were there and Nazi sentiments were arising — there were all sorts of things possible for a brief moment in those countries, good and bad. Possibilities that had never been breathed before in European society were being contemplated. They're not anymore, but five years ago they were. And I was there: I was there in Poland, I was there in Estonia, I was there in Russia, I was there in all those countries. So it was irresistible to try and do something with that.

I haven't written these stories politically. That is, I was more interested in Lander's problems. One could have turned around and written a story in a Kundera-like way, I suppose. And there is a novel that I plan to do down the line, sort of in a Czech/Hungarian way, or maybe almost in a Calvino-like way. Something about fictional countries. Countries that are, in a sense, like novels — you don't know how they're going to turn out.

TS: To my mind, *If I Were Me* in some respects recalls Joyce's description of *Dubliners* as "a chapter of the moral history of my country."

CB: Could be. Joyce is never far from — any of his various pronouncements, especially those in or involving either *A Portrait of the Artist as a Young Man* or *Dubliners*, are never far from — any writer, I think. He did lay out a particular kind of mode that we haven't veered from too much. Either you're going into the smithy of your soul to forge the uncreated conscience of your race or else you're doing a moral history of your place. Those are things that we haven't gotten away from. And why should we?

TS: [Laughter.] At the same time, there seems to be something substantially new about this book. Whereas in earlier work of yours I see the emphasis as being on the relationship between a child and his parents, here in this novel the emphasis is on the relationship between a parent and his children. Particularly in the sixth and seventh stories, "The Banality of Virtue," about Lander's adopted daughter, Rachel, and "White Children," about his son, Sam. That seems to be a new development. Or at least it seems to be given more emphasis than it was given in earlier work of yours. I'm wondering if this connects with Lander's double interest in memory and anticipation, in the past and the future. Looking in one direction at the generation of one's parents, but also looking in the other direction at the generation of one's children.

CB: It's about time, isn't it, that I start talking about it, since I'm now the old guy in the family. It would be unseemly, I think, to continue to write, as a man in his mid-fifties, about his parents. And also just having done the book on my father — and still being very much involved in the subject of my father because the book I'm writing right now is French-Canadian to its core. Here I wrote a book without a mention of the word "Canada," without a mention of the words "French Canada" or "French-Canadian," and in which the father is a very minor figure. He was just a dry-cleaner who had a rather typical lower-middle-class/middle-class mindset about profit and loss.

Obviously, it's Lander's mother who is the decent moral force in his life, the one who saw clearly through race and through everything else, who supported the adoption of a Black daughter and all the rest of it. So his attempt to redeem his mother's life — I talked about this a bit in "Meditations on Starch": the desire of the son to redeem his mother's life and to say that her life was meaningful — is really what I'm trying to do here. It's not like my mother's life, which was a little more public. Lander's mother had a fairly anonymous life. But she was a good person and is the direct inspiration for his theory and for everything in his life.

TS: His exploration of her Alzheimer's.

CB: Her "word-salad" as it's called, right.

TS: Your treatment of Lander's relationship with his son, Sam, is especially poignant.

CB: The only two first-person stories, "A Saint" and "White Children," are both about the boy. They're about the very difficult relationship that Lander had with the boy, the love that he had, the horrible failure of his relationship with the boy. I can't imagine, in a sense, a worse failure than to see your child who had all of these gifts and all of these qualities simply become a zombie in the service of a murderous cult. And even if you save him, even if you save the physical body of this boy, what do you have? He has lost something — he has lost his humanity in some way. And Lander believes it has something to do with himself. But he doesn't know what.

I don't know what either, frankly. But I think it does have something to do with going on a quest for ultimate understanding. In other words, clearly there is a Faustian bargain that Lander has struck. There is not a devil out there. Well, maybe there is a devil in the story. I don't know. There may be many devils in the story. Lander has struck a bargain. The devil has not taken his consciousness. The devil has not taken his intelligence or his wit. The devil has allowed him to play. But Lander has an enormous will, an enormous determination, an enormous discipline to allow him to do what he has done and still have a clear purpose. Whereas the son perhaps didn't have that will, didn't have that clear defining purpose. So when the son struck the same Faustian bargain, in his case with the Aum Shinrikyo, he was engulfed by it, his mind was taken over.

TS: That's staggering. There really is an extraordinary sense of descent at that point in the book with "White Children," the story set in Japan.

CB: It's the longest one — together with "Dark Matter."

TS: Yes. So after the first five brief pieces, there's the regular-size story "The Banality of Virtue" sixth, the much longer story "White Children" seventh, the regular-size story "Doggystan" eighth, the much longer story "Dark Matter" ninth, and the "Epilogue: Yahrzeit" tenth.

I was interested that in a couple of the earlier pieces — "A Saint" and "Kristallnacht," which come third and fourth in the book — Lander is not identified by name. "A Saint" is first-person and "Kristallnacht" is third-person, yet they are similar not only in their brevity but also because he is not identified by name in either one. I'm reading this novel in typescript after you have obviously gotten it where you want it. Still, I'm wondering if an editor, considering the matter I've just raised, could say, "Might there be an advantage, in terms of the readership of this work, not in changing the point of view anywhere, for there are reasons that you shift from third-person to first-person then back, but in some gesture ..."

CB: Towards continuity.

TS: Yes, particularly given the brevity of the first five pieces — that is, because the "Prologue: Strangers in the Night" and the second piece, "Salad Days," quickly set up certain expectations through identifying Lander by name.

CB: Could be. I hadn't thought of it, but this is why it's valuable to have someone read it. As I say, next to no one has read it, so I haven't been hearing critical or editorial voices. I just had a feeling that as soon as you name a character — as opposed to saying "he" or "I" — you've distanced him in some way, you've made him an object rather than a subject.

TS: Which you do in the first two pieces.

CB: Yes. So if Lander is hearing praise of the Nazis, which one did hear in Eastern Europe at that time — in the rush to throw off the Communists, the Russians, what other alternative do they have but to remember the wonderful days of the Nazis when the Nazis were so competent? The hatred of the Russians was for their sheer incompetence, their sheer mediocrity. The Germans at least represented a kind of technical proficiency, a kind of beautiful precision, that the Russians never had. But it seems to me that as soon as I would say "Lander," then, put in that position, Lander would have seemingly been called on to have said something. Whereas "he," just dazzled by the great good fortune that he has in being with a beautiful woman in the Estonian story — I didn't put Estonia down as a name but if you read between the lines, that's more or less where it has to be happening — "he" is willing to overlook all this. Maybe later in his life he wouldn't be. He remembers her in the Japanese story. And he remembers Ainu. But I didn't name her "Ainu" earlier, either. Could have, but didn't. I don't know.

TS: As a reader, one doesn't want to be led by the hand. And as a writer, I'm sure, one doesn't want to feel obliged to lead anybody by the hand. [Laughter.] Yet the possible value of a little more consistency — or, as you say, continuity — did cross my mind, given the variety of forms that you are employing here.

CB: There might be all sorts of structural and other kinds of flaws that I'm not aware of, or that I have in my own mind rationalized, about which a reader might say, "Now wait, hold on just a minute here, I don't get this," or "I don't follow this and I'm not interested in this." I really can't predict how people are going to respond to this book. Maybe you feel that way about every book after you've finished it. But this one is written with much less of a sense of reader involvement, much less of a sense of audience than anything else I've ever written. So maybe I've taken on less compassion for the reader or less empathy for reader response. I really don't know. I guess we'll have to see.

TS: I suppose the argument I would make is that while the various parts of *If I Were Me* definitely exhibit great delicacy and great power, I wouldn't want anything to detract from the book's overall impact by permitting a reader to float at occasional points a bit more than might be desirable. I raise this possibility partly on the basis of my own editorial experience as the publisher of Red Kite Press working with George Elliott on his story collections *The bittersweet man* and *Crazy Water Boys* and *Sand gardens on First Beach*, partly since I'm in the position of talking to you before this book goes into print, but just as much out of personal aesthetic interest.

CB: I have no interest in the book now. Quite literally, I have no interest in the book now. One could say just about anything about it and it would not really move me to do very much about it one way or another. It's as though it was written by someone else and it's out of my hands. I might say, "Oh, that's interesting." But I don't have the same proprietorial possessiveness. My paws aren't on this in the same way that might be the case with some other book in which I feel as though I know what readers are going to get from it, what they are going to say about it, and I know how to manipulate them into my corner.

Now, this is all said by someone who has never had *any* kind of commercial success — I mean, *no* kind of commercial success. So if in ten previous books or nine or whatever it is, with all the exquisite attempts at audience manipulation that I've tried, I've been such a failure at it, then if this time I'm not trying at all, maybe it will be a success. Who knows? I really can't say. I wouldn't know how to begin to go about making this book more reader-friendly than it is.

TS: Another way of viewing the structure of *If I Were Me* — much in the way that I look at a work of poetry like T.S. Eliot's *Four Quartets* — is to see it as the elaboration of a developing series of philosophical questions posed by Lander, including a question about Israel, "could I be happy here?" and the question that he imagines as determining the remainder of his life's work, "What does it mean, *to live in the moment*?" And I thought I might conclude by asking you: What does it mean for Clark Blaise, right now, to live in the moment?

CB: Well, I don't know. I think the accustomed meaning of the phrase is that you have somehow liberated yourself from drags and contingencies. Certainly from contingency, from consequence and antecedent. You're living in the middle, without a sense of a beginning or an end. I guess that's what it means. I don't live that way, so I wouldn't know. I would imagine truly living in the moment might be something that happens to some performers when they are performing outside of themselves — that is, when they have successfully impersonated a character on the stage. Or to certain athletes when they are, as they say, in the zone, when they are simply performing with all of the reflexes. They're not thinking. They're just performing at the highest possible, or the lowest possible, level of bodily instinct.

And I'm sure it has happened to all of us, that we've had moments in which all of the multiple contingencies that we are, all of the things that make us who we are, simply, for a moment, vanish. And we feel that we are simply a pair of eyes looking at something that need not be attached to Tim Struthers, need not be a scene in Canada, you need not have read a single book in your life to have had that response. It can be very liberating. It can be a very heady experience. I don't think it happens to most self-conscious people very often. And probably it shouldn't. But it probably is what is meant when you say, "living in the moment." It happened to Lander when he had that revelation of the beauty of mathematics. Or when he could listen to his mother's gibberish and suddenly have it make perfectly clear sense to him.

TS: I would like to thank you for these not-so-little moments.

CB: OK.

TS: Thank you.

To Do Justice to the Stages of His Life and to the Places That Formed Him: An Interview with Clark Blaise [2002]

J.R. (Tim) Struthers

TS: The last time we sat down together was in June 1996, in Iowa City, at an earlier conference in this biennial series of international celebrations of the short story. Two years after that, in 1998, you resigned from your position as Director of the International Writing Program at the University of Iowa, following nine full years of distinguished service and extensive travel, and moved to San Francisco. Could you describe for me your sense of San Francisco?

CB: It's an ideal place in the American landscape in many ways. I was just simply fortunate. My wife, Bharati, is a professor at Berkeley. She had come in 1989, when prices were already through the roof but nowhere near what they are now, so she was able to buy a house. She has a very fine-paying position with good benefits. It offered an opportunity to end the commuter marriage that we were in.

I had been working summer and fall in Iowa, keeping the program together and raising money for it. And when the thirty-five international writers were there in the fall, I was doing everything I could to provide seven-days-a-week, twenty-four-hours-a-day service for them. And then in the spring I was travelling around the world to recruit for the next year, attending various festivals, and meeting with officials and foundations in every part of the world to try to raise money — in their countries or in our country or in USIA posts, that is, United States Information Agency posts, around the world — to provide for the writers.

Gradually, as these things happen, the USIA was absorbed into the State Department. So there was no longer a cultural attaché in various countries. And the University of Iowa underwent its third regime change in my nine years there — the third new president and new provosts and new deans and new hierarchies and all the rest of it. Each time that happens, you lose a little bit of your edge. It takes two or three years for a program director to make a special case to a dean or to a new administration who is not at all aware of who you are. Especially if you are not bringing in money in an acceptable way or in a traditional way. Because our writers were independent people, we didn't have students as such. We didn't give degrees and we didn't run classes.

Twice I did it, and by the end of the most recent administration's three years I was on very good terms with them. But then I could see that this latest regime change had a very, very different operating principle: everything had to be tailored in a particular way to look the same, so that all departments in the liberal arts wing had to be pulling in the same direction. We were seen as the square peg and we were told that money which had always come to us was going to be pulled. And indeed it was. That meant the last bit of money I could expect to get was not going to happen. So I left.

They couldn't find a replacement. They pulled the program for a year. There was an international, national, state, local, and faculty uprising about the loss of this program. They learned what an important program it was, historically and in fact strategically, for the university's placement in the world. Then they had to go out and recruit a new person. And in the recruiting of the new person they had to guarantee that there would be sufficient financial coverage from the university and that he would be spared the necessity of doing all the kinds of fund-raising that I was having to do. So it's back on board, but it couldn't have happened if I had stayed. It had to have that bloodletting.

TS: Moving from Iowa City to San Francisco seems to me to be a big move. My big move was in 1985-86, from London, Ontario, to Guelph, Ontario. [Laughter.] I had set myself a goal of finding a tenure-stream job that was no more than a two-hour drive from London, Ontario, the place of my birth, of all my formal education, the place where I spent my first thirty-five years, where my by then aging parents still resided. So moving from Iowa City to San Francisco seems to me to be a big move! [Laughter.]

If I may, I would like to ask you about San Francisco. Do you have any favourite places there that you could visualize for me? And what do you think it would take for San Francisco to become material for your writing? Or would that even be possible?

CB: I don't think San Francisco will ever enter my writing world. It's too much of a completed, formed society for me to enter it. It would be like moving to London or something.

TS: The other London. [Laughter.]

CB: It has its intact hierarchies. It has its power centres and its institutions. They are so well established, so historically rooted. I am one of the drops of water that falls off the duck's back. San Francisco is the duck's back and I'm a passing rain shower. I can enjoy the city for what it is. It's a very, very pleasant place that's never too hot and rarely too cold. It allows me to work. It has wonderful restaurants. And a lot of good writers are there. It's a very highly literary society and it honours writers along with film makers and creative people of all sorts. It's funky and eccentric as a place. Also, it's rigidly establishmentarian in other respects. But the various features of the society seem to get along pretty well and that's all that I think I can ask for or hope for.

TS: So now we find ourselves here in New Orleans in mid-July 2002. I arrived on the 10th of July, Alice Munro's seventy-first birthday as a matter of fact. This is a city that I had never visited before and a city that you ...

CB: I've never been here before either. It's the largest city in North America that I had never seen. And I had never even been to Louisiana, strangely enough. This is the forty-ninth state that I've visited. Next month, in August, we do Mississippi. And that will be the fiftieth state.

TS: Wow. [Laughter.]

CB: For someone with Francophonic and Francophilic tendencies, it's very strange that I would have waited this long to get to New Orleans. But it was strange that I had waited so long to get to San Francisco, too. I mean, these are two hot destinations for an American and you would think I would have hit them earlier. I've still only been to Los Angeles maybe for one day in my life. I came down in the morning, spent an afternoon, and left in the evening. There are still some places that I'm not terribly familiar with.

TS: But isn't there some sense in which we have already visited certain places before we go there?

CB: Well, for someone like me, who is a Faulkner addict,

Mississippi and Louisiana are not at all strange concepts. I mean, the historical concept is very deeply impressed in me. And of course I've done a lot of research on the Acadian expulsion and *Evangeline* and Acadia in general. When I read through *The Times-Picayune*, the newspaper here, and I read the obituary pages, I see fully eighty per cent of the obits have French names. Even names that in this generation were Williams or something else like that, when they talk about the parents they're Duchesnes or Leblancs or whatever it may be. So if the individuals are not familiar to me, the names are at least reassuring in some way. It feels as if the footprints of ancestors are around. And the big ancestor is Faulkner.

In fact, I've written about Louisiana — in an essay I did for Ishmael Reed's on-line magazine, *Konch* — about how the only successful bilingual, biracial societies that were ever constructed in North America were in fact Louis Riel's Manitoba and the Creole world of Louisiana. Both of course were doomed, but ...

TS: From time to time I teach a course focussing on three different cultural sites, largely emphasizing three different periods of time, three different literary renaissances: beginning with Ireland with Yeats and Joyce early in the twentieth century — though I like to put Joyce together with Edna O'Brien, *Dubliners* with *Mother Ireland* — followed by the American South from the twenties to the sixties, focussing on Faulkner and Welty and O'Connor, and then contemporary Canadian writing, including work by Hugh Hood, Alice Munro, and yourself.

Two nights ago here in New Orleans, you and I attended a reception at Faulkner House Books, over in the French Quarter, on Pirates Alley ...

CB: Where they say that they can smell his pipe on a night in which a Faulkner celebration is coming. The owner says she smells the pipe. None of them smokes and yet the pipe smell is strong.

TS: The owner — that's Elizabeth, right?

CB: Yes.

TS: And her bookstore is housed in the building where Faulkner wrote his first novel, *Soldiers' Pay*.

CB: *Soldiers' Pay*. Right.

TS: My way of orienting myself for this trip was to pick up a couple of guidebooks. Of course, the first section I turn to in guidebooks to places I'm travelling to is the list of local bookstores. And I cannot adequately express my delight at discovering the listing for Faulkner House Books. I knew that if there was only one thing I was able to do outside of this hotel during this conference, it was to visit that store. And so I actually got over there the night before the reception, after closing as it turned out, just to orient myself, and then returned the next night.

But speaking of orienting oneself: If someone who didn't know where San Francisco is located asked you "Where's San Francisco?", how would you answer?

CB: Well, apart from the simple geography of it all, you could say it's at a confluence of the Pacific Rim. It's the focal point of Pacific immigration, of Asian immigration, to the United States without the same mix of Latino and Black admixtures that you have, say, in Los Angeles. Los Angeles is a more cosmopolitan place in some ways, in terms of its ethnic mixes. San Francisco is a little bit more fifty/fifty Asian/Anglo or Asian/non-Black. It's a city with no ethnic dominance, with no racial dominance. I think just about everyone is a forty/forty/twenty split, Asian/White/Latino. It's a city with a long history — by California standards, going back to the Gold Rush — of this form of curious integration, unique in the American experience at that time.

The constant trembling of the earth is a phenomenon that puts a point on one's contemplativeness. This is not the kind of place that you can retire to with the safe assurance that your house is going to be there tomorrow. If you get too rambunctious in that landscape, you've got fires to deal with, you've got mudslides to deal with, you've got floods to deal with, you've got drought to deal with. If you move twenty miles east of the city, you can go up forty or fifty degrees in temperature in a day. A person just in a simple commute from the eastern suburbs to downtown San Francisco will pass through maybe a fifty-degree range of temperature.
TS: And if someone who hadn't been to New Orleans asked you "Where's New Orleans?", what would you reply?
CB: I would say it's at the mouth of the Mississippi. It's where, again, a lot of rogue elements came together in American culture: slave, slave-holder, French, Creole, Spanish, Anglo, Confederate, corporate, and buccaneer all came together. And it has got such a long tradition of institutionalized corruption in its politics. There is an easy tolerance for most of that.

Both San Francisco and New Orleans are cutting-edge in certain ways in terms of social mores. San Francisco with its gay population and its open tolerance — in fact, almost encouragement — of the gay community, and with its leftward-leaning politics, is one thing. New Orleans with its Creole and Cajun populations and its biracial tolerances — they weren't always that way, this was a terribly segregated city at one time — nevertheless has kind of an easy racial adjustment. Racial accommodations are, I think, more visible here than elsewhere.

But it doesn't have the aspiring Black managerial middle class, say, that Atlanta does. It doesn't have the history of educated, politically integrated Blacks that Washington, D.C. has. It has, however, a kind of joint poverty, shared between the White and the Black. The classes are not racially divided as they are in Atlanta and Washington, D.C.

TS: When I was getting ready to leave Guelph for New Orleans, I told my wife, Marianne Micros, and our two daughters, Eleni and Joy, "It's an hour earlier than here." So it's a little past noon right now in Guelph.

CB: Well, if it's 11:15 here, it's 9:15 in San Francisco.

TS: That way of orienting oneself wouldn't have been possible except for the thinking done by the man, Sandford Fleming, whom you made the subject of your 2000 nonfiction book, *Time Lord*.

CB: Well, it's interesting about the Mississippi River. It's such a natural divider in the American imagination of the West and the East — such a centre, although it's slightly more eastern than western. There was a general consensus that there should be two time zones: there should be east of the Mississippi and west of the Mississippi. And west of the Mississippi was just a vague concept to most Americans in the middle part of the nineteenth century. But as the railroads developed and certainly after the Civil War and of course also with the earlier experience of the Gold Rush, the Pacific west had a place in the eastern imagination, but not the intermountain west and not the Great Plains. They were still sort of forbidding areas of buffalo herds and recalcitrant Indians and all that.

The Mississippi does chart a kind of unifying force, temporally. That is, St. Louis and New Orleans are on exactly the same ninetieth degree of longitude. So if you went up the Mississippi south to north, you didn't gain or lose even a minute. All the way up to Minneapolis you kept a fairly straight course. Solar time — you know, sundial time — was based on longitude. And so long as the Mississippi River charted the same longitude it seemed like it was a way of combining science and the Bible. The Mississippi did both for you, so that you could be one hour ahead, east of the Mississippi, one hour behind, west of it. And the Mississippi was as sharp a division as if you had drawn it with a straightedge or a ruler.

The obvious observation of Fleming, and others who were allied with him, was, "It's not enough. Two divisions of North America are not enough. You have to have a principle by which you divide the whole world." And this is where Fleming departed from all other standard time advocates in North America — in that he said North America is not enough, North America is part of the world, it doesn't end at the two coasts. And as part of the world, North America has to adjust to a Prime Meridian, wherever we decide to put it. It doesn't have to be Greenwich. But wherever we decide to put it, you start dividing the world into twenty-four zones from *there*. And then North America obviously becomes a four- or five- or maybe even five-and-a-half-zoned continent. And if you add Alaska, Hawaii, and the Aleutian Islands, you have nine or nine and a half zones for North America.

TS: Recognizing that North America has to be seen as part of the world isn't an observation that the author of a first story collection called *A North American Education* and a later story collection called *Man and His World* would find disconcerting.

CB: No, not at all. That's why Fleming was such an appealing figure to me. Even his allies, even people who counted themselves as Victorian progressives, didn't really think beyond the box — beyond the geographical box either of Great Britain or of the United States — as he did. I think it's largely because he was a Canadian, and therefore not perceived to have a particular geographical bias, or not perceived to have any strength to enforce it even if he did. He was a citizen of the British Empire, not a citizen of Canada — there was really no Canadian citizenship as such. He was part of a British Empire that was both boundless and represented in all twenty-four time zones with equal force. But at the same time he was rather sharply critical of the English part of the British Empire. England was never a particular favourite for him. He was a Scotsman. And he liked that, above all else.

TS: One of the topics discussed at this short story conference has been genre — and genre slippage. I was wondering, therefore, in terms of genre, how you would characterize *Time Lord*?

CB: I would call it "history of ideas." When I find it in bookstores in the science section, I think that's doing a disservice to science or a disservice to the book, because it's not science as such, it's history of ideas.

TS: Does meta-something begin to enter into it?

CB: Something about itself? No, I don't think so. I don't see it. And even though it won a couple of prizes as biography, I don't see it as a strict biography. In fact, I chose not to write it as a biography of a great Victorian, of an unknown Victorian, in which I would be tracking down every hint or sniff of indiscretion on his part. In writing that book, I was always driven by the idea of a man trying to bring about a revolutionary change that was essential to the unleashing of modernism — of the modernist spirit. It was both a reflection of those energies that were already in the air and a culmination in some ways of implications that could be drawn from many, many sources. So that was what I was trying to do. And to convey his personality. This would not have happened without his particular kind of personality and his particular kind of energy, confidence, and contacts. He would have been perceived as being too much the creature of the Greenwich advocates or the American advocates or whatever it may be. The Americans realized they couldn't bring it about and the Brits resisted trying to bring it about and the French of course dug in their heels about it. So you had to have someone who was a perceived neutral but who at the same time had extraordinary contacts and vision and energy. And that was Fleming.

TS: A striking quality in the book that I should have expected but that I still didn't expect — and therefore it both surprised and delighted me — was the strong autobiographical component to it, especially in the book's superb brief afterword, "The Ghost of Sandford Fleming." Not unrelated to that point, I would say, this afternoon I'll be presenting a condensed version of a new creative/critical essay entitled "Imagining Alice Munro's 'Meneseteung': The Dynamics of Co-Creation." That story is the only Canadian one included in *The Best American Short Stories of the Century*. [Laughter.] And it's a story that is not only part biography of a fictional character, the late-nineteenth-century Southwestern Ontario poetess whom Munro names Almeda Joynt Roth, but also, for the story's narrator and in some respects for its author, a veiled or perhaps not-so-veiled autobiography.

I was also wondering: If you were to put a few books together on a shelf with *Time Lord*, are there any that you think would be especially interesting to consider alongside it?

CB: Well, I think Michael Ondaatje's novel *In the Skin of a Lion* would be a strong parallel in some strange way, because they're both about the creation of a country and they're both about fascinations with words that create a country. The idea of an adolescent boy who is an accidental witness to a procession going past at the beginning of *In the Skin of a Lion*, or of the lumbermen going and touching the cattle as the cattle are coming in, belongs almost in Keats. Each of those is a *Time Lord*-ish kind of moment. And a young Sandford Fleming, still in Scotland, sketching castles and sketching roller skates and sketching batteries and sketching ideas for inventions that he had no money and no capital investment to experiment with — they were pure concepts of inventions that could not even be given a prototype spin.

I'm moved, always, by the idea of persons imprisoned by geography, or imprisoned just by chance, in a place that is as remote and as untouched by supposedly great events and centres of cosmopolitan thought. So on your own you have to fashion some sort of communion with the larger world. In the same year that Fleming devised standard time, the two greatest novels in the English language of that particular kind of thwarted or maybe even successful communion were written. They're still the greatest young adult novels ever written. Robert Louis Stevenson's *Treasure Island* and Mark Twain's *Huckleberry Finn*. They came out at exactly the same time and they are based on exactly the same thing. The avid child stumbling into an adult conspiracy. Either at the Admiral Benbow or listening to the fact that Jim is about to be sold and lighting out. There's a continuum there that strikes me as part of the great central myth of people from far away forcing themselves into the centre — the enduring centre of consciousness for the rest of us.

TS: That experience of the child, the adolescent, the adult is something we perceive both in the first volume, *Southern Stories*, of your ongoing *Selected Stories*, and in the second volume, *Pittsburgh Stories*. I would very much like to ask you about the way your conception of this continuing series, this group of story collections, evolved.

CB: John Metcalf wanted to have all my stories, or a selection of all my stories, kept in print, because they were all out of print, there was no way you could get any of them. The question was either to reprint the original books as they were or to find some other way of bringing them together. It was my idea to say that all my work falls within four geographical boundaries. As I've always said, geography is fate, geography is destiny. And it has always been a strong determinant in my life. That's why I say I don't think I will ever write San Francisco. I don't think I can enter it. It's scar tissue. It's sealed over.

TS: So the four centres ...

CB: The four centres. Well, there's the South. And Pittsburgh. And then Montreal or Quebec is the next one. I've just finished two new stories to go into that collection. But we'll have to cut back on that because there are many more Montreal stories than there are anything else. And then the fourth one will be the international stories. Largely Indian. But *If I Were Me* will be reprinted in there, more or less in its entirety. And one or two more stories that I had dropped from the original publication of *If I Were Me* will probably be included. That's the area in which I'm still working most. I'm working in stories that are set everywhere in the world now, with less inhibition than when I forced myself to go back to write Montreal and Pittsburgh and Southern stories. I'm looking forward in fact, probably next year, to writing some more international stories.

TS: You say that you have just finished two new Montreal stories. What are they called?

CB: One is called "Life Could Be a Dream (Sh-boom, Sh-boom)" and the other one is called "The Belle of Shediac."

TS: Something quite unique about this project, it seems to me, is that it represents an opportunity for you to do different kinds of things. For starters, you get to gather up previously uncollected stories that provide very strong material for each new volume. For example, "A Fish Like a Buzzard" — the opening story of *Southern Stories* and of the series — is, I think, vintage Clark Blaise.

CB: I wrote it when I was an undergraduate.

TS: And published it in a magazine...?

CB: In a tiny tiny little campus magazine.

TS: Do you remember the title of the magazine?

CB Oh, yes. It was called *Silo*, published at Bennington College.

TS: S-i-l-o? That sounds like a good agricultural metaphor. [Laughter.]

CB: I don't know why they called it that, because Bennington's hardly agricultural. The reason why it happened was that Bernard Malamud, my teacher at Harvard the summer before, had read the story and loved it. So when he went to Bennington to be a teacher and this young undergraduate — Nina Pelikan was her name — wanted to start this magazine, she asked Bern if he knew of any stories and Bern suggested that. She also got a poem out of Howard Nemerov. So she had a good start.

It was my first publication. I had written it in 1960 and it came out in 1962. Nina Pelikan became a famous person. She went on and married Roger Straus of Farrar, Straus and Giroux and they had a daughter named Tamara. Tamara Straus. And Tamara is now the editor of *Zoetrope* magazine in San Francisco, the magazine that Frances Ford Coppola brings out. And she is sitting right now on a copy of "Life Could Be a Dream (Sh-boom, Sh-boom)." And if Tamara brings that story out it would be a very strange forty-year spell in which mother and daughter were both editors of the same writer.

TS: Wonderful.

CB: She may say no, in which case the story would end. But it's very strange.

TS: I think the story is going to last. [Laughter.]

So it seems to me that in gathering together in this new series of yours important earlier uncollected work, in making selections for it of important already collected work, in reassembling those pieces, deciding on the order in which they will now be placed — all of this is tremendously exciting, tremendously significant. And I'm not sure that I can think of anyone else who has done that with a series like this.

CB: That's your kind of work, Tim. I just want to get them out. I do pay some attention to the order. They're not strictly chronological. In fact, in some cases I can't even sort out which ones were written exactly in what order. But to find excitement in the process you're describing, and to see it as something worthy of discussion or worthy of note, is exactly where my interest in it leaves off and yours continues or maybe even starts.

It's something that I saw rather brief notice of, in *The Toronto Star*, by Phil Marchand on the publication of *Pittsburgh Stories*, where he lamented the fact that by putting all of these stories together in one book you saw how similar they were and how sort of unadventurous and repetitive I could be. So there you go. It has, I guess, its upside and its downside.

I think it does perhaps force a reader into more creative acts of discrimination — a closer reading perhaps — in order to find the movements or the changes or the variations that are in them. But of course you run the risk of someone saying that all of his characters are horny adolescents or something else like that. What an overall, overarching view might say is that the author of these forty or fifty stories, when you take them all together, was a child in the South, an adolescent in Pittsburgh, an adult in Quebec, and an old man in the world. And that the stories represent four phases of a man's life. And that he is trying to be as scrupulous and honest and recollective as he possibly can be to do justice to the stages of his life and to the places that formed him.

TS: Could these four collections, as you envisage them, be regarded either as four quadrants on a map or as four sections of a mandala?

CB: Probably the latter more than the former. The South, Pittsburgh, Montreal, India are certainly quadrants on a map. But I would hope that the treatment of them would tend more to myth than to geography.

TS: I was speaking metaphorically, yes. Or as you say, mythically.

CB: So it's the myth of Pittsburgh, the myth of the South. See, I can't enter the New South. It repulses me anyway: the New South with its George Wallace-like politics cleaned up to look like Trent Lott politics. The New Republican South is, to me, even more hideous than the Old lynching segregated South of the Democrats. In other words, I sort of carry on a Faulknerian battle with the South in the sense that they still haven't come to grips with their original sin. However they try to pretty it up, they still haven't made the proper amends. It's like a Jew looking at modern Germany and saying, "Yes, you've done everything that you possibly can, you've paid as many reparations, you are unfailingly a friend of Israel, but still, deep in your dark heart, I'm sure you harbour things." It's that unforgiving quality that the writer has to keep mustering, it seems to me, to be successful or to come to grips mythically with a place. If you are reconciled totally with a place, then there's no need to write about it.

TS: And the metaphor or the analogy of the four sections of a mandala?

CB: To me, take any one of those out of the equation that made me and I wouldn't be a writer. Had I not had a Pittsburgh adolescence, with all the curious anachronisms and anomalies that Pittsburgh represents, I don't think I would have been able to have gotten through my adolescence. By that I mean it was an ideal place for me — with its inherited nineteenth-century institutions: museum, library, observatory. It gave scope to all the inchoate ambitions that I had. And at the same time it was sufficiently off the beaten track, kind of a joke to the rest of the country, so that I could take it seriously. If I had been in New York, I would have been overwhelmed. If I had been in just about any other large city, I probably would not have been able to survive the competition. But Pittsburgh was just about my speed. And I honour Pittsburgh. I like Pittsburgh very, very much.

The new Pittsburgh with its gleaming corporate headquarters and its closing down of the steel mills and its now tarted-up downtown, and its Andy Warhol Museum — I prefer the Andy Warhol who had to get out of Pittsburgh, who was hounded out of Pittsburgh, that's the Pittsburgh I like. I like the grime of it and the dirt of it and the squalor of it. And I liked the losing teams. The Steelers were terrible. The Pirates were terrible. Once they all became go-go franchises, I lost heart.

TS: Do you have working titles for the next two volumes of stories?

CB: Just *Montreal Stories* — or perhaps it will be *Quebec Stories* because there are some rural Quebec stories that are outside of Montreal. But they are all French-derived or French-influenced. The other one I might call *International Stories*. But I should probably come up with something else.

TS: It could be argued, I think, that we might read story collections in time, but conceive of them in space. In saying that, I suspect I'm echoing a view expressed by Northrop Frye in one place or another. But to pose a different question: I wonder if you have in mind an overarching title for all four collections?

CB: Well, my idea for all four was *Brief Parables of the Twentieth Century*.

TS: How appropriate. How resonant.

Learning To Read, Learning To Write: An Interview with Clark Blaise [2007]

J.R. (Tim) Struthers

TS: I would like to explore what you have learned over the years about the short story theoretically and practically speaking — from your own early writing teachers, from reading, from writing, from conversation and reflection — and consequently what you have chosen to pass on to others. By the time you completed your MFA in the Writers' Workshop at the University of Iowa in 1964 at age twenty-four, you had already experienced the benefits of working with a variety of important writing teachers and mentors. Beginning in your undergraduate days at Denison University in Granville, Ohio, with writing courses taught by Paul Bennett, for whose final collection of poems, *Appalachian Mettle*, you would later write an introductory tribute. Followed, immediately after graduating from Denison, by a very influential writing workshop conducted at Harvard in the summer of 1961 by Bernard Malamud, whose instruction and support you have gratefully acknowledged in a number of places, among them "The Voice of Unhousement," the opening segment of *Resident Alien*, as well as your superb essay "Mentors." And then, several months after working with Malamud when you were still just twenty-one, by the opportunity to study for the next two years with other stimulating teachers of writing and literature at the University of Iowa while enrolled in the Writers' Workshop, including the composition of your MFA thesis, "Thibidault et fils," supervised by Philip Roth.

CB: The teachers I had were admirable people, generally. Not Roth, though there were others at Iowa who were, like John Clellon Holmes, Kurt Vonnegut, etc. They were mentors, as you've noted, but their teaching-touch was very light. They said in effect, "You've got talent, just trust it, and I'll be here if I think you're abusing it in some way."

TS: Of course the writers to whom we give the most careful attention in our reading serve as important teachers, too. Are there particular writers you've known or read whose works you would say have the most to teach?

CB: I think, and it's hardly original now, that Alice Munro offers the most for any writer to learn from. You can learn from her the way you can from Chekhov or Joyce or Hemingway — they inspire a certain desire to fall in line with her. You can't say that of Mavis Gallant, who is *sui generis*, or Malamud.

TS: Still, I'm certain you would agree that Malamud and Gallant deserve special accolades as well. There are qualities in the works of each that I have no doubt touched, and very likely helped to shape, the core of your being as a writer.

CB: All that I meant, in an informal way, is that there are writers who inspire you to imitation, and others who inspire you to admiration. It's not a question of greater or lesser achievement, merely that there are those who knock you over but announce at the same time "Don't even try it." Writers like Hemingway, and Ray Carver, inspire actual imitative competitions. But no one can imitate Malamud or Gallant. And many others — Beckett, Kafka, Borges, etc.

TS: To proceed to an example of how you have approached teaching writing ... "Drama and Poetry in the Short Story" is the title you gave to a week-long course that you ran in September 2004 as part of the annual writers' workshop organized by *Zoetrope: All-Story* magazine at film director Francis Ford Coppola's lodge in Belize. Decades earlier, during the summer writing workshop that you took with Bernard Malamud, he likewise gave special attention to the importance of "dramatization" in fiction. As you recall approvingly in your essay "The Justice-Dealing Machine" first published in Maurice A. Lee's collection *Writers on Writing: The Art of the Short Story,* the description of the short story offered by Malamud one day in class was "the dramatization of the multifarious adventures of the human heart." And in the course outline for your own writing workshop on "Drama and Poetry in the Short Story," you direct attention specifically to what you call "dramatic standards," including the creation of an effect, in readers' literary experience of narrative time, close to our everyday experience of actual time.

The subject of "lyricism" in fiction has received rightful attention, too, beginning at least as early as Eileen Baldeshwiler's classic essay "The Lyric Short Story: The Sketch of a History," first published in the journal *Studies in Short Fiction* and then reproduced in Charles E. May's anthologies *Short Story Theories* and *The New Short Story Theories.* Certainly, single defining images — and as you know, Alice Munro actually calls one story in her first book "Images" — can serve an essential function in short story writing and in related forms such as "the prose poem" or "the vignette" or "short shorts" or "postcard stories" or "flash fiction." And throughout your own story writing from the title piece of your first full collection, *A North American Education*, to "Meditations on Starch" in *Man and His World*, to "Migraine Morning" in *World Body*, you in effect call attention to the crucial role that lyrical devices such as image patterns and/or key images can play in the short story.

The very title of your writing workshop in September 2004 in Belize, "Drama and Poetry in the Short Story," immediately gets people thinking about the functioning of much more than narrativity in the short story. Here I'll briefly interject that "theatricality," "narrativity," and "lyricism" are three terms that to me seem very useful for describing the rich mixture of qualities working in the short story. Say, for example, in the title piece of *A North American Education* or in Alice Munro's "Royal Beatings," the first story published by her in *The New Yorker* and the story chosen to begin the Everyman's Library selection of her stories, *Carried Away*. Therefore I'm wondering if you would elaborate a little on your own sense of these qualities of the short story.

CB: In my essay "The Craft of the Short Story" — originally in *Proteus*, but later reprinted in *The Southampton Review* and then in *Canadian Notes & Queries* — I locate the story somewhere on the tree of utterance where poetry and drama in some way intersect. I think of the story as an expanded moment, not a contracted one, therefore the role of drama is somewhat diminished. Drama is a succession of encounters, generally. But I'm not particularly interested in laying down laws of composition, for they will vary according to the author and according to the author's desired effects.

TS: In connection with the elements that play a part in

the creation of what Eileen Baldeshwiler has termed "The Lyric Short Story," a tradition that I believe is extended and enhanced by writers like Alice Munro and yourself, may I ask you to give some examples of poets whose work has impressed you, has reached you, at one time or another?

CB: It should be predictable that Keats was a favourite, and Yeats, and, in my later years, Whitman. I'm not at all an addicted reader of poets, nor do I feel inferior to them.

TS: Keats's "Ode on a Grecian Urn," yes, definitely. The embodiment in that poem's form and technique and style of the idea of the frozen moment or frozen motion. The significance of that method for Faulkner, one of your great influences, in his novel *Light in August*, his story cycle *Go Down, Moses*, and so forth. This moment in turn has served as a stimulus for you, in your reflections on time and your work with the short story form.

In the case of Yeats, we might cite "Coole and Ballylee, 1931": his proud, sad, arresting statement that "We were the last Romantics...." I've always relished the irony conveyed there, indeed made possible there, as in many of your stories, by the not so simple use of the simple past tense.

And certainly Whitman's "When I Heard the Learn'd Astronomer," from which you quote a few lines in *Time Lord*, your study of Sandford Fleming and the idea of standard time.

Furthermore, your overall purpose of making each work that you write "forever fresh" or "forever fertile," as you remark in "The Voice of Unhousement" in *Resident Alien*, is an aim that evokes Whitman. And I would infer that the point of your comment about not feeling inferior to poets is that freshness and fertility are definitely qualities attainable as much through the construction of one good sentence of prose then another as through the construction of one good line of verse then another.

Indeed, the following pair of lines from Whitman's "Song of Myself" might well serve to capture the heart of your own accomplishments, especially your individual enrichment of the tradition of the short story: "In me the caresser of life wherever moving ... backward as well as forward slueing / To niches aside and junior bending."

Perhaps the artistry of each line of a poem, because it possesses the form of verse rather than prose, is more readily discernible to the eye and hence to the mind than the artistry of each sentence of a short story. Of course this is not to say that one of these is better than the other, for the ease with which readers comprehend a work is in itself no indication of its quality.

More importantly, I believe the craft of a short story is just as discernible to the ear and thus to the mind as the craft of a poem. In order to understand a short story on the printed page — just as when we are reading music — we must therefore look closely and listen intensely, at the same time.

But to move on to the two writers — poets in prose, one might say — whose stories you asked the members of your writing workshop in Belize to consider most fully ... What do you think a story writer like Ernest Hemingway was intent on accomplishing formally, technically, stylistically — say in his story cycle *In Our Time*, since that was the book you listed by him in the "Suggested Readings" for that workshop? And what about Alice Munro — say in her story cycle *The Beggar Maid*, originally published in Canada, as you are well aware, under the more complex not to mention feisty title *Who Do You Think You Are?*, or her later collection

The Love of a Good Woman, since those were the options you listed by her?

CB: I think that the story is most beholden to energy, and most of the techniques employed by writers over the years have been calculated to jolt up the energy level. Certainly that's what Hemingway did, cutting out the fat, chopping down the backstories, the motivations, etc. That's basically all there is to it; Alice has jolted the story in different ways — by flooding the narrative with competing closures, among many other things.

TS: To expand our discussion here to some broader insights of yours about the history and the possibilities of the short story form, I would like to reproduce at this point, as if it were a direct answer from you, the characteristically perceptive course description which you prepared for your writing workshop on "Drama and Poetry in the Short Story" and which you recently forwarded to me.

CB: The "classic" short story is a marvel of unified effect: it elapses (or collapses) in "real time" in a single setting, with a constricted set of characters. Think of many early Hemingway stories ("Cat in the Rain," "Soldier's Home," "Hills Like White Elephants," and "A Clean, Well-Lighted Place") as familiar models. The same can be said of Raymond Carver, Joy Williams, Updike (his famous "A&P" and dozens of others), Chekhov, Joyce ("Ivy Day in the Committee Room"). Even Thomas Mann, known for his expansive novels and orchestral novellas, holds fast to convention with "Disorder and Early Sorrow." While the action of Cheever's "The Swimmer" occurs over several hours — and can be read in about forty minutes — it's a near-"real time" experience (as is Carver's "Cathedral" or Flannery O'Connor's "A Good Man Is Hard To Find"). It's good to keep these dramatic standards in mind when we're tempted to stray too far from them and turn the story into a kind of novelistic, leisurely narrative, a fictionalized memoir, or a lyrical, poetic experience.

Thinking about the unforgiving form of the classic story allows us to appreciate certain contemporary deviations from it. Alice Munro stands at the centre of the modern rebellion (although she's the most "conventional" of stylists and hardly a bomb-thrower in anything but story form); her stories introduce numerous, competing plot-lines, "end" many times in a thematic sense before they end narratively. The same can be said of many Ann Beattie stories; they are dramatically "loose," they find their unities elsewhere. Let's find them, and see which model of story works better for our time and our needs.

So, the major aspect of this course will be the study of the "single effect" story, using Hemingway's *In Our Time* and other stories mentioned above, including a couple of mine, contrasted with unconventional forms, as represented by Beattie, Munro, and others.

TS: Immediately following this course description, and directly before your "Suggested Readings," you provided a summary of the imaginative and personal challenge faced that week and, I would suggest, thereafter. "The critical question is: At what cost do we adhere to convention, and for what advantage do we stray?" That would bear considerable contemplation.

But let us move on to certain specifics that you would have discussed during the workshop. In your brief essay "To Begin, To Begin" first published in 1972 alongside your stories "A North American Education" and "Eyes" in John Metcalf's anthology *The Narrative Voice*, you state that "The most interesting thing about a story is not its climax or its dénouement—both dated terms — nor even its style and characterization. It is its beginning, its first paragraph, often its first sentence." Further, you explain, "the story seeks its beginning, the story many times *is* its beginning, amplified." And of the first sentence in each story you remark: "It is an act of perfect rhythmic balance, the single crisp gesture, the drop of the baton that gathers a hundred disparate forces into a single note."

I would therefore like to ask — starting with Ernest Hemingway because he is the earlier of the two story writers highlighted in your "Suggested Readings" for the workshop — if I could obtain your responses to some story openings by him. Say to the first sentence of each of the three stories Hemingway included in his first book, *Three Stories & Ten Poems*: "Up in Michigan" and "Out of Season" and "My Old Man," the second and third of which he also included in the volume by him named in your "Suggested Readings," *In Our Time*. Here are the sentences ...

From "Up in Michigan," identified by Hemingway in his preface to *The Fifth Column and the First Forty-Nine Stories* as the first story he wrote: "Jim Gilmore came to Hortons Bay from Canada."

From "Out of Season": "On the four lire Peduzzi had earned by spading the hotel garden he got quite drunk."

And from "My Old Man," a title that for you I'm sure has a magnetic effect: "I guess looking at it, now, my old man was cut out for a fat guy, one of those regular little roly fat guys you see around, but he sure never got that way, except a little toward the last, and then it wasn't his fault, he was riding over the jumps only and he could afford to carry plenty of weight then."

Could you comment on what registers most powerfully for you in these three first sentences or in any other favourite openings from Hemingway's stories?

CB: One of my favourite Hemingway beginnings is from "Cat in the Rain" and I think I used it in Belize. I called attention to the first paragraph in "Cat in the Rain," showing how much information was imparted with so very few commas to interfere. It is comparable in its informational overload to Alice's "Walker Brothers Cowboy" or Mavis's "An Autobiography."

TS: I find it odd that such a fine story as "An Autobiography," which you and John Metcalf had selected for your landmark 1977 anthology *Here & Now: Best Canadian Stories*, and which John and I had subsequently reproduced, along with a second Gallant story, "Irina," in our anthology *Canadian Classics*, was not one of the fifty-two works chosen in 1996 for the nearly nine-hundred-page *The Selected Stories of Mavis Gallant*, or, as the American edition was called, *The Collected Stories of Mavis Gallant*. Maybe "An Autobiography" didn't seem to fit within any of the categories into which it was decided to divide that volume. And after all, Gallant has published over a hundred stories.

But to continue with Hemingway, I can't help but think a life-long border-crosser like you would be greatly intrigued by the opening line from "Up in Michigan" involving Canada.

CB: I've always been attracted to versions of North America that include the whole continent. My beloved uncle, Ed Russenholt, a former CBC weatherman in Winnipeg — look up his book, *The Heart of the Continent* — played in a cross-border sandlot baseball league that led him from his native Estevan down to Montana and North Dakota. Ross Macdonald, an old Canadian, appeals to me — Winnipeg figures at one point in his early work. Kenneth Millar was his real name, and he too had a working-writer wife, Margaret Millar. Faulkner

— with Shreve McCannon, the Alberta-Harvard room-mate of Quentin Compson — appeals to me. Alberta in 1910, at Harvard! What is he trying to say? I've always been geographically sensitive, if not acute, a fact that you, doubtless, can document. So, Hemingway's interest in "the North," or Canada, is interesting to me because it represents the first instance of his own form of inter-nationalism: Cuba, Europe, Africa, etc. It might also be mine — i.e., American borders do not represent the end of diverse characterization.

TS: Could you tell me what strikes you about the open-ing line from "Out of Season" in terms of Hemingway's approach or technique as seen or heard there, the syn-tax or phrasing or choice of particular words, your sense of what's stated or unstated there, the line's impact?

CB: In the sentence you've isolated, the clear Heming-way voice is in "quite." This would be a Wayne Booth type observation. Who is interjecting that little adver-bial modifier? The author of course, and so a plane of irony is introduced, a plane from which the action un-folds. There are two Hemingways: one that is pure, one that sneers or at least mocks and bullies. Think of "Mr. and Mrs. Elliot."

TS: And what about the opening line from "My Old Man" — or whatever stands out personally for you in that story?

CB: Actually, it's the last line in "My Old Man" that ap-peals to me even more. "Seems like once they get start-ed they don't leave a guy nothing." I repeat it to myself frequently and feel better for it.

TS: Because the other story writer highlighted in your "Suggested Readings" for the workshop was Alice Munro, I would also like to direct attention to some story open-ings by her. Say to the first sentence of each of the first three stories in her first book, *Dance of the Happy Shades*: "Walker Brothers Cowboy" and "The Shining Houses" and "Images." I'll reproduce the sentences, then add a brief question that I hope will allow you to say something comparable to your comments about Hemingway.

From "Walker Brothers Cowboy": "After supper my father says, 'Want to go down and see if the Lake's still there?'"

From "The Shining Houses": "Mary sat on the back steps of Mrs. Fullerton's house, talking — or really listening — to Mrs. Fullerton, who sold her eggs."

From "Images": "Now that Mary McQuade had come, I pretended not to remember her."

Could you comment on what registers most powerfully for you in these three first sentences or in any other favourite openings from Munro's stories?

CB: I've done long riffs on the first paragraph of "Walker Brothers Cowboy." It is a model of nuance and insinuation.

TS: And can you name a particular Alice Munro story where you have found the ending to be of special force or interest for you?

CB: I don't think of Alice as having striking endings; as I've said, she proliferates her closings so that they tend to say — to me, at least — this one is as good as any other one. That makes its own philosophical point, the one I think she's driving at in all her writing, a balance of equivalences.

TS: To complete the course outline for your writing workshop on "Drama and Poetry in the Short Story," under the heading "Suggested Readings," you began by recommending Hemingway's *In Our Time* and either Munro's *The Beggar Maid* — known in Canada, I mentioned, as *Who Do You Think You Are?* — or her *The Love of a Good Woman.* You also asked the workshop to read a couple of stories and four essays of your own that you don't name on the outline — the four essays presumably including your recent essay "The Craft of the Short Story" along with the three brief essays by you — "To Begin, To Begin," "The Cast and the Mold," and "On Ending Stories" — collected in *How Stories Mean*, the book co-edited by John Metcalf and myself that you listed next. Of *How Stories Mean* you observed, not a little wryly, "This is a collection of essays on the art of the story, written by practitioners. (The fact that all of them happen to be Canadian should not be daunting.)" Finally, at the bottom of the "Suggested Readings," you noted almost as an afterthought though this remark in fact resonates powerfully: "It would be beneficial for anyone to read the annual *Best American Short Stories* volumes, and to have as a matter of shared knowledge the works of Chekhov, Carver, O'Connor, Cheever, Oates, Babel, Updike, and dozens more."

No doubt, given your close attention lately to Nathaniel Hawthorne, you would now add his name to such a list. For myself, as a means of acknowledging the profound importance both professionally and personally of the teacher and scholar who has encouraged so many men and women of successive generations to recognize the significance of Hawthorne's stories in particular and the power of the short story form in general, the teacher and scholar honoured by the volume *Creative and Critical Approaches to the Short Story* edited by Noel Harold Kaylor, Jr., it pleases me greatly here to mention another name, Dr. Mary Rohrberger. With admiration and with gratitude, you and I and numerous other writers or critics speak of the vision, enthusiasm, leadership, understanding, and warmth Mary brought in recent years to planning and hosting several Society for the Study of the Short Story international conferences and to founding and editing the creative/critical journal *Short Story*. But decades earlier, in 1966, there she was as well, publishing her pioneering book called *Hawthorne and the Modern Short Story*.

CB: I would be interested in reading Mary's book, since that's where my recent reading, and inclinations, have led me.

TS: I have a line on an extra copy and was wondering who would most appreciate it. I should have known the answer; so consider this done.

To continue discussing the short story, I would like to mention an idea of mine about the function of all the man-made or natural containers I've noticed you and Alice Munro and others using as settings, as devices, in your stories ... Public spaces or institutions or buildings, commercial properties or stores or offices; personal dwellings such as houses, cottages, trailers, shacks, apartments, hotel rooms, hospital rooms; occasions and places of ceremonial gatherings; wherever people are born, live, mourn, die; secret niches and hiding-places. Spaceships and airplanes, boats, trains, buses, trucks, cars, wagons, motorcycles, bicycles, wheelchairs and baby-strollers; marches and parades and walks on the sidewalk, through the dirt, through fields, into swamp-scapes; drawn-out moments on bridges, dramatic moments on beaches. All the inland waterways and lakes, river systems and canals, declivities and holes, underground caverns, which in being explored grow more, not less, mysteriously potent with meaning. Aren't these containers actually a means of reinforcing the concentrated nature of the short story and thus a means of making possible the powerful effects it so brilliantly achieves?

I'm thinking, for example, of the frogboat that the two young brothers, Escal and Foley, occupy on their gar hunt right up to the last dramatic scene of "A Fish like a Buzzard," the opening story of *Southern Stories*, and also the final room, known as the Court Room, of the underground caverns visited by Frankie Thibidault in "Giant Turtles Gliding in the Dark," the second story in that volume. Or in "Sitting Shiva with Cousin Benny," the second-last story in *Pittsburgh Stories*, the beach-front bungalow in Sri Lanka that Cousin Benny has rented, on whose walls he has already put seven hundred self-portraits he has taken each morning with his camera — and, in "The Waffle Maker," the closing story of that volume, the airplane that sixty-year-old script-writer and playwright Lew Morrison sits in, reflecting, right up to the last dramatic scene of that story. Don't these containers function as tropes that contribute significantly to, and indeed represent, the concentrated form and style and impact of the short story itself?

CB: That's an interesting observation; stories do make us think of shelters, and they are often about confinement. I can't take it much further, but I agree with its general tenor. A short story is something of an animated doll's house.

TS: For whatever reason, I find myself recalling your comment about how you would repeat to yourself the final line from Hemingway's "My Old Man" — "Seems like when they get started they don't leave a guy nothing." — and feel better for doing so. And when I imagine that, I laugh and laugh. Then again, I regularly invoke to myself, my family, my friends the distressing circumstances of Thomas Hardy's characters in order to generate the kind of private or shared ironic chuckle that makes me feel better. Would you have any thoughts about what this might say concerning you and me? And could you help me out by suggesting an adjective or two that would identify the type of humour represented by the story of yours about repeating that line by Hemingway?

CB: In "My Old Man," the last line is not meant to be funny, or even consoling — it's condemnatory — so there's a kind of humour that strikes a note of ultimate despair but allows someone else to crawl out from under it, with a sense of relief. It's a kind of "Thank God I don't live in a trailer park" humour, or "It could always be worse," but you have to have a very clear sense of what "worse" is like. It's essentially Jewish, I think; there's doubtless a Yiddish word to describe it, but I don't know it. My closest friend, Murray S. Davis, the expert in humour, died recently, so I'm fresh out of advisers. Kafka approaches it.

TS: Might I ask if there would be any works by your friend Murray S. Davis that you would recommend in particular?

CB: *What's So Funny?* is a great book, especially with so many jokes included. He put another, *Aphoristics*, online for anyone to read free. You can locate it at his website: www.apennyformythoughts.com.

TS: From that website title alone, I can sense the wit he must have brought to everything, including conversation with you. And, having now checked out his website for myself as you suggest, I can see from the "About the Author" section how he characterized himself, again good-humouredly, not as having retired after many years of university teaching but as being "a free range sociologist living in San Francisco."

The "Publications by Murray S. Davis" section announces the forthcoming release, supposedly this year, 2007, of a new book entitled *That's Not Funny!: The War between the Serious and the Humorous* — a companion, I assume, to the earlier study you mentioned, *What's So Funny?: The Comic Conception of Culture and Society*. I would be interested to learn if he gave you a draft of *That's Not Funny!* to read or if he at least outlined his ideas for it to you. And have you heard anything about its present status?

CB: Murray was one chapter short of finishing that book when a sudden and virulent cancer claimed his life in May 2007. We got to see *Borat* as his last public outing. He sent me one chapter, but I don't think there's anyone out there who can complete Murray's thoughts. He was unique, a genius, a wit, but not good-humoured. His father, our local pharmacist, was a classmate of the actor/pianist Oscar Levant in Pittsburgh, and Murray's father was very much a Levant-style wit: sour, mordant, aggressive, a punster. Think of Groucho Marx — that's Murray as well. One of his last observations to me was how cheap it is to die, with the proper insurance.

TS: I would say that the wit involved in such a comment was a testament to its author's desire to keep "being alive," to borrow the title of a book of poems by the late Al Purdy. In any event, I have been wondering if you could tell me which writers of fiction meant the most to Murray Davis — and if the two of you shared any favourites.

CB: Murray went to the University of Chicago, while I went to Denison. He was thus exposed to the Great Books while I was in geology labs. During the Christmas break of our freshman year, the last time I was in Pittsburgh before my parents' break-up, he told me to read *Lolita*. He was of course reading Saul Bellow and Philip Roth and other Chicago writers — Dick Stern, notably. We intersected on Thomas Mann — *Death in*

Venice was a wonder to both of us. He loved Kafka. But he was not really a fiction reader. He was a sociologist, psychologist, philosopher. In later years, I think I was the only fiction writer he attended to.

TS: Concerning Thomas Mann, did you ever make a pilgrimage to see for yourself the landscapes, the seascapes, that formed part of the inspiration for Mann's creations?

CB: While I was working in Germany with my girlfriend as a twenty-two-year-old, I visited "Buddenbrooks Haus" in Lübeck, and also made my *Tonio Kröger* tour of the Danish and German Baltic shore. I have toured all the Baltic cities from København to Eckernförde, Kiel, Lübeck, Rostock, along with Bremerhaven, Bremen, Hamburg, and the Polish coast from Sopot up through Riga and Tallinn, the site of Lander's love-making in "Kristallnacht," and Helsinki and Turku, Stockholm, Visby, and back to Göteborg. It's what led me to say the Baltic seems a peace-inducing sea, contrasted to the Mediterranean.

TS: And could you say something about Mann's status as an influence on you?

CB: I have made very conscious use of Mann, and his region, in many stories. Particularly the Lander sequence in Poland — Gdańsk and Sopot. And very early when Mann was a heavy influence — see "Continent of Strangers" in *A North American Education*. You'll find a lot of references back to Mann in that story: stumblers at the dance in *Tonio Kröger*, etc. At the end of that story, the sight of the nude Finnish girl in the cold Baltic waters of Gotland is a conscious counterpoint to Tadzio on the Lido in *Death in Venice*, as well as Danish children at the beach resort in *Tonio Kröger*.

As an admirer of the Baltic cultures, I also regard

Günter Grass as an influence. You might dig up my *New York Times* review of his Calcutta book, *Show Your Tongue*.

TS: Yes, I've read your review of that book: a volume containing a mixture of journals, drawings, and a poem, and expressing a kind of prophetic rage, that caused you to liken *Show Your Tongue* to the work of William Blake. And looking at your review again now, I find myself obliged to come to terms with your approving quotation of Grass's statement, made about the cow-dung patties evident everywhere around Calcutta, that "All framed and pedestaled works of art should be forced to compete with such scenes from reality." But I also find myself reflecting on the transcendental, since those who exhibit a kind of prophetic rage also possess, necessarily I would think, a vision of the transcendental. For an artist like Blake or Grass or Hawthorne or yourself, how does a vision of the transcendental work into, enlarge, alter the devastating reality which works of art must take fully into account?

CB: I'm not anywhere near their league. I was simply recalling my own feeling about Calcutta, and other common scenes from Indian life, that you had better have a transcendent vision in your art, a motive — otherwise, you're just dabbling. It's a common enough young man's feeling after returning from a war, or Asia or Africa, etc.

TS: To continue with Thomas Mann, did you connect with him on some personal level as well as on an artistic level? Not that these are separable.

CB: As a young aspirant to a writing career, although wrapped up in a geology major, and as the son of an immigrant shop-owner in a provincial city, I caught a whiff of brotherliness with Mann — especially with my mother's long-term residence in Weimar. I started reading the novels right after the stories, and was always impressed by those Knopf "Borzoi Books" imprints, with the pages at the end dedicated to Mann's long bibliography. I wanted that for myself. At Iowa, we studied *Doctor Faustus* very carefully, under R.V. Cassill's guidance. I tried to read *Der Zauberberg* in German, but it was too monumental for me, and I went back to the translation, *The Magic Mountain*.

TS: And can you recall the circumstances when you first read *Death in Venice*?

CB: I read *Death in Venice* during the Christmas break of my freshman year in college, 1957-58. I read *Der Tod in Venedig* in German after learning the language in the summer of 1962 when I was working in Germany.

TS: How would you describe the appeal for you of Mann's *Death in Venice*?

CB: It was the integration of a personal aesthetic with history. See my story in *Pittsburgh Stories* about the furniture restorer and my mother.

TS: "The Unwanted Attention of Strangers," for which Mann's portrait of Tadzio in *Death in Venice* serves as a backdrop. A story first published along with some other interview material of ours, you will remember, in *The New Quarterly* in 1993. To quote briefly from that story, "I felt the truth of Ted Zablonsky's old lesson: Europe was a dead whore crawling with maggots. I went back to reading Thomas Mann. And suddenly I knew who Ted Zablonsky was. More to the point, I knew who Ted had been and what he represented. ... He was Tadzio, one of the immortals." It's truly a superb story, "The Unwanted Attention of Strangers" — speaking of the integration of a personal aesthetic with history. But could you elaborate a little on your sense of a personal or artistic connection with Mann in terms of *Death in Venice* in particular?

CB: I would say it was the romantic, or maybe sentimental, attraction to the notion of a diseased artist,
mute sexual longing, dedication to a classical sense of
beauty, to the classical references that I had to learn in
order to appreciate it, and the idea that fiction could
be supported with a shaft of classical allusion.

TS: Formally, technically, stylistically, how would you
describe Mann's achievement in *Death in Venice*?

CB: When I first read it, I wasn't reading Mann, but
Lowe-Porter, so I can't speak then of "style."

TS: That is to say, you were reading the 1936 "Borzoi
Books" edition of H.T. Lowe-Porter's translation of
Mann's stories entitled *Stories of Three Decades*. Upon
doing a little research after learning that Murray Davis
and you shared an enthusiasm for *Death in Venice*, I was
delighted to discover that an earlier translation of it
and two other novellas by Mann, *Tristan* and *Tonio
Kröger*, had been published in 1925 by none other than
Murray's and your fellow distinguished Pittsburgh boy,
the literary critic and man of letters Kenneth Burke.

CB: I'm well aware of Kenneth Burke and Malcolm Cowley having lived a kind of Blaise/Davis life fifty years
before us. Check out Malcolm Cowley's *Exile's Return*
and his role in re-establishing Faulkner's reputation in
the Viking Portable that led directly to his Nobel Prize.
It was a matter of Pittsburgh, not the two characters.
A notion that Pittsburgh could play in all the terms—
economic, historic, musical, literary, scientific—that are
used to establish a major city. I was unaware of the Burke
translation, although nothing surprises me about Kenneth Burke, the superstar of American literary criticism.

TS: I see from a little more digging that Kenneth Burke's
first book was a story collection, *The White Oxen and
Other Stories*, published in 1924—the same year that

Hemingway published his story cycle *In Our Time*. It would be instructive, perhaps even startling, to compare them. An expanded edition of Burke's stories was published in 1968 under the title *The Complete White Oxen: Collected Short Fiction of Kenneth Burke*. Have you read any of Burke's stories?

CB: No, I haven't, but it doesn't surprise me. The New Critics felt the need to practise the arts they theorized upon. The only comment I've made about Burke was remarking that he died of heart failure at age ninety-six. "Heart failure?" I snorted.

TS: To continue discussing your own reading, I would also like to ask you about Kafka, a great favourite of Murray Davis's and apparently also an interest of yours. Earlier you cited Kafka as being one of a select group of writers — Malamud, Gallant, Beckett, Kafka, Borges, amongst various others you say could be identified — whose work is impossible to imitate. Could you recall in what period of your life, or on what specific occasion, you read Kafka most carefully? And could you name those works by Kafka that particularly caught your attention?

CB: Kafka was part of my "You Must Know Everything" — i.e., read everything — phase, to take Babel's title personally. I read everything by him I could find. I even had an old English — actually, Canadian — orange-backed paperback of *America* which earned me great envy in Iowa. In those years, my early twenties, the early sixties of the last century, having a British Penguin was a real sign of sophistication. It meant you had actually gone to England — no one thought of Canada as having bookstores, probably.

TS: The phase of extremely intensive reading covered your early twenties, you say. That would include at least your final year as an undergraduate, the summer right after graduating from Denison when you took Bernard Malamud's writing workshop at Harvard, the next few months while employed at a bookstore there in Cambridge, on through your MFA in the Writers' Workshop at the University of Iowa, to the start of your teaching career.

CB: The two years I was in the Workshop, from ages twenty-two to twenty-four, and the two or three years immediately preceding were my book-a-day years. After that, I became a bit more selective since I was teaching and fathering.

TS: More specifically on Kafka, could you suggest one or two works by him that exemplify the type of humour you've been describing? And could you elaborate on precisely what is involved?

CB: I would have to say "The Metamorphosis" is at the centre of that particular kind of humour — "Well, you could always be a bug" — and on a slightly more esoteric level, "A Hunger Artist." There's a humour that recognizes an art that can only be helplessly performed anyway; the hunger artist and Samsa can only be what they already are; it's for others to frame their performances. I think of Malamud's "The Jewbird" of course in the same way.

TS: To pursue a little further the subject of humour that Murray Davis continued to make his own as he wrote all but one chapter of his final book, *That's Not Funny!: The War between the Serious and the Humorous*, could you also explain the way Beckett would fit into this discussion? How would you characterize his tone? Do you have favourite works or scenes or lines by him?

CB: In Montreal I always taught *Watt*, *Molloy*, or *The Unnamable*. I'm especially fond of *Watt*. I can't characterize his tone except as "mocking." I mean that positively: mocking academese, mocking nationalism, mocking the narrative voice of traditional fiction, that is, concentrating minutely on everything "narrative" overlooks, and overlooking everything "the novel" tries to attend to. I love the sequence in which Watt imagines Mr. Knott walking in the room above him, or Watt watching lovers on a bench, the gentleman inserting his tongue into the lady's mouth, etc. I suppose the humour is of the "man from Mars" quality: deep alienation from anything familiar, forcing us to investigate things scientifically, as oddities, or absurdities, that we take for granted.

TS: I was pleased to obtain recently the four-volume set of Beckett's collected works, *Samuel Beckett: The Grove Centenary Edition*, published in 2006 as part of celebrations honouring the centenary of his birth. I'm looking forward to reading that — item by item and as a whole, exhilarating if chastening as the experience will surely be.

CB: Further on Beckett: I think narrative convention places high value on inference; namely, you give one pertinent detail, or action, and the reader should be able to infer the rest. In Beckett's early novels he overthrows that convention. Mr. Knott gets up in the morning and retires in the evening, he paces his room, and we go through every permutation of his ritual. That is, the ritual itself becomes ritualized — like the kissing couple, or like the members of the research examination committee whose every gesture, every question, every paper-shuffle are described exhaustively. By excluding the areas of interiority, the minute inspection of emotions, feelings, etc., all those Jamesian properties, and inflating the so-called automatic responses and treating them with Jamesian intensity, Beckett creates a new humour, and a new literature.

TS: And Beckett certainly exhibited an extraordinary gift for paring down what he wanted to say. Would you see some version of what excited Murray Davis about "aphoristics" as giving force and definition to the work of an artist like Beckett?

CB: It has always been my experience that the more you cut, the more you get. Too many words means you're not using them effectively, only decoratively. A long time ago Ford Madox Ford summarized it in a familiar algebraic expression: $(a + b)$ squared. When you expand it you get a squared $+ 2ab + b$ squared. He termed that middle term, $2ab$, "an unearned increment," meaning that if you were a mathematical idiot you would expect to get only a squared plus b squared. If you're an artist you know that if you remove the plaque from the language, new relationships open up. That has something to do with the power of gnomic or condensed phrasing; it cuts immediately to a fresher connectedness, because it eschews the tedious and familiar.

TS: In looking up Murray S. Davis's *Aphoristics: What Makes an Idea Interesting* at www.apennyformythoughts.com, I found — not surprisingly I should have realized, but still intriguingly — that he was as fascinated with form or style as with ideas or perceptions. As he explained on his website, "Except for a standard introduction, my book is written entirely in aphorisms, the most succinct form of interesting ideas. It seemed fitting, at least to me, to employ interesting ideas to analyze interesting ideas — in short, to write aphorisms about aphorisms. Unfortunately, this procedure turned out to be too avant-garde for the academic presses and too esoteric for the trade presses I approached. But I hope my web readers will come to see that my book's form really is appropriate for its content."

I would like to suggest that Murray Davis, in the way he conceived of and wrote his book *Aphoristics*, appreciated and articulated the interrelatedness of form or style and ideas or perceptions — as aphoristics — much in the way you have viewed and crafted the short story. Perhaps most notably in the first five stories of the Gerald Lander sequence first published as *If I Were Me* and subsequently re-collected with one new story, "Migraine Morning," as the first half of *World Body*. Stories that are highly compressed yet extremely expansive — or compressed and therefore expansive, as I believe you would say. Even explosive, I might add. Like the bomb-blast reported to have ended the life of the protagonist of that sequence. And, more to the point, like the way you treat so powerfully Gerald Lander's split second of suddenly intensified and rapidly widening consciousness between the bomb-blast and his reputed death.

I assume you would agree that Murray Davis was on to something of considerable consequence both intellectually and creatively in his concern with and approach to aphoristics. Do you see a connection between aphoristics and the short story?

CB: Murray and I had a special relationship of more than fifty-five years in which we probably talked almost every day. Even in high school we could finish each other's sentences. I spoke to him about aphorisms, which I consign to my always-present notebook, because I feel an aphorism has to arrive exactly as it's written. In other words, an aphorism arrives as something fully formed, which includes the rhythm of the sentence. He felt it was something chiselled, worked over. I find that I can import nearly any of my "aphorisms" from the notebooks into any story I'm writing — they are not specific to any context; they simply exist in the ether and come to rest.

TS: The especially concentrated nature of much contemporary short story writing is a quality no doubt most evident in experiments with stories of far less than conventional length by, for example, Kent Thompson in what he has termed his "postcard stories" or Margaret Atwood in similar pieces. Striking instances are also provided by the first five of your Gerald Lander stories. Yet I would consider it fair to say that this quality is achieved in such works and in stories of more conventional length as much by especially concentrated handling of beginnings and endings, scenes or paragraphs, lines, phrases, images as by choosing to work within a much shorter overall length. How would you characterize what a piece of this kind is meant to do? What is most important to allowing, to making, such a piece — say, "Strangers in the Night" or "Salad Days" or "A Saint" or "Kristallnacht" or "Drawing Rooms," any one of these first five Gerald Lander stories — do all that it's meant to do?

CB: If we say length or brevity is the hallmark of the genre, then it's inevitable that some will fall short of the standard length and others will exceed it, and there are good reasons for it. Kent's postcard stories or Robert Olen Butler's *Had a Good Time* and some of Hemingway's stories and Bharati Mukherjee's "Courtly Vision" in her volume *Darkness* all have strong thematic reasons for their brevity. In the Lander stories, I was moved by incremental notions, not wanting to get into back-stories until I'd staked out the main themes: travel, memory, language, sex, Jewishness, etc. So I felt that I could treat those ideas briefly and discreetly, then combine them in longer later stories or chapters.

TS: To consider a little more deeply the connection between aphoristics and the short story, I wonder if you could say why handling form and style in this way would be important to writers as seemingly different but so strongly connected as Murray S. Davis and yourself?

CB: I really don't have anything I could say about it. "About those things we cannot speak, we must remain silent" (Wittgenstein).

TS: Concerning Bharati Mukherjee's four-and-a-half page story "Courtly Vision," a work that you point to as one illustration of this especially concentrated kind of writing we've been discussing, I do find it interesting to look at that story not only in itself but also in terms of the effect of the placement of that type of story at the end of her volume *Darkness*. The choice of "Courtly Vision" as the closing story for her first collection strikes me as having a similar rationale to Faulkner's choice of finishing his first collection, *These 13*, and later his *Collected Stories*, with his five-page visionary monologue or lyric short story or prose poem "Carcassonne." Stylistically and formally, I would say that your contemporary apocalypse story "The Love God" functions in much the same highly concentrated and magical way as an ending to your collection *Man and His World* and later to *Southern Stories*. Would you have any thoughts on this generally or in terms of the three stories I mention?

CB: Nice try. I still don't have an answer. I write what I have to write, and this is where I'm connected to aphoristics. Those story ideas arrive fully formed, in much the way an aphorism does. As you know, I'm much attracted to Pascal's *Pensées*, in much the way Murray was to Nietzsche and Kafka.

TS: About how aphoristics and the short story are related, about why handling form and style in this way has been important to Murray S. Davis and yourself, I find myself thinking about the topic of time that you researched and thought about so fully in preparing your book *Time Lord* and about the topic of visionary thinking that you discussed in one of my favourite pieces by you, the itself visionary address "The Subtle Contingencies of History" that you presented in June 2004 on the occasion of receiving your honorary doctorate from McGill University and published the following year in *Canadian Notes & Queries*. There you cite the interconnectedness a hundred and twenty years earlier, in 1884, of such seemingly disparate events as Sandford Fleming's creation of standard time and Long Island serial killer Charles Rugg's slaying of eight people and Mark Twain's completion of his classic novel *Adventures of Huckleberry Finn*. You then explain: "What I am suggesting is that the model of history, of an arts education, is not the ability to see historical events as discrete happenings on a linear time-line, but the vision that animates us to see every moment of history in a living cross-section, a flow-chart of wildly discordant elements." Hence, as you conclude, aphoristically it might be noted: "The challenge of the truly educated is to see the subtle contingencies of history in every moment of every day of our lives."

When we reflect on how aphoristics and the short story are related, on why handling form and style in this way has been important to writers as seemingly different but so strongly connected as Murray S. Davis and yourself, aren't we making a case for the importance of a concentrated, non-linear, visionary mode of perception of the sort that aphoristics and short stories like the three I named embody? Aren't we saying that there's a fundamental point to be made about how we should view time and history and thought and art, how we should think, how we need to imagine?

CB: I agree with the thrust of the question. Anyone attuned to the contemporary intellectual environment has to be aware of the bombardment of news-bits, the "crawls" that dump unedited wire service bits on an endless loop, of popular movies with an intellectual message, like *Syriana*, that jump over the world with discontinuous storylines. We've come to equate acute insight with discontinuity. I've always favoured the short story for its energy, a result of its confinement, and for the fact that its length reflects the author's ability to hold it entirely in his/her head, like a musical note. You can't do that with a novel. Holding everything, meaning the syllables, the rhythms, the balance of scene and narration, long sentences and short, in one's head naturally leads to aphoristic thinking.

Where Murray and I disagreed, since we were both notebook-carriers who couldn't go to the bathroom without our notebooks, is that my entries come to me entirely formed, perfectly balanced, sometimes using words I don't know and have never used, but I recognize that something higher than coherence demands that it be a five-syllable word starting with a "d" and I take that to be part of an aphorism, that it just drops in on you, out of the ether, as though I have no role in it. Murray saw it as a small idea to be polished, but that probably speaks to the difference in intellectual orientation, being a critic and analyst with large ideas that need a great deal of documentation, or being relatively unburdened by anything or anyone outside of personal experience.

TS: Further to the matters I raised about the form, the style, the placement, the function of a work like Faulkner's "Carcassonne," I find myself thinking — in the context of an observation you made thirty-five years ago in your rightly still often-quoted brief essay "To Begin,

To Begin," where you remarked that "climax" and "dé-nouement" were both dated terms — that maybe we need to view the form, the style, the placement, the function of such a work rather as an "apotheosis," which I'll define as a transformation or a transfiguration into the godly, the divine, the eternally mysterious. The last of the Gerald Lander stories, "Yahrzeit," where at the end of the story — that is, at the end of the sequence — the possibility is raised that Lander's death may never be proven in actual fact, represents an additional example. In short, if stories, like aphorisms, come from the ether, isn't it fitting for a writer, in deciding on the type of story to employ last in a collection, to signal by that choice how stories, we, all things, don't simply return there but how, through immersion in art, we can participate here and now in that "apotheosis"?

CB: Clearly, I was trying to indicate Lander's eternity, that seeing one's double is not the end of life but only a new beginning. All collections try to make their final story a *summa*. Always, Joyce is the model. This is especially true if you start with brief stories.

TS: Before concluding I wanted to say that I greatly appreciated hearing about your friendship with Murray S. Davis, as well as about your fondness for your uncle Ed Russenholt. Starting just about twenty-five years ago, following the death in 1983 of my own beloved uncle, Jim Kemp — a bomb-disposal expert and gunnery officer for the Canadian Navy during the Second World War and later head of publicity and advertising for the London Life Insurance Company, but just as importantly a very accomplished painter and a delightfully knowledgeable conversationalist — I began saying of people very close to me whom I have lost, "He's still talking to me" or, as appropriate, "She's still talking to me." The publisher of my wife's, Marianne Micros's, first book of poems, *Upstairs Over the Ice Cream*, and an inspiration to me in starting my own small press, Red Kite Press, Win Schell, a continuing, exceptionally supportive, jovial friend to us and our two daughters and my Mom and Dad, died suddenly, shockingly, of an aneurysm on the 2nd of September 2004 at only age sixty-one. So I repeat: "He's still talking to me" or, as appropriate, "She's still talking to me."

Very interestingly, my Mom, Jean Laurie Struthers (née Bowley), in the six months prior to her, for me, basically unexpected death this 4th of July 2007, considered it important to reiterate more than once to me what she said had been her own mother's final words to her: "I will always be with you." We recognize the source of that statement, know why people of certain beliefs hope others will take heart, at the time and later in memory, from hearing that statement by Jesus repeated. Consequently, while I do want to extend my sincere condolences for your recent loss, I also want to express my belief that Murray, like your uncle, will be with you always. And I want to assure you that as a result of your speaking of them as you do, they will also continue to be with others like me.

And in terms of endings that represent beginnings — Beckett, for the final words of his novel *The Unnamable*, chose, as you well know, the now immortal "you must go on, I can't go on, I'll go on." Words echoed by our dear friend and your fellow Montreal Story Teller the late Hugh Hood in one of my favourite stories by him, the uncharacteristically bleak yet more than usually revealing "Every Piece Different," a work dedicated to yet another Montreal Story Teller, John Metcalf, and appearing in Hugh's collection *August Nights*. And so perhaps we all end, and begin, by repeating "I can't go on, I'll go on."

However, there's a different line by Beckett, one from his play *Waiting for Godot*, that I merrily imagined Hugh Hood repeating each time I accepted his friendly invitation and turned up for a few days to relax and visit at his and Noreen Mallory's home in Montreal or at their cottage on Charleston Lake near Athens, Ontario, on which occasions Hugh and I would often tape-record another interview. It's a line that I now merrily imagine you repeating not just when I arrive to do another face-to-face interview at the time of the release of a new book by you or during a short story conference we're both attending, but any morning, afternoon, evening when you check your e-mail and find a new query from me. The line reads: "There you are again...."

And so I am. And so you are. And for your constant welcome I thank you.

To Elevate Experience into Metaphor: An Interview with Clark Blaise [2012]

J.R. (Tim) Struthers

TS: Here we are again. To quote Beckett. [Laughter.]

CB: OK. Fire away.

TS: Yesterday, here in North Little Rock, Arkansas, at The 12th International Conference on the Short Story in English, I gave a paper that I called "Seeing a Line Through the Circles: The Role of Metaphor in Reading Stories, Collections, *Oeuvres*." In my choice of metaphor for the title of this paper I was echoing, as you would immediately have recognized, a description in Mavis Gallant's story "An Autobiography," which I first encountered in the landmark anthology that you and John Metcalf co-edited for Oberon Press in 1977, *Here & Now: Best Canadian Stories*.

A line through a set of circles, as you will remember, is the way that Erika, the protagonist/narrator of "An Autobiography," describes the design of the village in Switzerland where she teaches: a village consisting of concentric circles or rings of successive types of dwellings — hotels, chalets, private schools — but with a single road, "one straight street" Erika calls it, running through the circles. And I think it's fair to say that the road or line running through the circles of the village in Gallant's story serves as a metaphor for the individual narrative — "An Autobiography," as the title says —

that Erika, and equally each reader of her story, constructs out of the circles of her life.

What I was doing in my paper was borrowing Gallant's metaphor to develop a theory that posited the existence of five concentric circles representing the different dimensions or worlds in our lives and in the lives of the characters whose stories we read. And then extending this theory to suggest that we view the act of memory or perception, of reflection or interpretation, as a single line of definition drawn through the great complexity of the lives of the characters and through our own lives as well.

Of Gallant's story "An Autobiography" I argued as follows ... If it seems reasonable to propose that the largest or outermost of the story's five concentric circles stands for the epic panorama of political and socio-cultural and literary history throughout Europe from the time of Goethe through the time of Freud to the time of Mavis Gallant, and if it seems reasonable to suggest that the second-largest or fourth circle represents the importance to Erika's formative childhood years of what I am terming the legacy of Freud, then it would, I believe, be reasonable to say that the third or middle circle might be seen as consisting of Erika's brief early adulthood romance with Peter and that the second circle represents time present some years later when Erika is teaching elementary botany at a girls' school in a village in Switzerland and unexpectedly encounters Peter and his new wife at the local train station. Leaving us to identify the story's first or innermost circle: the act of narration, the act of self-definition, the all-important act in the first person — looking from the present to the past and to the future — of, let us say, personal salvation, if using such a phrase is not to push a Mavis Gallant story far too much in the particular allegorical direction of, say, a Hugh Hood story.

After my paper, when we spoke about what I had proposed, you suggested that some of the ways in which I think about stories differ from the ways in which you think about stories. I believe you said that you were more of a sentence by sentence by sentence guy. And I was wondering if you could elaborate on your response to what I had proposed.

CB: You're suggesting a kind of conical slice. With the line going through a cone, or a cone-shaped object, or maybe five cones. It may be that way. I think if you're writing an autobiography, probably you *are* involved with five or more cones. You're having to place yourself within a historical continuum of some sort, so probably the five that you enumerated come into play. Maybe there are ten or maybe there are fifteen. Various things come into play. There's your family, there's your education, there's your nationality, there's your place of birth and place of upbringing, there are your various loyalties in various directions. There are your failings. There are your yearnings. There are your thwarted dreams and thwarted desires. All those things are part of an autobiography.

It just seemed to me that I would see more discontinuities between the line and those five or more cones or concentric rings. Even in Mavis's story, the line is a broken line. It's sort of like the line in the middle of a highway. It's discontinuous. It's *there*, but it's discontinuous also. It allows you to pass, if necessary. It's not a solid line.

That was just an offhand thought. I don't want things to get prescriptive, that it must be this way or it is always that way. I'm prescriptive enough anyway in my own writing — what I hold myself to or what I think will make for a better story. I try to bend the last sentence back to the first sentence, and I feel that the surprise elements, or the revelatory elements, in a story are the disclosure, the full disclosure, of the opening.

The opening fully explored will give you the ending, as in the story I read today, "The Kerouac Who Never Was." It's the two brothers talking about how life will open up for you when you have a paper route, and the whole world opens up because of the paper route. It's that kind of thing.

TS: A comment I tossed out while presenting my paper had to do with the fact that while I might choose to talk about a single line through the circles, others might prefer to think of there being many lines through those circles. If, for example, you were to start at some point on a circumference and work your way around, having different lines running towards the centre with one degree between them, you would have 360 different possibilities.

CB: The sense I got from your description is that the concentric rings are sort of fixed on a grid. They are fixed points, whereas the line is the narrative thrust. The line is growing and lengthening if you wish, whereas the other parts of the grid are fixed.

TS: In terms of that title, "An Autobiography," when one first looks at it one might easily assume that by far the most important word is "Autobiography." But perhaps the word "An" has equal weight in that title.

CB: It's one out of many.

TS: Yes — so that very conceivably there is a calculated ambiguity in Gallant's choice of the word "An" for that title. How did the title of the story that you read today, "The Kerouac Who Never Was," come to you?

CB: Well, there were other titles that I had in mind. The story that I had done just before that was called "We Are All Illegals." I was a little looser in the title here. "The Kerouac Who Never Was" is of course the brother who will die, and who is clearly the inheritor of Kerouac, would have been the next Kerouac. But all of these other elements come into play that keep him from being that Kerouac.

Kerouac has a very, very strong presence in Franco America — and in Quebec for that matter. Among French Canadians, Kerouac is just about the only legitimate folk hero. So I wanted to evoke the Frenchness of the story immediately by talking of Kerouac, although most Americans reading it would probably think of Kerouac the Beat writer, and *On the Road*, not the Kerouac of *Doctor Sax*.

Doctor Sax is probably the epic story from French Canada, from Franco America anyway. It's a very complicated book, and a crazy book, but a very moving book and I wanted to pay homage to that part of Kerouac. I've been a little hard on some other aspects of Kerouac, the late Kerouac. But the early Kerouac strikes me as being painfully sincere, and painfully aware of all the frailties of Franco-American life, of Catholic life, of French life in America. And unflinching in many ways, without the sentimentality that I think harms so much of Kerouac's writing.

TS: You seem to be summoning up — not summing up, I don't think you will ever do that [laughter] since you're always going forward, but summoning up — a great deal here. You indicated in the discussion period after your reading that your awareness reached back to about 1640. I think that was the year you mentioned.

CB: 1640 was the year when Pierre Blais was born in

Angoulême. And he came over from France to Canada in 1662. 1668 is when he picked up his wife, Anne Perreault. She was *une fille du roi*, arrived in Quebec City, married Pierre the next day. They had, I think, ten children, she died in 1682 giving birth to the last, and he immediately married a second wife with whom he had six more. He got a special dispensation from the local priest on Île d'Orléans to remarry immediately because he had this baby that survived the mother's death. So he had to marry the next day, two days, three days later, and he married a woman named Elizabeth Royer, his neighbour's daughter. She outlived him. And she herself ended up remarrying right away and going off to Montreal after Pierre died in 1700. She lived until 1715 and died in Montreal.

TS: You were born in 1940 — exactly three hundred years after Pierre Blais. What relation was he to you?

CB: There must be nine "greats" in front of Pierre's name.

TS: Île d'Orléans is the place where short story writer George Elliott settled in the late eighties and lived for the rest of his life, until 1996. I had the pleasure of working with George — in what, sadly, proved to be the very last years of his life — on editing three books of his stories for publication by my small press, Red Kite Press: *The bittersweet man* in 1994, *Crazy Water Boys* in 1995, then *Sand gardens on First Beach*, which we planned to release in 1996 and which I finally completed in 2010.

CB: I wasn't aware that he was living in Quebec. My father's family lived on Île d'Orléans for about four generations before they finally jumped ship and moved to the Eastern Townships, to what had been called les Cantons-de-l'Est — l'Estrie it's now called — and made their way slowly, slowly, generation by generation, as tenant farmers, down through Beauce, then through Frontenac, and finally ended up in Lac-Mégantic.

TS: Now, in terms of the workings of the story "The Ker-ouac Who Never Was" that you read today ... During your reading I picked up on a phrase you used and in the discussion period afterwards I asked you a question about that which I would like to repeat here. It was a phrase about the God in the fog, or the God coming out of the fog, referring to a moose. If you would elaborate on that, I would appreciate it.

CB: Well, I don't think it's a particularly original idea. I think probably every writer has the sense that a story must contain some element that allows for transcend-ence, that there must be some *thing*, not necessarily a person, not necessarily a living object, some *thing* — a mountain, a tree, a flower, whatever it may be — that elevates experience into metaphor. Otherwise, it's just a recitation of a series of events and experiences, it's little more than journalism, it presents itself as a flat surface. Where is the elevation here? Where is the thing that becomes unmatchable, untouchable, transcendent, that transforms a character into a caring individual or, let's say, an entity into a person? It's like asking the question, What do you care for? What is it in the story that you as a character want, what is it you care for, what is it you would die for? What is it that you would cry for, at least? Those are all questions that are ger-mane, I think, to any story. And if this element is lacking, then the story is lacking, and certainly the character-ization is lacking.

TS: The sense of it coming out of the fog, as if it were materializing — that excited me.

CB: Yes, that excited me too. And the idea that if you have that much fog, you've got to have something com-ing out of it. Literary fog is not fog until it yields a speci-men of something. You know, you bump into something, or something falls on you, or a creature or a person comes out of it. And it seems to me that this is part of the gamesmanship of fog. Otherwise, you're just a lone kid with a sled struggling to find the next corner.

But suddenly something has come on to you that thinks you're its mother, and you have to act accordingly. Either you swat at it and get away, as his brother had told him — don't mess with the moose — or else you feel somehow that maybe you are a moose yourself, maybe you are somehow responsible for it.

What happens to an eleven-year-old? Eleven-year-old kids can be very cruel, but they can also be very tender. They can want to take responsibility for things or they can want to avoid responsibility for things. A kid on any given day under any given conditions might want to take out a shotgun and shoot himself a moose. On another day he might want to give his life to protect it.

That's more or less what is happening here, I think.

TS: You speak of this in terms of an experience on the part of a character in the story. But that experience is felt equally, I think, by the story's readers — or, today, by the story's listeners — who have a similarly strong sense of something materializing for them.

CB: I hope so. Certainly the intent is.

TS: And there's a great excitement in that, whether it's in listening to the story, as your audience had the satisfaction of doing today, or, in reading the story, as would normally be the case. I was trying to get at something like that when I spoke about drawing the line through the circles. It can be an act of perception on the part of a character, but it can also be an act of perception on the part of a reader.

CB: To apply your formula to the story, there are those implacable circles: Catholicism, Frenchness, illness, asbestos, the police, any number of things. The grandparents, the parents, the kids in Lambert Park, all those things have to be driven through, if you wish. And this kid has been given, say, the vehicle for getting through it — a sled in the winter, a wagon in the summer — and he's trying to make his way being told, sort of like in a board game, don't go here, don't go there, don't mess with this, don't mess with that, don't let Father Beaubien get you. But will he make it through? Will he make it through the day, will he make it through his route? And then there's the disease.

So I think your formula works to a certain extent here. But there are obstacles to the straight and narrow. And keeping to the straight and narrow is not always possible.

TS: "The Kerouac Who Never Was" represents the first story in a planned "novel-in-stories," if I may call it that, which you are thinking of calling *Entre-Nous*. Just before you began reading the story today, you alluded to the idea that I had put forward in an essay on your first published story, "A Fish Like a Buzzard," the story that you placed first in your collection *Southern Stories* and therefore also first in your four-volume *Selected Stories*: the idea that the opening piece in a story collection is often a disguised essay about how a writer wishes to write and wishes to be read. And then you added, "Or perhaps a disguised autobiography." I was very, very interested to hear you make that comment and am wondering if you would elaborate on it.

CB: Well, as I say, it's not my autobiography in the least — I've never even been in Winooski, Vermont, where the story is set. But certainly there is the brother with the disease, the disease itself, the fact that the narrator has escaped the disease. All of these things obviously relate vaguely to my own autobiographical problems with the disease and to my older son's condi- tion. And the guilt that I feel and all that sort of stuff is there. So it's a deeply disguised autobiography if it's an autobiography at all.

But I am aware of the tentative relationship that I have to French Canada or Franco America, the absolute irreligiosity of my background. I have no religious feel- ing at all, but this has to be a deeply Catholic kind of story. There are things that I've had to reach deeply back for — that I know of but have never experienced first-hand.

In some ways, I am imitating my father's feeling about the Catholic Church, which was vicious. I mean, he would have castrated the priests and then hung them, as in the Spanish Civil War. His hatred of the church was deep and never yielded — not even when he was in terrible shape later in life, morally shaken to the core. I said, "I can take you to a priest." And he almost got out of bed and swatted me for even the idea that a priest would have anything to help him with.

TS: Whenever questions of autobiography come up, I remember an observation made by Keath Fraser in his essay "Notes toward a Supreme Fiction," written for the one hundredth issue of the journal *Canadian Literature* and later anthologized by John Metcalf and me in *How Stories Mean*, where he points out that in many respects writers are at their most profoundly autobiographical when they're being most fully imaginative — that is, when they're operating at the transcendent level you were talking about earlier.

CB: The next story in this series is totally non-autobio- graphical. It doesn't even share the same degree of grief or moral hardship or anything else like that. It has some physical hardship, but it's totally imagined and I don't think it has any autobiography in it, except that it draws on a book called *Histoire de Lac-Mégantic* by Jean-Pierre Kesteman. It was published thirty years ago. I read it, I still have it. It speaks of the founding of the village and all that sort of stuff. It's good historical writing. It offered me a framework for imagining French-Canadian rural life in the nineteenth century. It's the scaffolding for fantastical events in the fiction, which is Franco-American (an imagined Winooski, Vermont) not French-Canadian. So I'm appropriating for my fictional purposes a historical record that I've had to absorb.

TS: And the title of this second story is...?

CB: "Betsy Robitaille."

TS: And who is she?

CB: Richard Fréchette says, "If I were a knight, Betsy Robitaille would be my quest."

TS: In answer to the question that I asked following your reading, about the God coming out of the fog, you said, "I've come to the conclusion that every story has a God. In fact, a story *better* have a God [laughter] to lift it from experience into metaphor." And you also gave the example of a favourite Hemingway story.

CB: "Cat in the Rain," yes. Just the inclusion of a waiter, standing silently in a doorway of a restaurant, waiting for the rain to go away, because the rain has totally wiped out his business. But he's there and, as I said, there's no reason why he should be there in the story. The story is eloquent enough with just the rain conveying that it's a desolate urban scene.

But putting him in there alters the relationship of everything. It gives a third point, it allows for a triangulation of the rain and the desolation. It's there. And I've always felt the presence of that waiter. He has no role in the story. He disappears and we don't see him again.

Nevertheless he has made his entrance, he has stood there looking out over the rain. Probably, I can imagine, with the insolence of the normal Italian waiter. But I guess he goes back inside.

TS: And that sort of detail would come to you in the writing from some very deep level and not be inserted in any conscious way.

CB: You don't plan it. See, what happens here is when the young, dissatisfied, and unfulfilled wife is looking out over the rain herself from the window of her room, where her husband is lying in bed writing, she sees the waiter. This is not in the story at all — but in my mind she sees the waiter and since that is a forbidden kind of vision for her she sees the cat trying to stay dry and focusses on "I want a kitty," "I want a cat." It's probably not what she wants. But she can't articulate, or doesn't know, what it is that she really wants.

TS: So that sort of interpretation is left to the reader.

CB: You've given the reader one more thing to think about, one more thing to focus on. That this experience is seen through another set of eyes. That she has got her eyes looking out at it, but there's another pair of eyes, maybe more transcendent, maybe less personally involved, that are — how should I say? — looking out at the world dispassionately or with almost Buddha-like indifference. We can carry this too far, I suppose. But that's my sense of it.

TS: We conducted our first interview almost twenty-five years ago: in Guelph, Ontario, on Saturday the 12th of November 1988, the morning of the final day of the four-day conference of writers and critics that I organized to celebrate the ongoing achievements of Canadian story writer, editor, and critic John Metcalf on the occasion of his fiftieth birthday — and the ongoing achievements of other major Canadian story writers who participated, including Hugh Hood, Alice Munro, Leon Rooke, and yourself. I would like to thank you heartily for this opportunity to sit down and visit together once again. I always appreciate it.

CB: I wonder how many more there will be.

About the Writer

CLARK BLAISE is one of the most accomplished, most exciting, most prophetic writers in North America — the author of some twenty books of fiction, autobiography, and nonfiction beginning with the richly textured and dramatically powerful story cycle *A North American Education* (1973). His considerable qualities as a writer are exhibited supremely in *If I Were Me* (1997), the four-volume *Selected Stories of Clark Blaise* (2000-06), and *The Meagre Tarmac* (2011), in *I Had a Father* (1993), *Time Lord* (2000), and his *Selected Essays* (2008), and in many other titles. Along with his signal achievements as a writer, Clark Blaise has enjoyed a profoundly influential career as a writing and literature teacher in universities throughout the world and as a major arts administrator — Director for nine years of the prestigious International Writing Program at the University of Iowa and, before that, founder of the graduate program in Creative Writing at Concordia University in Montreal. Clark Blaise holds honorary doctorates from Denison University (1979), McGill University (2004), and Concordia University (2013) and was made an Officer of the Order of Canada in 2010. He now lives in New York City with his wife, the writer Bharati Mukherjee.

About the Artist

RON SHUEBROOK is a Canadian artist who is Professor Emeritus at OCAD University in Toronto where he served as President from 2000 to 2005 and as Vice-President, Academic from 1998 to 2002. He has taught and been an administrator at six other Canadian universities and art schools and is a former President of the Royal Canadian Academy of Arts and a former President of the Universities Art Association of Canada. He received an Honorary Doctorate from OCAD in 2005 as well as a Queen Elizabeth II Diamond Jubilee Medal in 2012. He is currently Senior Artist in Residence at Boarding House Arts in Guelph, Ontario. Shuebrook exhibits nationally and internationally and is represented by Olga Korper Gallery as well as other galleries. His work is in more than sixty public and corporate collections, including the National Gallery of Canada and the Art Gallery of Ontario, and in numerous private collections. An image of an untitled painting of his from 1989 (in the Art Gallery of Guelph collection) is reproduced in *Abstract Painting in Canada* by Roald Nasgaard. He lives in Guelph, Ontario and Blandford, Nova Scotia.

About the Editor

Highly respected nationally and internationally by scholars and creative writers for his work as a bibliographer, an interviewer, a literary critic, an editor, and the publisher of Red Kite Press, J.R. (TIM) STRUTHERS has edited some twenty-five volumes of theory, criticism, autobiography, fiction, and poetry — including works in honour of, or by, such important writers as Clark Blaise, George Elliott, Jack Hodgins, Hugh Hood, John Metcalf, and Alice Munro. For over forty years he has been writing about Canadian literature, particularly the short story, including, in 1975, the first two scholarly articles published world-wide on Alice Munro. He has conducted some forty interviews with Canadian writers and has been described by W.J. Keith, FRSC, as "probably the best literary interviewer in Canada." An enthusiastic teacher, he has taught English full-time at the University of Guelph for over thirty years. Tim lives in Guelph with his bride of forty years, poet and scholar Marianne Micros, inspired and delighted by the company of their two daughters, Eleni and Joy, and their four grandchildren, Matteo, Rowan, Asher, and Reed.

Contributor Biographies

BRIAN BARTLETT has published many collections of poetry, including *The Watchmaker's Table* and *Wanting the Day: Selected Poems*, recipients of the Acorn-Plantos Award for People's Poetry and the Atlantic Poetry Prize. He has also written a book of prose, *Ringing Here & There: A Nature Calendar*, and edited volumes of selected poems by Don Domanski, Robert Gibbs, and James Reaney. He edited *Don McKay: Essays on his Works* for Guernica's Writers Series, and essays of his appeared in the P.K. Page and Richard Outram volumes in the same series. Since 1990 he has taught Creative Writing and many fields of literature at Saint Mary's University in Halifax, Nova Scotia.

CATHERINE BUSH is the author of four novels: *Accusation*, an Amazon.ca and *NOW Magazine* Best Book of the Year; the Trillium-Award-shortlisted *Claire's Head*; *The Rules of Engagement*, chosen as a *New York Times* Notable Book; and *Minus Time*. Her work has been critically acclaimed, published internationally, and shortlisted for literary awards. Her nonfiction has appeared in the anthology *The Heart Does Break* and elsewhere. She coordinates the University of Guelph Creative Writing MFA.

BARRY CAMERON is a retired professor of English and Film. He taught at both the University of Toronto and the

University of New Brunswick. His seminal monograph, *Clark Blaise and His Works* (ECW Press, 1984), was the first substantial critical consideration of Blaise's writing.

GEOFF HANCOCK, in the barn-board studio beyond the gravelled drive, under a pale pool of simple lamplight, contemplated the invisible literature of Canadian short fiction and emerging or neglected writers. His special interest in the unexplored extremities resulted in several anthologies of magic realism, illusion, fables, fantasies, the gothic, surreal, and grotesque, fiction and physics, and alchemy in fiction. He edited *Canadian Fiction Magazine* for twenty-five years. Other publications include *Canadian Writers at Work* (1987) and, with Eric Henderson, *Short Fiction and Critical Contexts* (2010), both Oxford University Press titles. Most recently he guest-edited *The Visionary Art of Sharon Butala* (2013), a special issue of *Prairie Fire*.

NICHOLAS JOHNSON was born and raised in Iowa City, Iowa — the United Nations' "City of Literature" that also gave birth to the Iowa Writers Workshop and Director Clark Blaise's International Writing Program. Johnson's legal career includes a degree from the University of Texas, a U.S. Supreme Court clerkship, corporate practice, three presidential appointments, teaching (U.C. Berkeley and University of Iowa law), and characterization in *The Yale Biographical Dictionary of American Law* as one of 700 individuals described by the publisher as "leading figures in the history of American law, from the colonial era to the present day." He has also been an author, TV host, public lecturer, radio commentator, syndicated columnist, congressional candidate, co-director of a public health public policy institute, and school board member. Web page: www.nicholasjohnson.org; Blog: FromDC2Iowa.blogspot.com; Contact: mailbox@nicholasjohnson.org.

ALEXANDER MacLEOD is an Associate Professor of English and Atlantic Canada Studies at Saint Mary's University in Halifax, Nova Scotia. His research is focussed on theories of literary regionalism, social space, and cultural geography. He is the author of the short story collection *Light Lifting*, which was shortlisted for the Scotiabank Giller Prize and The Frank O'Connor International Short Story Award.

JOHN METCALF stands as one of the most important figures in the history of Canadian literature. In addition to obtaining and readying for publication hundreds of books for such distinguished literary presses as Oberon Press, The Porcupine's Quill, and, most recently, Biblioasis, he has edited or co-edited dozens of anthologies and textbooks — including a pair, *Canadian Classics* and *How Stories Mean*, with J.R. (Tim) Struthers — and now nearly twenty volumes of the annual *Best Canadian Stories*. Metcalf has produced a very substantial and wide-ranging body of his own powerfully crafted, uniquely textured fiction: short stories such as "Gentle as Flowers Make the Stones," novellas such as "Polly Ongle," and the novels *Going Down Slow* and *General Ludd*. In 2016, five previously published novellas were collected under the title *Vital Signs*, while a dazzling brand-new sequence of linked novellas and stories was released under the title *The Museum at the End of the*

World. "Words deployed like cut diamonds on black velvet trays," as Clark Blaise describes Metcalf's writing. As well, John Metcalf is the author of two major literary memoirs, *An Aesthetic Underground* and *Shut Up He Explained*, he has written numerous incisive essays, many of which have been collected in his books *Kicking Against the Pricks* and *Freedom from Culture*, and he has now completed a monumental new critical study called *The Canadian Short Story* (forthcoming in 2017).

CATHERINE SHELDRICK ROSS is Professor Emerita at Western University, where she taught in the English Department and in the Faculty of Information and Media Studies (FIMS) and also served in various administrative roles including Acting Dean of Graduate Studies and Dean of FIMS. Interested in texts, authorship, and reading, she has published articles on Canadian writers as well as interviews with Canadian writers, including authors of children's books. Her published books include four information books for children, two books on communication and interviewing written for practising librarians, a biography, *Alice Munro: A Double Life* (1992), and two books on the experience of reading for pleasure: *Reading Matters: What the Research Reveals about Reading, Libraries, and Community* (2006) and most recently *The Pleasures of Reading: A Booklover's Alphabet* (2014).

Bibliographer, interviewer, literary critic, editor, and the publisher of Red Kite Press, J.R. (TIM) STRUTHERS has conducted some forty interviews with Margaret Atwood, Clark Blaise, George Elliott, Imogen Knister Givens, Douglas Glover, Jack Hodgins, Hugh Hood, Penn Kemp,

John B. Lee, Daphne Marlatt, John Metcalf, K.D. Miller, Alice Munro, John Newlove, James Reaney, Leon Rooke, Diane Schoemperlen, Ray Smith, Audrey Thomas, Kent Thompson, and Rudy Wiebe. Many of these interviews have been published in books or periodicals, while others await editing and publication. He has had the pleasure of interviewing Clark Blaise more times than any other of the stellar writers — most especially, short story writers — whose work he seeks to honour. His essay on Blaise's story "A Fish Like a Buzzard" was featured in 2011 as the lead essay in the inaugural issue of the British journal *Short Fiction in Theory and Practice* and a companion essay on Blaise's story "The Birth of the Blues" appeared in 2016 in *Clark Blaise: Essays on His Works*.

SHERRI TELENKO, M.A., became a writer and editor after graduating from the University of Guelph with a master's degree in English literature. Currently, she teaches English and Communications at Mohawk College in Hamilton, Ontario, and writes travel, lifestyle, and interview articles for magazines, while developing two on-line pet blogs about travel, horses, and dogs.

ALLAN WEISS is Associate Professor of English and Humanities at York University, where he has taught since 1990. His research interests are in Canadian fiction and fantastic literature. He is Chair of the Academic Conference on Canadian Science Fiction and Fantasy and has edited three collections of proceedings from that conference, most recently *The Canadian Fantastic in Focus* (2014). Among his publications are articles on Canadian literature, science fiction and fantasy, and the short story. He is also the author of about two dozen short stories; his story cycle *Living Room* appeared in 2001, and another collection is forthcoming in 2016.

Acknowledgements

Barry Cameron's "To Create Histories Around Little Things: An Interview with Clark Blaise" was first published under the title "A Conversation with Clark Blaise" in *Essays on Canadian Writing*.

Geoff Hancock's "Clear Veneer: An Interview with Clark Blaise" was published first under the title "An Interview with Clark Blaise" in *Canadian Fiction Magazine* and subsequently under the title "Clark Blaise" in his book *Canadian Writers at Work* issued by Oxford University Press.

Alexander MacLeod's "Too Canadian for the Americans and Too American for the Canadians: An Interview with Clark Blaise" was first published in *Essays on Canadian Writing*.

John Metcalf's "Texture and Voice: An Interview with Clark Blaise" was first published under the title "Interview: Clark Blaise" in *Journal of Canadian Fiction*.

J.R. (Tim) Struthers' "In the Beginning: An Interview with Clark Blaise" was first published under the title "Angles of Vision: An Interview with Clark Blaise" in *The New Quarterly*.

An earlier version of J.R. (Tim) Struthers' "Learning To Read, Learning To Write: An Interview with Clark Blaise" was published under the title "An Expanded Moment, Not a Contracted One: An Interview with Clark Blaise" in *Short Story*.

J.R. (Tim) Struthers' "Looking East: An Interview with Clark Blaise" was first published as a portion of "Part of the Myth: An Interview with Clark Blaise" in *Carousel* [U of Guelph].

J.R. (Tim) Struthers' "Part of the Myth: An Interview with Clark Blaise" was first published as a portion of "Part of the Myth: An Interview with Clark Blaise" in *Carousel* [U of Guelph].

Sherri Telenko's "Room for Anything: An Interview with Clark Blaise" was first published under the title "Face to Face: An Interview with Clark Blaise" in *Matrix*.

J.R. (Tim) Struthers wishes to thank Ph.D. candidate Alec Follett and undergraduate students Kelsey McCallum, Will Wellington, and Kelly Wighton at the University of Guelph for their conscientious and very good-humoured service as research assistants at different stages while he prepared the companion volumes *Clark Blaise: Essays on His Works* and *Clark Blaise: The Interviews* for Guernica.

MARQUIS

Québec, Canada